155367

1-29-90

W9-CKH-255

COMIC VISIONS

Media and Popular Culture

A Series of Critical Books

SERIES EDITOR
David Thorburn
*Director of Film and Media Studies and
Professor of Literature,
Massachusetts Institute of Technology*

In recent years a new, interdisciplinary scholarship devoted to popular culture and modern communications media has appeared. This emerging intellectual field aims to move beyond inherited conceptions of "mass society" by recognizing the complexity and diversity of the so-called mass audience and its characteristic cultural experiences. The new scholarship on media and popular culture conceives communication as a complex, ritualized experience in which "meaning" or significance is constituted by an intricate, contested collaboration among institutional, ideological, and cultural forces.

Intended for students and scholars as well as the serious general reader, **Media and Popular Culture** will publish original interpretive studies devoted to various forms of contemporary culture, with emphasis on media texts, audiences, and institutions. Aiming to create a fruitful dialogue between recent strains of feminist, semiotic, and marxist cultural study and older forms of humanistic and social-scientific scholarship, the series will be open to many methods and theories and committed to a discourse that is intellectually rigorous yet accessible and lucid.

Communication as Culture
Essays on Media and Society
JAMES W. CAREY

Myths of Oz
Reading Australian Popular Culture
JOHN FISKE, BOB HODGE, and GRAEME TURNER

Teenagers and Teenpics
The Juvenilization of American Movies in the 1950s
THOMAS DOHERTY

Comic Visions
Television Comedy and American Culture
DAVID MARC

Forthcoming

Shakespearean Films, Shakespearean Directors
PETER DONALDSON

Dateline the Sixties:
Reporting the Counterculture
RICHARD GOLDSTEIN

Additional titles in preparation

Ban # *6440*

1811

COMIC VISIONS

TELEVISION COMEDY
AND AMERICAN CULTURE

DAVID MARC

Boston

UNWIN HYMAN

London   Sydney   Wellington

Copyright © 1989 by David Marc.
This book is copyright under the Berne Convention. No
reproduction without permission. All rights reserved.

Unwin Hyman, Inc.
8 Winchester Place, Winchester, MA 01890, USA

Published by the Academic Division of
Unwin Hyman, Ltd,
15/17 Broadwick Street, London W1V 1FP, UK

Allen & Unwin (Australia) Ltd,
8 Napier Street, North Sydney, NSW 2060, Australia

Allen & Unwin (New Zealand) Ltd,
in association with the Port Nicholson Press Ltd,
60 Cambridge Terrace, Wellington, New Zealand

First published 1989

Library of Congress Cataloging-in-Publication Data

Marc, David.
  Comic Visions : television comedy and American culture / David
Marc.
    Bibliography: p.
    Includes index.
    ISBN 0-04-445284-5. ISBN 0-04-445285-3 (pbk.)
    1. Comedy programs--United States. 2. United States--Popular
culture. I. Title. II. Series.
PN1992.8.C66m35 1989
791.45'09'0917--dc19

                                                                88-27780
                                                                     CIP

British Library Cataloguing in Publication Data

Marc, David
  Comic visions: television comedy and
  American culture.- (Media and popular culture)
  1. United States. Society. Effect of television
  programmes. Sociological perspectives
  I. Title II. Series
  302.2'345'0973
ISBN 0-04-445284-5
ISBN 0-04-445285-3 pbk

Set in 10 on 12 point Palatino
Printed in Great Britain by
Billing & Sons, London and Worcester

In loving memory of S.J.K.

Contents

Acknowledgments

Parts of the section on *M*A*S*H* in Chapter Five were re-searched and written in collaboration with Paul Buhle, as part of an article that appeared in *American Film*.

I would like to thank the following people for their help in the preparation of this book: Daniel Barnett, Barry Bergman, Daniel Czitrom, Richard Goldstein, Jerry Lee Keller, Franco Manai, Robina Moyer, Jeffrey Moyer, John Semivan, Ron Simon, Robert Thompson, David Thorburn, and Kathleen Welch.

I would like to thank the following institutions for their encouragement and support: the Museum of Broadcasting, New York; and the Annenberg School of Communications, University of Southern California.

Author's Note

Television, in the manner of most popular media, paints pictures of life with broad brushstrokes. In America, the country that Walt Whitman called a "teeming nation of nations," this has meant the creation of an entire mythology of ethnic and racial stereotypes. The minstrel show, which offered white audiences a set of Afro-American stereotypes that helped justify state policies of racial subjugation and separation, was the most popular form of theater in nineteenth-century America. The turn-of-the-century vaudeville stage resounded with stereotypical—and sometimes vicious—jokes about Italian passions, Irish drinking, Jewish business practices, German problems with the English language, and so on.

Television, via the movies and radio, has inherited this mantle. In a sense, any discussion of television history—and especially any discussion of a representational genre such as the situation comedy—is an examination of how these popular stereotypes have been exploited in the late twentieth century.

Throughout this study, I have referred to the portrayal in television comedy of various groups, including WASPs, blacks, Jews, women, and others. In no way do I intend to imply that these fictional portrayals are accurate pictures of their subjects or even realistic renderings. The idyllic picture of WASP life created by Joe Connelly and Bob Mosher in *Leave It to Beaver* is not to be taken as any more "realistic" than the picture of black life in Harlem created by Freeman Gosden and Charles Correll (two white Southerners) in *Amos 'n' Andy*.

In a culture where racial and ethnic tensions remain never far beneath the surface of day-to-day life, this is a point worth reiterating.

David Marc
Annenberg School of Communications, U.S.C.
Los Angeles
May 2, 1988

CHAPTER 1

What's So Funny about America?

Vulgarity, or at least what a certain community terms so, does not necessarily impair certain mysterious characteristics, a fay grace. . . .

—Vladimir Nabokov[1]

Though more culture than ever is intended for millions of people, "mass culture," a special culture for the unwashed that dirties everyone, is in many ways a hopelessly outmoded phrase. It implies that hidden behind the glitzy facade of modern commercial entertainment there remains *Kultur*, "the best that has been known and said," separate, incorruptible, truthful, and beautiful. If this was once so, it no longer is. Culture has become too large and diversified a business to be identified by any one of its market constituencies. The "consciousness industry," as Hans Magnus Enzensberger calls it, has a high end, a low end, and a vast sagging middle, to be sure, but this is the same marketing configuration that challenges automobile manufacturers, shoe companies, the makers of artificial breakfast drinks, or any other industry doing large-scale business in an advanced capitalist society.[2] The legacy of mass culture persists, however, as a peculiarly American dream: a vast population composed of functional robots survives the hours between work and sleep sprawled out across Naugahyde couches, its glazed eyes fixed on *The Love Boat* and *Fantasy Island*, while back in the city, a few crazed bohemians and diligent bookworms, mostly recruited from a barely visible class of surviving WASP gentlefolk and from

1

refugees from Nazi Europe, keep the flame of *Kultur* lit with tortured readings of Kafka and Pound. This is a transcendental dream that serves those who see the shoddiness of the twentieth century as its greatest evil. It is a nightmare, however, for those who hold out any hope for a future or for a role for democracy in it.

In 1924, just as promotion was beginning to surpass production as the central problem of industry, Waldo Frank observed that "America is European dada."[3] This comment may be helpful in explaining Marcel Duchamp's immigration to the United States; it is essential to an appreciation of Jerry Lewis's promotion to the rank of Commander of Arts and Letters by the French Ministry of Culture sixty years later. Little has happened since the 1920s to contradict Frank's contention: with neither a genetic aristocracy nor a socialist bureaucracy to assert balancing prerogatives, entrepreneurship has flourished relatively unfettered by questions of taste or propriety. An environment shaped by mass-production technologies has evolved in the service of corporate visions of mass consumption. This has yielded a unique form of cultural democracy that aspires to the ideal of every citizen having the right to buy anything that he or she believes will bring happiness—or at least some measure of relief from the pain of existence. Those with enough money can actually have the thing; those without sufficient credit can have a schlock imitation of it. In a short while, the haves may tire of the item and the have-nots are likely to find theirs broken. But what better conditions could be imagined for the introduction of new products? Madison Avenue has waged a relentless campaign to portray even the most bizarre and ethereal whims and notions as essential human culture in a struggle against nature; every odor, trait, and inclination has been improved upon at a reasonable price. Hollywood has offered an emphatically realistic art whose model is precisely this consumer utopia.

Looking out at the hamburger strip from behind the windshield in mounting traffic, a carefully targeted hit dictating the rhythm, one finds it difficult to ignore the parody of traditional European *Kultur* that throbs beneath the debris of day-to-day life in what Edmund Wilson called "the real, the live America of motor traffic."[4] McDonald's is, after all, a restaurant. A motel is a kind of hotel. An evening at a drive-in movie cannot fully escape the heritage of an evening at the theater. A shopping mall, though resplendent in ample parking, can trace its lineage to the downtown commercial district that was the center of community life during the urban era. Even a mobile-home park, easily accessible to the Interstate, with its laundromat, 7-Eleven store, and pay phone, owes a debt to the idea of a city. What happened to these nineteenth-century middle-class cultural institutions that caused them to mutate in such bizarre fashion in twentieth-century America? Is the physical environment spawned by a new technology always driven to mock the culture of the technology that preceded it? Is there an inherent disjunction in the evolution of cultural form that automatically turns the new into a crazed imitation of the familiar?

At the dawn of the industrial revolution in eighteenth-century Britain, several writers, notably Alexander Pope and Jonathan Swift, were among the first to realize that the age-old balance of cultural power that had isolated most people from literate expression was threatened by a radical shift in the technological environment.[5] The new economic order of mercantile capitalism demanded a broad-based clerking class in possession of the requisite skills to process contracts and keep the books. But while this made it necessary to train increasing numbers of people to read and write in order to conduct business, there was neither economic need nor sufficient social inclination to teach the newly literate to read Homer, St. Thomas Aquinas, the Elizabethan poets, or any of the writers whose works were considered essential to a genteel education. Denied access to the classical canon, the aesthetic energies unleashed by literacy shopped elsewhere for satisfaction. The "penny press" that grew up around London's Grub Street became, in effect, the first Hollywood—a primitive commercial community devoted entirely to the production of inexpensive, mechanically reproducible appeals to the emotional and imaginative urges of any and all who would pay for the product.[6]

The old literati watched in horror as advances in printing technology turned the written word from a rarefied treasure of the court elite into a marketplace commodity. Not surprisingly, "serious" writers (those educated in, and loyal to, Western literary traditions) responded to the "scribblers" with the weapons at hand, producing wild satires of the new literature. Pope, a translator of Greek classics and an editor of Shakespeare, was merciless in his attacks on the "babbling blockheads" of Grub Street.[7] In *The Dunciad* (that is, "The Epic of the Dunce") the poet imagines the fate of the life of the mind during the millenial rule of the Goddess Dullness (a personification of what would later be called mass culture):

> Beneath her foot-stool, *Science* groans in Chains,
> And *Wit* reads Exile, Penalities and Pains.
> There foam'd rebellious *Logic*, gagg'd and bound,
> There, stript, fair *Rhet'ric* languish'd on the ground.[8]

In *Gulliver's Travels*, Swift parodies a burgeoning pop literature that prefigures modern American supermarket tabloids such as the *National Enquirer* and the *Star*, publications whose readers are no strangers to encounters with midgets, giants, talking animals, and aliens. Voyaging to Balnibarbi, a nation populated exclusively by scientists, Gulliver visits the exalted seat of higher learning, the Academy of Lagado. The Balnibarbians, who maintain their country on a cloud suspended above the earth so as not to get contaminated by germs, are busily engaged in research aimed at scientifically processing human feces into reusable food. The relationship between economy and taste implied by the academy's experiments in high-tech nutrition anticipates the dilemma of the modern consumer reading the ingredient labels of the products for sale in a gleaming state-of-the-art supermarket.

Those twentieth-century intellectuals who are still able to prescribe distinctions between culture and consumption are, like Pope and Swift, put on the defensive when confronted by evolving communications technologies. Throughout the nineteenth century, a culture of subsistence literacy prolif-erated as basic reading skills extended across class lines. The realistic prose novel displaced the verse epic, carrying the read-ing of imaginative fiction outside the walls of the palace. This phenomenon reached what can be seen as its popular apogee with the publication of Dickens's novels as mass-circulation newspaper serials in the 1880s. In the realm of nonfiction, daily newspapers and popular magazines created a rhetoric for the mass discussion of politics, history, and culture.

In the twentieth century, however, even as the number of leisure hours was increasing, nonvocational usage of literacy went into decline. The narrative motion picture relieved the novel of the lion's share of popular storytelling duties, while radio gradually established itself as the clearinghouse of public information (that is, rhetoric). Since the end of World War II, television has synthesized these functions into a single medium. While Pope, Swift, Henry Fielding, and Laurence Sterne were provoked to their eighteenth-century satires by the "bad reading" made possible by the historical marriage of inexpensive printing and cheap literacy, the worst-case scenario for contemporary intellectuals is not so much bad reading as the prospect of no reading at all. Peter Conrad expresses the tone of highbrow response to this problem in his book *Television: The Medium and Its Manners*:

> In the Oxford college to which I belong, a television set has been supplied for the delectation of the brain-weary dons. It's hidden away in a musty chamber, bottling up the fug of defunct cigars, called the smoking room. In a corner of that room, it stands, masquerading as a Gothic cocktail cabinet, concealed behind panels of fretted wood which have to be opened out like an altar diptych to disclose the screen. People sometimes scuttle across the quad after dark to watch it, conscious (in their furtiveness) that in doing so they're neglecting their pedagogic chores, and the set they watch is as ashamed as they are.[9]

As the cultural primacy of reading continues to diminish, the literary priest class of professors and critics, sensing the disintegration of its constituency, begins to dote on the very form of the printed word. Daniel Defoe's *Robinson Crusoe*, the melodramatic adventure that inspired Swift to the barbed parody of *Gulliver's Travels*, is now itself piously enshrined in the curriculum as a "classic"; after all, it is centuries old and its "adventure" qualities might capture the interest of nonmajors. Though an occasional movie or even TV program of quality may be discovered—usually as if by accident—the chief effect attributed to the electronic nonprint media is theft of the cultural limelight from books. As punishment for constituting this barbaric threat to civilization and tenure, the popular arts are categorically exiled from the continuity of cultural history to the shadowy sociological twilight zone of mass culture. Intellectuals of strikingly diverse political orientations—from Dwight Macdonald to Herbert Marcuse on the left, from T. S. Eliot to José Ortega y Gassett on the right—have assured the twentieth century that mass culture stands outside the continuity of the history of human expression as a kind of evil anticulture, a monolithic hypnotist whose purpose is to homogenize our taste (Macdonald), rob us of our traditions (Eliot), lobotomize our erotic impulses (Marcuse), and steal prerogative from the worthy (Ortega). This perception of "culture" and "the mass media" as separate adversarial entities dueling for the attention spans and the souls of the audience is widely held among intellectuals and educators. It has only served to increase the intimacy of the relationship most Americans enjoy with their sets. Barbara Tuchman spoke for many modern intellectuals when she related in the New York *Times*, with great mortification, a story concerning an English teacher at an "affluent suburban" high school who devoted a week of class time to the study of television. "This," wrote the outraged Tuchman, "in the literature of Shakespeare to Mark Twain, Jane Austen to J. D. Salinger!"[10] One wonders if Tuchman is aware that Twain and, indeed, American literature itself were dismissed as "pop culture" and kept out of most American college curricula until well into the twentieth century. Would she have sided with the radicals who founded the Modern Language Association in the 1880s?

Tuchman's position is at the heart of the refusal of most university humanities departments to allow the critical study of the American electronic arts, despite the fact that they have become the major vessels of the language. The life, death, or revised meaning of a word, phrase, construction, or inflection is today largely determined by its usage in mass communications. This is especially true of English, a language that has never been under the formal direction of an official academy, but has instead depended upon the evolving conventions of common parlance for its grammar. An English department that

6

limits the definition of the language to the sum of its (well) written documents is clinging to an honorific title; it could more honestly call itself a literature department.

In *Media and the American Mind*, Daniel Czitrom describes the reaction of American intellectuals to new communications technologies in terms of a ritual: A new invention—the wireless radio, the movie camera, television—is patented. At first, intellectuals welcome it as a panacea that will universalize the distribution of information, bringing democracy, at long last, to full blossom. Entrepreneurs, however, soon get hold of the marvel and commercialize it for the sale of popular fantasies. The common denominator prevails. Millions are seduced; none are uplifted. Angered and frustrated, the intellectuals get revenge by refusing to confer the status of art upon the burgeoning form. Instead, they relegate it to the humanistic scrap heap as a "communications technology" whose "messages" are best left for study to psychologists and sociologists who specialize in the analysis of the "mass mind." But the medium is finally saved from this fate when a new invention spawns a new medium that is even more contemptible than the one it is about to replace as the central narrative instrument of the culture. The social scientists, whose only text is "the masses," move on to explore the "effects" of the new medium. As public interest in the old medium decreases, however, a suspicion grows among certain partisans of the humanities that there may be an aesthetic dimension to it after all. The grandest example of this is the elevation of the movies to the status of a respectable art form in America—a development that took place in direct correlation to the rise and proliferation of television during the 1950s.[11]

Throughout the country's history, many American writers—Henry James, Henry Adams, Ezra Pound, and T. S. Eliot among them—have voiced their disdain in no uncertain terms for both the substance and symbols of the mindless semiliterate mass society to which they believe America lost its cultural possibilities. Finding none of the joy in heterogeneity that led Walt Whitman to exclaim, "The United States themselves are essentially the greatest poem,"[12] such writers turned their hearts and souls away from the formlessness of the New World and dedicated themselves to the cultivation of Old World attitudes and the critical recovery of Western civilization. Eliot, the Missouri-born poet who repatriated himself to the United Kingdom in the 1920s, wrote a manifesto for this point of view in his 1948 essay, "Notes Towards the Definition of Culture." Culture, Eliot concludes, can thrive only where there is cosmic tribal consensus based on national religious unity and a serene social order built upon universal respect for class hierarchy.[13] America, a nation founded with the energies of religious eccentricity and built upon an economic system institutionally dependent on universal dissatisfaction with personal status, is structurally doomed to become a grotesque cultural monster.

Other writers, while mindful of its dangers, have displayed a more bemused ambiguity toward American culture. There is an inkling of this in so conservative a novel as *The Great Gatsby*. F. Scott Fitzgerald's narrator, Nick Carraway, is a recent Yale graduate from an old Minnesota family. When confronted with modern culture in the form of a wild party in Harlem, he comments, "I was within and without, simultaneously enchanted and repelled by the inexhaustible varieties of life."[14] Though Fitzgerald paints a picture of emerging twentieth-century mass society that is as bleak as Eliot's wasteland, Nick's ambiguity is a significant departure from Eliot's ineluctably tragic vision of modern life. Beneath alienation and denial there is at least the possibility of celebration.[15] Since 1945, many of the best American novels, while dutifully painting a frightening enough picture of modern life, betray a profound appreciation of the culture's absurd charms: "To any other type of tourist accommodation," sighs Vladimir Nabokov's Humbert Humbert, "I soon grew to prefer the Functional Motel—clean, neat, safe nooks, ideal places for sleep, argument, reconciliation, insatiable illicit love."[16]

As is the case with Lolita herself, America's disjunction from culture is as seductive as it is exasperating. In *On the Road*, Jack Kerouac's Dean Moriarty does not forfeit his individuality to mass society but instead becomes an avatar of the erotic possibilities of the machine age. The automobile, in addition to destroying the city, the land, and the respiratory system, becomes both the way and the place to get laid. Among recent American writers perhaps no one has shown as much contempt for mass culture or as much taste for what it has to offer as Norman Mailer. His biographies of Marilyn Monroe and Gary Gilmore are nothing less than epic sagas of redneck America's life in the electronic theme park, of mass communiculture. In the final chapter of *An American Dream*, Mailer's Stephen Rojack—Harvard graduate, former congressman, professor of existential psychology, and TV talk-show host—takes a cancerous trip "out West, driving through the landscape of Super-America . . . freeways, motor lodges, winged motel inns, the heated pools."[17] In the outskirts of Las Vegas, the very Mecca of modern schlock, Rojack pauses at the heart of ambiguity, seeing before him "a jeweled city on the horizon, spires rising in the night, but the jewels were diadems of electric and the spires were the neon of signs ten stories high."[18]

The capacity to experience, even for a moment, the comic beauty of America as "a jeweled city" before falling prey to the tragedy of the poison gases lurking beneath the surface is what allows Rojack to keep his sanity. Though the end of the novel finds him planning to leave techno-America in search of the unspoiled root of the New World in the jungles of the Yucatán, Rojack, like Humbert and Dean, has the strength to claim some measure of personal-erotic satisfaction and thus survive the deadly inanities of the machine-made society.

For these would-be survivors of the twentieth century, America becomes, simultaneously, a dehumanized, cultural concentration camp and a fecund surrealistic junkyard—two prismatically related possibilities fighting for control of consciousness. When the barren, lonely vision of the former dominates, it is some comfort to remember that while each continent has had its share of both, America has managed the greater reputation for junkyards, while Europe has shown a genius for the camps. At the same time, if the gorgeousness of the automobile stereo giving good bass at seventy miles per hour get out of hand, one can always switch on The News.

The News

While earlier discoveries of the world by Western imaginations may have required the excitement of the epic to order their exhilarations or the reversals and recognitions of tragedy to give meaning to their anxieties, the latest discoveries have been so completely depressing, so utterly baffling to any remnant of optimism that may still reassert itself in youth like some vestigial second heart, that laughter has become the mark of courage. The News makes itself available twenty-four hours a day by radio, by television, by newspaper, and by everyone who listens to, watches, and reads it. Logic compellingly dictates how this mammoth narrative must climax. With such a vast stockpile of weapons poised to do the job, gravity itself is likely to depress the button if no one beats it to the punch. Son marries mother? Prince fails to avenge father? What are these to those of us facing *The Day After*?

The freak show that freely emerges beneath the sword of Damocles while cruising down superhighways through crumbling cities, or watching special "theme" episodes of *Family Feud*, or listening to descriptions of the day's murders to pass the time in traffic jams, or hopelessly scanning the cable channels by remote control is, like any carnival, at once insulting to the learned traditions of Western sensibility and a release from the deathwatch that modern life has become. The choice between tragedy and comedy is underlined by this problem of selective perception. While fictive tragedy has been trivialized by descriptive reportage, the joke's the thing that puts despair in the service of endurance.

It is perhaps in this spirit that Dr. Derrick de Kerckhove, the director of the Marshall McLuhan Program in Culture and Technology at the University of Toronto, has characterized thermonuclear weaponry as "the ultimate information medium."[19] Indeed, the message of this hottest of media is straight to the point and easily decodable without the aid of semioticians: The capacity for murder has not only survived the current level of technology but has found in it a realistic scenario for the delivery of a pièce de résistance. All that is familiar sits squarely in the sights of a loaded gun. Culture and nature, estranged since the exile of Adam, are ironically reunited as victims of this common threat. In 1945, only several months after the atomic attacks on Japan, the editors of *Reader's Digest* perceptively observed that all of humanity had become "fused unbreakably in the diabolical heat of those explosions."[20]

With civilization at the other end of a burning fuse, the burden of individual mortality can no longer be mitigated by a sense of participation in a grand, permanently accreting cultural history. Religion, which suffered during much of the industrial revolution as an antagonist of both unbridled technological expansion and the pursuit of leisure-time sex, is enjoying a comeback among human generations that know they are capable of the ultimate sin. Nineteenth-century humanists, such as Matthew Arnold, held out the hope that culture might act as a fortress to protect what is beautiful and noble from the brutal storms of history. But what fortress is likely to withstand the firestorm? The creatures frequenting the libraries left standing on a nuclear winter's day may be more disposed to eat the books than read them. "You can't do what you want with the bomb," notes Dr. de Kerckhove. "The bomb does what it wants to you."[21]

The market value of comedy ascends in the face of a plausible end to history. Religions offering their subscribers the happy ending of Heaven have surely benefited from this introduction of a permanent state of crisis concerning a future for the earth. Secular humanists, on the other hand, have defined themselves by their preference for art over religion. Is the imagination capable of finding a force short of an omnipotent, omniscient being that can save humanity from committing suicide? The bomb, as those of us who live at its disposal so familiarly call it, stands guard over civilization. Humor, not tragic empathy, offers would-be survivors the possibility of catharsis. What will it be while waiting for the end? Faithful contemplation of the hereafter? A nihilistic rediscovery of the satisfactions of personal violence? The pursuit of amnesia? Or the laugh that the victim reserves for the tormentor? All of these strategies have their advocates.

Stand-up and Sitcom

A drama—comic or otherwise, live or recorded—asks an audience to willingly suspend its disbelief, to forget that what it is seeing is artifice and contrivance. In return for the sacrifice of its better judgment, the audience is promised psychic transportation to a dimension of consciousness where terror, chaos, insecurity, and other fearful states are always experienced through the cushions of identification and sympathy and where laughter and other expressions of pleasure are relatively safe from humiliation and guilt. Relieved for a few hours of the relentless primacy of the biological urge to survive, normally suppressed aspects of the imagination may emerge from hiding to recreate the self. When both artist and audience are up to the task, humankind is to be congratulated for its stunning capacities; the high prices of theater tickets, movie seats, and cable services suddenly seem trivial. But, of course, not very many dramas are that good, and it is particularly hard to achieve a total experience with an illusion that is repeatedly deflated by commercial punctuation. This is the tremendous sadness of television and, to varying degrees, all of popular culture. Supply-side art is offered at a bargain, but—*caveat emptor*—you get what you pay for.

Among the forms of comedy that have publicly flourished in the United States under the conditions that have emerged since 1945, two general types have come to dominate: stand-up comedy and situation comedy. Aesthetically at odds, these two genres of mass humor form a Janus face of American culture. Stand-up is a surviving bastion of individual expression. The comedian confronts the audience with his or her personality and wins celebration—the highest form of acceptance—or is scorned and rebuffed as a pitiable outsider. The heckler, the mood of the audience, or the temperature of the room cannot always be handled through quality control. Even when presented electronically, the jokes of a stand-up monologue cannot be underlined by canned laughter without the manipulation thoroughly exposing itself. In *The Entertainment Machine*, Robert Toll recalls how this became evident in the early days of radio:

The first major adjustment all stage comedians faced in radio was the empty studio. All their performing lives they had learned to play to live audiences, responding to laughs, adjusting their timing and material, and catching the audience up in the infectious quality of laughter. So, in early radio, comedians demanded live studio audiences, which allowed comics like [Ed] Wynn and [Eddie] Cantor to retain their physical humor and to assume that if they made the studio audience laugh they would also make the folks at home laugh, even though they couldn't see what was happening.[22]

The sitcom, by contrast, is the technology of the assembly-line brought to art. Even when live audiences are used, their reactions are "sweetened" with carefully calculated titters, chortles, and guffaws. Large sums of investment capital must be assembled to produce a sitcom; all factors must be controlled by recognized experts. The sitcom has no tank towns to tour, but is always a nationally marketed product whose "effects" are tested on "sample" consumers and refined accordingly. A complex system of checks and balances among advertisers, networks, and production companies continuously negotiates problems of textual dissent while the audience is kept at arm's length. A sitcom cannot suffer the massive sting of active rejection; its audience cannot boo or throw tomatoes. It is canceled only by indifference, and a perceived or projected indifference (the ratings) at that.

Stand-up comedy continues to expose itself to human contact, and there is a heroic quality to this in the nuclear age. It is an art of the bravado personality in a world being organized to and for death. The cult of the wiseguy is brought to the formal dimensions of art. If the threat of atomic doom has reduced us to powerless resentful children awaiting punishment, it is difficult to resist the bigmouth who can spit in the eye of civilization with a bit of grace (though the wince is unbearable when the attempt is feeble). Without the protection of the formal mask of a narrative drama, without a song, dance, or any other intermediary composition that creates distance between performer and performance, without even, necessarily, some remarkable physical trait or ability to gratuitously display, the stand-up comedian addresses an audience as a naked self, eschewing the luxury of a clear-cut distinction between art and life. Good actors can be singled out of bad plays; good singers can put over bad songs. But in the case of the stand-up comedian, there is no dividing medium from message. When performing stand-up comedy, Steve Martin is Steve Martin is Steve Martin. ("Many people ask me, 'Steve, are you a ramblin' kind of guy?'")

Owing largely to the extra tensions created by the purposeful confusion of "play world" and "real world," few spectacles in modern show business are as compelling as the successful stand-up controlling the physical responses of a large group of people with the power of language. A monologue, like a sermon, asks the anonymous members of the assembly to spontaneously merge into a single emotional organism capable of reacting uniformly to the metaphor, wisdom, and worldview of one appointed personality.[23] By the same token, because of the massive investment of ego by the comedian, few public spectacles are as pathetic as the stand-up laying an egg—straining with the very inflections of the voice for the unambiguous response of the laugh, while suffering the brutality of mass rejection.

Though it can be argued that all public figures are vulnerable to grand expressions of public acceptance and rejection, the exposure of the stand-up comic to public judgment is extraordinarily raw and personal. The politician, by contrast, may cloak his or her ego in the defensive armor of party, ideology, or nation. Richard Nixon's resignation, for example, was played this way.[24] It was not Nixon who had performed poorly, but rather an ever-widening collection of supporting players. The hardworking, competent, innocent star had been victimized by a bunch of clowns from central casting, his only crime a benevolent failure to exercise full artistic control. The closing of the show was not a bowing to the demands of the critics, nor was it an admission of guilt; the hero assures us he would have preferred to stay in office and clear his name. The resignation was, rather, a selfless attempt to maintain the credibility of the institutions and policies with which the man had identified himself: the Republican party, international "détente," benign neglect of domestic civil rights, and the office of the presidency of the United States. The show must go on. Nixon painted a picture of himself as a veritable martyr to these causes in his 1977 television interview series with David Frost.[25] More than a decade after his resignation, the only president in American history to resign from office continued to explain his victimization at the hands of others, even making orchestrated public appearances in front of friendly crowds. Don Rickles, however, cannot walk off stage after a failed routine pleading a higher devotion to insult humor. The audience either laughs at the jokes or leaves the monologist to die.

Most dictionaries, including the usually authoritative *Oxford English Dictionary*, offer no definition at all of stand-up comedy.

14

The supplemental *Oxford American Dictionary* does contain a brief secondary reference to the phenomenon under an entry for "stand-up" (as in "He's a real stand-up guy"): "3. (of a comedian) performing (often while standing) alone on stage." This definition is inadequate and potentially misleading. If accepted, such performers as Marcel Marceau, David Copperfield, and the Amazing Kreskin would have to be classified as stand-up comedians. But though mimes, magicians, mind readers, and other assorted specialty acts do perform certain types of comedy while standing alone on a stage, they are not performing stand-up comedy.

The lack of a workable definition of stand-up comedy is a serious problem that undermines what little criticism of the art form has been written. In a 1985 article in the *American Quarterly* titled "Stand-up Comedy as Cultural and Social Mediation," Lawrence Mintz writes that stand-up comedy is arguably "the oldest, most universal, basic, and deeply significant form of humorous expression."[26] The readers's hopes that a Neanderthal stand-up comedian has been uncovered remain, however, unredeemed. The critic's assertions lose their meanings as we see the term "stand-up comedy" used as a catchall for a wide range of comic forms. Examples of stand-up comedy cited in the article include Jackie Gleason's Poor Soul (a dramatic pantomime), Bob Hope's character in the *Road* movies (a fictive dramatic persona), and Robin Williams' performance in *Mork and Mindy*.[27] At one point, Mintz writes of a "legion of transvestites" who are stand-ups, but offers no examples. While he could have pointed to Flip Wilson's Geraldine as one instance of this, female impersonation is almost always presented in the form of a parodic musical showcase and could only be called stand-up comedy in the loosest sense.

A useful definition of stand-up comedy must go beyond both the *OED*'s perfunctory gloss and Mintz's belief that a definition should merely "stress relative directness of artist/audience communication."[28] I would argue that the *absolute* "directness of artist/audience communication" is the definitive feature of the art and that its primary structural element is the comic monologue, a collection of verbal jokes that may be augmented by physical gags. The component jokes and gags of the monologue are tied together either by a common textual theme or, more often, by a series of tangential connectors called segues. Most important, the monologue is a freestanding presentation rather than a part of a narrative drama. While, as Mintz notes parenthetically, the informal telling of jokes surely can be dated to the advent of human linguistic competence, professional joke telling that is utterly divorced from any narrative or larger oratorical context is a rather recent phenomenon, historically tied to the rise of mass culture. Born in the larger contexts of minstrelsy, vaudeville, the medicine show, and the public lecture during the late nineteenth and early twentieth centuries, stand-up comedy came to form in the resort hotels and urban nightclubs of the mid-twentieth century, gradually adapting to the technological refinements of radio, phonograph records, and television.

Previous to the cultural dominance of the mass-production marketplace, the formal requirements of classical discourse had put severe limits on the gratuitous telling of jokes by demanding that all public speeches, comic or otherwise, justify themselves by the didactic promotion of ethical or religious lessons. Adherence to this guideline—at the threat of censure—not only prevented orators from directly mocking the policies of the state or the mores of the ruling class and its culture but also precluded the presentation of a speech whose sole purpose was to make an audience laugh. As early as the fifth century B.C., however, these restrictions on comic discourse were being circumvented in spirit by Greek dramatists. Playwrights, including Aristophanes and Euripides, managed to work politically satiric references into their plays by allegorizing current events (that is, The News) into fictional settings, a convention well understood by the audience. By swaddling jokes in the blankets of a drama, an artist could get away with things that would be considered vulgar or even mortally offensive had they been presented to the audience in direct first-person address. To this day, drama has a better time of it than stand-up comedy in totalitarian and authoritarian societies.

Though it has never quite achieved the status of the epic or of tragedy in Western culture, comedy has certainly been valued and admired by critics when "properly" presented as drama, satiric poetry, or (in recent times) the novel. But the bald-faced telling of jokes in public—divorced from these traditional contexts—has, like most mass-culture phenomena, generally been considered a vulgarity not even worthy of back-row admission to the hierarchy of forms. This exclusion may be motivated by several factors. The stand-up's refusal to respect sharp distinctions between the play world and the real world results in the violation of a primary convention of Western theater. The audience is explicitly asked *not* to suspend its disbelief. Instead, it is challenged to hold fast to both its literal and figurative assumptions and to test the comic's wit against them. The audience knows that Joan Rivers has a plain figure and a distaste for Britain's equestrian royalty; that Lily Tomlin is a feminist; that Richard Pryor is a black man living in America; and that Robert Klein, Richard Lewis, and Richard Belzer are crazed, hyperactive Jews with high IQ's from New York. As is the case with professional wrestlers, the mask cannot be pried loose from the face of the performer. There are no perceptible differences in the personae of any of these stand-ups when they are "speaking candidly" in interview situations, as opposed to when they are "performing." This may be particularly distressing for the sensibility that continues to hold out hope of discovering order in the universe through art.

Another aspect of stand-up comedy that may put off honorable critics is the totalitarian imagery suggested by the stand-up comedy spectacle. By addressing the audience directly and demanding its personal response, the stand-up comedian may appear to be a formal cousin to the feared circle of TV news reporters, game-show hosts and commercial pitchpeople who daily address the viewership-citizenry as the voices of information, authority, power, and connection. The mass hysteria engendered by a particularly successful (that is, hilarious) monologue may even conjure hallucinations of Mussolini working the crowd from a terrace. But this is a bum rap. These and other hobgoblins of mass culture take advantage of institutional masks to manipulate the viewer: a TV reporter is presented as a conduit for The News and, as such, is above responsibility for its content (that is a responsibility that can only be pinned on fate or God); a game-show host simply presides over the playing of the game and cannot be held responsible for the champion's performance during the big-money round. Who can say if a commercial is lying? After all, it's on television and there must be some truth to it, or they wouldn't let them say it. Dictators mask their lusts for power as the duties of divine missions and appointments with destiny. But the honesty of the stand-up comedian is tested with each joke every bit as much as the honesty of the novelist by each sentence and the honesty of the painter by each stroke.

As a consequence of the stand-up's direct address to the audience, the layerings of person and persona are more difficult to unravel than in representational drama. Just as an actor wears a costume in a play, a stand-up can present an image by dressing like a beatnik (George Carlin), like a businessman (Bob Hope), like a well-to-do aunt at a bar mitzvah (Joan Rivers), or in whatever style or demographic uniform he or she chooses. However, for the stand-up, self is text to a much greater degree than for the dramatic comedian. Fatness, skinniness, shortness, tallness, beauty, ugliness, race, class, ethnicity, and/or whatever other visible or audible baggage the comedian carries in life is not merely fair game for exploitation on the stage but a textual feature of the act that demands use—or requires avoidance. A talented young stand-up named Louie Anderson, for example, is about fifty pounds overweight and he "uses" this in conventional stand-up style. Waiting an extra two beats before coming out on stage after his introduction, he opens with this apology: "Sorry I'm late folks, but I'm in between meals." Anderson makes quick use of the tensions of obesity—tensions that he cannot strip off like makeup after the show—to galvanize the audience's focus on him. Like a medieval eunuch who flaunts his sexual impotence by wearing a hat of flaccid jingling phalluses, a modern American fat person demonstrates a powerful mastery over social convention by actively calling attention to his presumably deviant and deficient condition. This might be compared to the Zuni Indian shaman who opens his presentation by drinking urine.[29] Such a personality seems to know no fear of humiliation and thus appears to be dangerously outside the boundaries of social control. Anderson doesn't restrict himself to fat jokes. But by opening his act with one, he indicates to the audience that he is a psychological daredevil capable of saying things that most of them would not consider saying in public.

The contrast between the boldness of stand-up comedy and the ameliorative structure of dramatic comedy had a significant impact in shaping the character of American commercial television in the 1950s. The rise of early TV stand-up comedians such as Milton Berle, Jack Carter, Martha Raye, and George Gobel in stage-show variety formats was meteoric but brief. By the mid-sixties the comedy-variety show—the great vehicle of these pioneer stars—was disappearing from prime-time television. Of the few successful TV variety shows that have aired since that time, most have been hosted by singers (for example, *Sonny and Cher*, *Tony Orlando and Dawn*, *Donny and Marie*). Stand-up comedy was to a great degree exiled from prime-time to late-night talk shows and morning game shows (genres at the margins of the daily television schedule), while the sitcom became the most enduring and popular of all prime-time television genres.

In the early days of network television, before the stratification of commercial TV forms had crystallized, several shows toyed with mutant forms that crossed various elements of stand-up comedy with situation comedy. For example, the insertion of satiric stand-up monologues into self-consciously banal dramatic plots was a prominent feature of *The George Burns and Gracie Allen Show* (CBS, 1950–58). Ralph Levy, one of the show's creators, remembers its humble genesis: "We evolved the idea for the show: a simple situation comedy with the cut-out set of the Burns's house, and another one for their neighbors, and, downstage, an area where George could stand and talk directly to the audience, to explain about his wife, Gracie, predict what was going to happen, and to comment on his daily life in and around their neighborhood."[30] But the results were far from simple. Though *Burns and Allen* presents itself as a comic drama, it denies the gap between art and life. George Burns appears in the program not only as sitcomic husband, father and neighbor but also as cynical self-reflexive narrator as well. In the opening credits, he stands in front of a proscenium arch, puffing cigar smoke at the superimposed titles, as if to make fun of the flimsiness of representational illusion. After the first commercial, however, George and the viewer have been transported into the familiar cosmos of 1950s

19

Southern California sitcomland. Here, George and Gracie are indeed played by Burns and Allen, but their next-door neighbor Blanche is played by second-banana Bea Benaderet. Moreover, Blanche's husband Harry Morton could very well be any one of four actors who played the part, depending upon what phase the syndication cycle is in. We learn that Harry Von Zell (playing himself), a frequent visitor to George and Gracie's comfortable if modest sitcom home, is the announcer for something called *The Burns and Allen Show*, which may or may not be the same television show the viewer is watching.

On its narrative surface, *Burns and Allen* seems very much like any of a dozen sitcoms of the era. The archetypal domestic setups are all in place: women versus men, neighbor versus neighbor, young versus old. Among these situations, as is the case in most domesticoms, spouse conflict dominates. Like Lucy in *I Love Lucy*, Gracie schemes and plots to get her show-business husband to buy her mink coats and take her on vacations. The chaos that Lucy delivers with body language, Gracie accomplishes verbally. Blanche, like Ethel, functions as sidekick, sounding board, and one-woman support group for the machinations of the terminally zany female star. Harry Morton is a snobby, genteel accountant from Boston, generally alienated from the other characters, all of whom are "normal"—that is, satisfied, Californianized customers of mass culture. Harry's high culture sensibility is especially exasperated by George, a proud veteran of vaudeville who gladly admits ignorance of the classics. (It is interesting to note that the *Burns and Allen* writing staff included Paul Henning, who would bring the just-plain-folks versus pretentious gentility conflict to ground zero several years later as creator and producer of *The Beverly Hillbillies*.) George and Gracie's son, Ronnie (Ronnie Burns), rounds out the regular cast of characters. He is cut from the same sitcom cloth as a Ricky Nelson or a Bud Anderson—an all-American teenager who loves cars, sports, and going out on dates with girls but whose youthful enthusiasm can land him in awful fixes. None of these problems, however, is too big for the bottomless well of love and understanding that is the heart of middle-class sitcom America.

All of this is adequately inane. It's a whole different story, however, when George turns away from the other characters to address the viewer directly. Punching a hole through the proscenium, he motions to the camera for a close-up. Sitcomic drama lapses into a state of suspended animation as George is instantly transformed from character to narrator, from third-person representation to presentational personality. Placidly puffing his cigar, he offers the audience a stand-up routine that usually begins as a bit of impromptu *explication de texte* on the narrative development of the episode, then segues to an associative digression, and ends with a joke whose relationship to the studied suburbo-realism of the plot is utterly subversive:

> So Ronnie wants ten dollars for "books." I know he just wants the money to take out that pretty Bonnie Sue McAfee. Ten dollars! When I was a kid that's how much your old man gave you to get married—and he expected you to open a business with what you had left over. Anyway, I'll give him the ten bucks. If I don't, the plot will fall apart and we won't be able to get on with the rest of the show and that means the sponsor'll kill me.

The Burns and Allen Show reaches the height of its surrealistic confusion of presentation and representation when George retires to his den and turns on the television to see what the other characters are up to: Gracie is over at the Mortons' house, telling Blanche and Harry Von Zell how she's going to get George to take her to visit her mother in San Francisco.

"Gracie's having an awful lot of trouble explaining this scheme to Blanche. Maybe I'd better save everyone—including me—some trouble," George wonders aloud. He reaches for the telephone and dials. Blanche picks up the receiver on George's little TV screen within a TV screen. But before she can say a word, he matter-of-factly says, "Tell Gracie she doesn't have to convince me that there's going to be an earthquake in Beverly Hills this weekend; I'll take her to visit her mother in San Francisco." George smiles at the camera as an astounded Blanche tells Gracie the wonderful news on the tiny TV screen.

"I'm glad that's over with," announces George, "but now there's no story and we've still got some time left on the show.

Maybe there's something else on." He turns the channel to a cowboys-and-Indians movie; the cavalry is chasing thousands of screaming warriors on horseback. We watch this with George for about five or so seconds. Cut to commercial. The episode ends with Gracie stepping across the proscenium and joining George in a reprise of a Burns and Allen vaudeville routine.

The sudden switching of *The Burns and Allen Show* from radio (where it had played on NBC for seventeen seasons) to the CBS television schedule in 1950, a feat nonchalantly accomplished in a matter of months, may have contributed to the dislocated, absurdist tone of the series. But it was by no means the only early TV show that exploited the purposeful confusion of the "real lives" of its stars and their dramatic personae. *The Jack Benny Show* (CBS, 1950–64; NBC, 1964–65), another transplant from NBC radio, takes similar liberties with its mode of presentation. Benny opened his show each week standing in front of a curtain in classical stand-up style. After the first commercial he reappeared, still as Jack Benny but now "at home" (that is, in a sitcom), being attended to by his valet, Rochester (Eddie Anderson). *The Adventures of Ozzie and Harriet* (ABC, 1952–66), which had its beginning as a radio show in 1944, played yet another kind of balancing act with the art-life ratio. Like a troupe of professional wrestlers, the Nelsons transcended the conventions of the "fourth wall": "Ozzie, Harriet, David, and Ricky Nelson resided in a television house modeled on their real Hollywood home. On television, Ozzie was never acknowledged to have a job. He just seemed to hang around the house all the time, although we all knew he was an actor."[31] *The Stu Erwin Show* (ABC, 1950–55; syndicated as *The Trouble with Father*) an otherwise prototypical nuclear-family sitcom, provides yet another type of example. Its star, Stu Erwin, is played by Stu Erwin, but other members of the Erwin family are actors who play characters with fictitious names.

The practice of identifying actor and persona as a single entity in comic drama had almost completely died out by the 1960s, with the continued use of a star's first name (Danny Thomas as "Danny Williams," Andy Griffith as "Andy Taylor," Lucille Ball as "Lucy Ricardo," "Lucy Carmichael," and "Lucy Carter") surviving as a kind of legacy until the end of the decade. Though several subversive narrators were tried in sitcoms after *Burns and Allen*, the power of the device was sacrificed as it was stretched to hyperbolically absurd extremes. On *The People's Choice* (NBC, 1955–58), Socrates Miller (Jackie Cooper) plays an ecology-minded resident of a mobile-home park who gets elected to the city council and falls in love with the conservative mayor's daughter, eventually marrying her and becoming a real estate agent. Cleo, Sock's pet basset hound, serves as the cynical narrator, pointing out the silly foibles of the human beings while directing plot traffic. Cleo's messages to the audience are delivered by a kind of mental telepathy that is signaled with a close-up of her droopy-eyed face beneath a female voice-over. NBC tried a similar vehicle, *Happy*, in 1960–61, with a baby in the dog's role, but it didn't last the season. In the 1970s, Jim Henson revived several of these long-dormant TV techniques in *The Muppet Show* (syndicated, 1976–1981). Knotting representation and presentation, *The Muppet Show*, like *Burns and Allen* or the *Benny* show, is essentially a sitcom whose characters are the stars of a TV variety show and whose plots are based on the problems of preparing material. Kermit the Frog serves as self-reflexive narrator.

Other pioneer TV comedians, such as Jackie Gleason, Sid Caesar, and Red Skelton, made use of the blackout sketch on their comedy-variety hours to move back and forth between stand-up and sitcom. Each created, in effect, an anthological collection of ongoing situation comedies. Skelton's characters included Freddie the Freeloader, Sheriff Redeye, and the Mean Whiddle Kid. Usually, an entire episode of the *The Red Skelton Show* (NBC, 1951–1953, 1970–71; CBS, 1953–1970) was given over to a playlet involving one of these characters, with Skelton appearing in stand-up before and after the representational drama as a kind of framing device.

Sid Caesar tended to perform in front of the curtain more than Skelton. Characters such as the German Professor and Giuseppe Marinara, the Italian film critic, gave Caesar the chance to display his considerable talents as a mime and a dialect comedian. But *Your Show of Shows* (NBC, 1950–54) is best remembered for the sitcomlike sketches that paired Caesar with Imogene Coca as the middle-class suburban couple Charlie and Doris Hickenlooper. "The Hickenloopers," whose writers included Neil Simon, Woody Allen, Mel Brooks, and Carl Reiner, pioneered such soon-to-be-standard sitcom fare as the dented fender and the forgotten anniversary.

Similarly, Gleason achieved singular recognition for his portrayal of Ralph Kramden, though originally *The Honeymooners* was but one segment of a variety hour that included half a dozen sketch characters as well as stand-up sequences. It was only because this particular sketch was repackaged as a sitcom for a single TV season (CBS, 1955–56) that it was allowed the opportunity to enter the eternal TV pantheon in syndicated reruns. If it had not been, the Honeymooners might well have become as obscure to most viewers as other Gleason characters, such as the Poor Soul or the Bachelor. It is interesting to note that while the fat jokes delivered by Norton and Alice provide much of the energy that powers the *Honeymooners* scripts, obesity is a subject that is rarely broached by Gleason in the stand-up format.

Experiments notwithstanding, the sitcom has generally upheld the sanctity of the proscenium, and producers working in the genre have taken pains to respect the age-old tradition of grafting humor to moral suasion. This is as true of *Maude* and *WKRP in Cincinnati* as it is of *Diff'rent Strokes* and *Father Knows Best*. The stand-up monologue, despite its formal similarities to a church sermon or a political address, strays into the realm of didactic lecture only occasionally, and when it does, it produces the most ideologically charged work in all of American popular culture. But stand-up, unlike sitcom, retains the right to thumb its nose at didacticism. In most cases the comedian promises the audience nothing other than laughter and his or her performance is measured solely by this standard. The resulting spectacle is a highly intellectual effort aimed solely at stimulating the id.

Whereas sitcoms depend on familiarity, identification, and redemption of popular beliefs, stand-up comedy often depends on the shocking violation of normative taboos. Frank, intimate, first-person accounts of sex and sexuality, unabashed toilet talk, brutal self-deprecation, critical commentary on consumerist culture, and the relatively uninhibited airing of racial and ethnic stereotypes are just a few of the subjects at the center of stand-up discourse. The sitcom, despite several attempts to push it in deviant directions, insists on a portrayal of reality that can best be defended with statistics. It is worth noting that in the early 1970s, with the successes of *The Mary Tyler Moore Show*, *M*A*S*H*, and the Norman Lear programs, the sitcom went through a significant expansion of subject matter. But the character of that expansion tends to highlight the genre's unflappably centrist political psychology. Compare, for example, Don Rickles insulting a member of the audience on *The Tonight Show* to Archie Bunker making a racist remark on *All in the Family*:

Rickles, scanning the crowd with microphone in hand, walks up to a brown-skinned man and asks him to stand up, ostensibly to play "Stump the Band." "You're a Mexican-American, sir, a Chicano, aren't you, sir? Personally, I think the Chicanos are a very important people. My doctor told me that I've got to eat lettuce every day in order to stay regular. Without you people, everything comes to a halt—if you know what I mean." The line between outrage and catharsis remains momentarily blurry before the conventional recognition of Rickles' privileged status as a jester invokes itself. The audience—including the insulted person—laughs with great gusto. A moment of danger has passed: Rickles has broken taboo in mass-culture rhetoric. He has trivialized racism but in so doing has confirmed its normalcy.

In an episode of *All in the Family* titled "In-Law Indigestion," Cousin Oscar, a ne'er-do-well, dies while visiting Archie and Edith. Louise Jefferson, the Bunkers' black neighbor, comes over to pay her respects. Soon, several other neighbors ring the doorbell. "Edith, we got people coming," whines Archie. "See if you can get *her* [pointing at Mrs. Jefferson] to put on an apron and maybe they'll think she's the maid." The "live" television audience rhythmically responds, underlining the joke with a hearty laugh. There is, however, neither danger nor comfort. Archie's attitudes toward blacks, Mrs. Jefferson, and toward most of what he is likely to encounter are known entities. These attitudes ritually trotted out in the course of each episode, demonstrated for the public, and reverently put away. Archie . . . black woman . . . company coming . . . Louise . . . maid. Certainly!

Whatever one thinks of Don Rickles, it is difficult to ignore the powerful forces that are unleashed by his act. Race is the barometer by which daily spiritual pressure is measured in America. Apologizing one minute ("Of course, sir, you know I'm only kidding . . . "), undermining his apology the next (" . . . would you mind showing me your green card?"), Rickles dances back and forth across the lines of propriety in a charged mythopoeic field. Several years ago, at a restaurant in Little Italy, New York, I witnessed the comedian exercise his jester's privilege in "real life." The owner of the restaurant came out to personally present Mr. Rickles with the bill. Not missing a beat, Rickles took the check, held it high up in the air and announced in a booming voice to the entire restaurant, "See this? You'd better pay up around here or else it's a swim in the East River with the concrete shoes." The dozen private tables in the room were instantaneously galvanized into an audience. The moment of nervousness waxed and waned. The owner had his picture taken—hugging the star. Everybody laughed.

In *All in the Family*, racism is embedded as a character flaw of Archie, who is ultimately sympathetic, even lovable. There is an implicit assumption, fostered in part by Archie's constant malapropisms, that the audience—both the audience at home and its "live" surrogate—knows more than Archie and is therefore laughing at him and not with him. We can be confident that Norman Lear will punish Archie Bunker for his sins. Who will punish Don Rickles?

Acting and Acting Out

An art of the middle, the sitcom rarely reaches the psychological or political extremes that have been commonplace in other popular American comic genres such as the minstrel show, the silent film, or the stand-up monologue. Situation comedy tends to establish a range of comfortable emotions and familiar logics in whatever subject matter it addresses. This is most obvious in domesticoms—from *The Donna Reed Show* and *Father Knows Best* to *Family Ties* and *Kate and Allie*—where that comfort is offered both literally and figuratively in a physically spacious yet spiritually warm home.

But home in the sitcom is where the producer makes it. Relaxed domesticity is a state of mind, as casually effected at the front in World War II as in a single-unit detached dwelling on a suburban lane. The crew of *McHale's Navy*, bearing the mythic baggage of the cast of the film *Guadalcanal Diary*, spends the war water-skiing behind its PT boat. The boys meet nurses and even shelter a Japanese prisoner of war who becomes their beloved houseboy and chef. When they (the writers? the actors? the audience sample?) get tired of the South Pacific islands, they pack up the PT boat and move to occupied Italy. *Hogan's Heroes*, set smack in the middle of the European theater of war, imagines a World War II devoid of Nazis and Jews: a bit of Teutonic high jinks doomed to failure at the hands of a bunch of fair-minded, fun-loving guys from the Allied countrjes who just can't wait to get the darned thing over with and get on with the Marshall Plan, NATO, and the baby boom. Even aliens from outer space, who had caused such mass terror and panic in the cinema of the 1950s, were not to be feared in the sitcom. *My Favorite Martian*, playing in prime time when Steven Spielberg was still contending with junior high school algebra, turns out to be not only as demure a houseguest as ET, but he also speaks good English and levitates the heavy furniture while vacuuming. *Mork and Mindy* go Tim and Uncle Martin one better: after a proper modern live-in courtship, they marry and are blessed with the birth of Jonathan Winters. In the proto-yuppiecoms of the seventies (*Mary Tyler Moore*, *M*A*S*H*, et al.) reassurance comes in the form of a dramatic illusion in which humane values successfully cope with the burdens of modern life by means of ironic wit. This may be the most surrealistic vision of all. Even at the psychic edge of what has been possible in the sitcom—in the sanctum sanctorum of the Kramden apartment—there is steadfast, if slim, affirmation: overlooked for endless promotions, a failure at a hundred get-rich-quick schemes, penniless, childless, hopelessly overweight, aging without automobile, telephone, or furniture, Ralph survives on the strength of his "love" for Alice, a woman who does not hesitate to remind him that she is physically disgusted by him.[32] Though the restoration of harmony has traditionally been the denouement of comic drama, it is the sitcom's unfortunate mandate to be sloshing through the mud of postbomb cynicism with the happy ending strapped to its back.

Committed to a cordial relationship with a society that it must simultaneously depict and solicit, sitcoms are full of barbs at day-to-day human foibles. Penetration, however, is carefully measured. With roots in the millennia-old traditions of dramatic comedy, the sitcom first established an independent identity during the heyday of narrative radio. With the commercial abandonment of radio drama in the fifties, the genre was transplanted directly to television, which has been its sole medium of transmission ever since. Thus, throughout sitcom history, production has been kept under strict corporate patronage.[33] There is no such thing as a "small-time" sitcom; a show either makes it coast to coast or disappears into the effluvium (though we keep hearing that cable might change this).

Because of this system, the creators and performers of sitcoms are structurally separated from immediate human reactions to their work. This is true even of sitcoms "taped before a live audience." To attend such a taping is to witness the preparation of a drama, not its performance. Crew and equipment, heedless of a nonpaying audience's prerogatives, move in and out of the line of vision at will. Second takes are by no means unusual. Most important, the members of the audience are more conscious of being a part of a television program than of seeing one performed, and this creates an almost irresistible incentive for enthusiasm. The audience knows that its negative reactions are irrelevant and that its only possibility for participation is tied to its approval. The effectiveness of the script, the jokes, and even the tiniest bit of comic business will finally be measured by ratings rather than by whatever human laughter might or might not be provoked.

The rise of the popular cinema in the early twentieth century signaled the coming isolation of most dramatic performances from visceral, dialectical audience contact in mass culture. It is worth noting, however, that the early film comedians had come to Hollywood with talents that had been thoroughly shaped in the presence of live audiences on the vaudeville circuits. As diverse a group as Chaplin, Keaton, Lloyd, Laurel and Hardy, W. C. Fields, Abbott and Costello, and the Three Stooges were able to make films using gestures, routines, and instincts that had been honed by the cheers, catcalls, bravos and boos of actual people. The best of the silent comedians, deprived of realistic sound, transmuted the American vaudeville stage and the British musical hall into cinematic space: Chaplin rudely awakened in the arms of a giant monument as it is unveiled to the throng; Keaton racing down a hill pursued by a hundred brides in wedding gowns; Lloyd dangling from a skyscraper flagpole above busy downtown Los Angeles. With the introduction of sound, however, it became easier to impose quality control than to encourage the radical re-imagination of the world as cinematic stage. Given the miracles of vocal dialogue and synchronous music, audiences would settle for realistic imitations of theater on film.[34] This was theater, however, performed without an audience.

The destruction of vaudeville by the technological jugger-naut of the movies and broadcasting would eventually spell the end of live dramatic entertainment on a truly mass scale.[35] At this early juncture in the transition from audience to machine, marketing surveys had not yet eclipsed the age-old sequence of imagination, memory, and action as the modus operandi of artistic creation. *The Jazz Singer* (1927), the first commercially released sound film, featured vaudeville star Al Jolson in the title role. Given the unprecedented expense of the new tech-nology—and the untested attitude of audiences toward it—the project was a risky one for Warner Brothers, then a small, financially unstable studio. Synchronous sound, according to the shooting script, was to be used only for the musical numbers. Al Jolson, however, with twenty years behind him as a Dockstader minstrel, a Jewish dialect comic, and a vaudeville headliner, was not accustomed to limiting his performances to the dictates of a script. During the key scene in which the Jolson character is reunited with his mammy, the man billed as the World's Greatest Entertainer "interrupts the song midway to steal a kiss, to promise her a new pink dress, to offer her an apartment in the Bronx, to assure her of a trip to Coney Island, all the while vamping suggestively."[36] This collision of stage and screen, as J. Hoberman has written, "destroyed the silent cinema":

The Warner Brothers had not really intended to make "talking pictures" as much as to automate the music that accom-panied silent films. It was only after witnessing the larger-than-life projection of Jolson's personality run amok—he had, out of nervous tension on the set, concocted this routine off the cuff—that the Warners realized what they had wrought. . . . The 1927 audience, which had already experienced the Show Biz epiphanies of Lucky Lindy's trans-Atlantic flight and the Bambino's sixty homers, attained a new plateau of hysteria. Their ecstatic response to Jolson's sudden improvisations in this scene was indicative of the immediate response that audiences would have for the revelation, as opposed to depiction, of personality on the screen.[37]

The richness of the techno-aesthetic cusp period that immediately ensued is perhaps best exemplified by the careers of the Marx Brothers. Born in vaudeville's proverbial trunk, Groucho, Harpo, Chico, and Zeppo, like Jolson, remained stage performers throughout the silent film period. They made their first movie, *The Cocoanuts*, between daily live performances of their hit stageplay *Animal Crackers*, shuttling back and forth between a Broadway theater and a Queens soundstage. "Sometimes I'd get so punchy," recalled Groucho, "that I'd find myself spouting the dialogue from *Animal Crackers* in a scene I was doing in *Cocoanuts* and vice-versa."[38]

Cut off from their live audience in the new medium, the Marxes created one out of whoever was available on the set:

"The shooting would be interrupted every time we started improvising," Harpo recalls in his autobiography. "The trouble was [Director Robert] Florey couldn't help breaking up. When he laughed, he laughed so hard he drowned out everything else on the sound track. . . . We played to Florey. . . . When he flew into a fit of silent convulsions we knew we had done something good. It was the weirdest audience we ever played to."[39]

Even after completing several pictures, moving to Hollywood, and decisively committing their careers to film work, the Marx Brothers continued to thrive on—in fact, to require—the timing adjustments and perhaps the spiritual authenticity of performing in front of a live audience. Early Marx Brothers films such as *Animal Crackers* and *The Cocoanuts* were finished stage pieces, having been performed in theaters hundreds of times and brought to the screen with only minimal alteration. In *The*

Marx Brothers at the Movies, Zimmerman and Goldblatt point out that much of *Horsefeathers*, another early film, is based on "Fun in Hi-Skule," a vaudeville routine that the act had toured with for years.[40] "We weren't like other [film] comedians," remarked Groucho. "We had to try everything out first."[41] But how could the Marx Brothers maintain a tactile relationship with their audience while working in the West Coast movie factories three thousand miles from Broadway?

Following the box-office disaster of *Duck Soup* (arguably their greatest cinematic achievement), the Marx Brothers were, in effect, dropped by Paramount. Irving Thalberg, a poker buddy of Harpo's, signed the brothers to a new contract with MGM and was sympathetic to their need to play to people: Thalberg's "brainstorm was a rather simple one on the surface, but it revealed a deep understanding of the essence of the team's comic gift. He proposed that the brothers take five big scenes on the road as a vaudeville show to put their jokes under the practical fire of a live audience."[42] Thus, *A Night at the Opera*—as combination vaudeville show and film-in-progress—made a four-city swing of Seattle, Salt Lake City, Portland, and Santa Barbara before shooting began. A 1935 article in *Reader's Digest* described the system this way: "When the patrons failed to laugh at a gag, that line came out. When they laughed late, the line was sharpened to take effect more quickly. When they laughed mildly, the line was sent back to the workshop. When they roared, the line was okayed for the film version."[43]

"If we had shot *Opera* with the material we opened with in Seattle," claims Groucho, "it would have been the end of all of us."[44] Indeed, the Thalberg scheme proved so successful in terms of *A Night at the Opera*'s box-office superiority to *Duck Soup* that it was expanded for the next Marx Brothers picture, *A Day at the Races*. This time, the cast embarked on a grand six-thousand-mile tour, theater-hopping the large industrial cities of the northern Midwest with a show consisting of a collection of proposed scenes for the new film.

An ominous innovation was added to the tryout system by Thalberg on the *Day at the Races* tour: at every performance, cards were handed out that asked each member of the audience for comments on the "funniness" of various lines, gags, and other particulars of the show. Using these audience-response cards, Thalberg and director Sam Wood selected the 175 jokes that the audience "enjoyed" most. An MGM news release, describing this advanced scientific process that the studio had instituted for the production of comedy movies, assured the public that only those jokes with "the highest laugh ratings will be used in the picture."[45] Though not yet fully recognizable, the industrial technique of postmodern electronic dramatic comedy—the sitcom—was falling into place.

Fifty years later, the sitcom is presented as a finished work without so much as a whiff of the greasepaint or a peep from the crowd. With no appreciable boondocks to play, the genre has developed without the aid of an idiosyncratic dialectic of refinement. Instead, piles of data suffice for a track record. It would be misleading, however, to say that the sitcom-in-progress is totally isolated from all audience reaction. Far from it. As Todd Gitlin writes, "Walk through Farmers Market in Los Angeles or Rockefeller Center in New York in the early spring and you are likely to see a cheerful youth passing out tickets for a free screening of a television program. The point is to net tourists, deemed a more representative national sample than everyday Angelenos or New Yorkers. But anyone except bag ladies and drunks can get tickets."[46] The coded, multiple-choice reactions of one of these "sample audiences" to a sitcom pilot will ultimately have more "effect" on the fate of a show than a gang of ill-tempered drunks with a case of rotten vegetables might hope to impose on a vaudeville act. The feedback that will reach the artist, however, will not consist of the vital reactions of people, but rather of a set of abstract ciphers on a page that smugly proclaims their accuracy with little concern for the truth: "60% of white housewives in Cleveland living in households making less than $20,000 per year thought it was either moderately funny, funny, or very funny." This mechanical relationship with its audience places the sitcom among the purest of mass arts.

If a human audience is little more than an optional sound effect in sitcom-making, direct contact with people remains a defining aspect of stand-up comedy. Stand-up must be understood as more than merely the structural setup of an individual telling jokes to an audience. Each performance is a variation on an epic challenge made by the group to the individual: Make us laugh, be the cause of our involuntary behavior, make us living proof that you can control us, conquer us psychologically and physically—or die.

We Are Having Fun

An American tradition of direct-address oral comedy can be traced to diverse nineteenth-century sources: the Down East yarn spinners of Maine, the traveling medicine-show barkers who offered monologue-like spiels as come-ons for the sale of health tonics, and the tale-tellers of the Missouri Territory are among the prominent contributors. The most popular form of entertainment in nineteenth-century America, according to cultural historian Robert Toll, was the minstrel show, a bizarre spectacle of racial confusions that contained several forms of proto-stand-up comedy.[47] The ritual opening section of the minstrel show had the entire cast onstage in a choral semicircle offering a comedy-variety review. The interlocutor, or master of ceremonies, adorned in both blackface and formal attire, introduced the acts, interpreting—and mocking—them in direct address to the audience. By pompously correcting the malapropisms and pointing out the stupidities of the "plantation niggers," he acted as a kind of missing link between the "superior" audience and the low characters being portrayed onstage. As actual black entertainers began to dominate minstrelsy in the years after Reconstruction, the Uncle Tomish interlocutor increasingly came in for a razzing from the endmen. These latter characters, known as Brudder Tambo (for his tambourine) and Brudder Bones (for his sticks), traded one-liners from opposite ends of the ensemble. But the closest antecedent of modern stand-up to be found in the minstrel show is the "stump speech":

> Over the years, the stump speaker became one of the major minstrel comedy specialists. Each of these stars had his own special style and topics. While some limited themselves to "nonsense," others used their ludicrous verbosity to express "serious" social criticism. Ad Ryman, for example, regularly "lectured" on education, temperance, and women's rights.

But whatever their content, stump speakers regularly got laughs by combining the physical comedy of endmen with [an interlocutor's] verbal pomposity.[48]

Toll offeis an excerpt from a typical stump speech:

Feller-feiier and oder fellers, when Joan of Ark and his broder Noah's Ark crossed de Rubicund in search of Decamoran's horn, and meeting dat solitary horseman by de way, dey anapulated in de clarion tones of de clamurous rooster, de insignificition of de—de—de—de hop-toad am a very big bird—du da—du da day—does it not prove dat where gold is up to a discount of two cups of coffee on de dollar, dat bolivers must fall back into de radience of de-de—anything else, derefore at once and exclusively proving de fact dat de afore-mentioned accounts for de milk in de cocoa-nut![49]

The roots of the double-talk practiced by such comedians as Al Kelly, Professor Irwin Corey, and Norm Crosby can be found in this kind of monologue. The speech often ended with the comedian falling off the "stump" (a natural platform) onto the floor.

Radio, the first great agency for the day-to-day depositing of regional and other subcultural styles and types into a central commercial myth bank, created a model of assimilation that remains intact. The medium was a basic force for the synthesis of popular local and ethnic comedy into the national genres that would eventually dominate electronic culture. Certainly, *Amos 'n' Andy*, the most popular program in radio history, borrowed much from the minstrel canon. Performed on radio by white actors affecting hyperbolic black dialect, the show transposed the racist preindustrial rural and small town stereotypes of minstrelsy into modern racist urban stereotypes. Black performers took over the roles in the TV version (CBS, 1951–53), but with so few black faces on television, the show carried unmistakably derogatory overtones, whatever intentions lay behind it. Especially odious, for example, was the character of Lightnin' (Nick O'Demus), a cotton-mouthed, cretinous janitor who eclipsed the excesses of Stepin Fetchit. Another early black TV comedy effort was *Beulah* (ABC, 1950–53). Originally spun off from *Fibber McGee and Molly* as a radio sitcom (with a white man playing the title role of the black maid), *Beulah* came to TV starring Ethel Waters, with Butterfly McQueen in the role of her best friend, Oriole. The protests of civil rights organizations led to the cancellation of both shows at the end of the 1952–53 season. As a consequence, however, blacks virtually disappeared from television comedy during the developing years of the medium. There were minor exceptions, such as Willy the Handyman in *The Stu Erwin Show* and Louise the Maid in *The Danny Thomas Show*, but black comedians would not be featured in starring prime-time roles for almost two decades.

NBC was the only network that showed concern over what amounted to the industry's lockout of black performers. As early as 1956, it tried singer Nat King Cole in a fifteen-minute variety series. Despite guest appearances by such white stars as Peggy Lee and Tony Bennett, not a single sponsor would buy commercial time during the show's thirteen months on the air. The commercial ice would not be broken until the premiere of *Julia* (NBC, 1968–71). This show was a painfully self-conscious reversal of the traditional black stereotypes of *Amos 'n' Andy* and *Beulah*. The title character, played by Diahann Carroll, was a straight-arrow nurse and mother, a Vietnam widow bringing up her young son. *Julia* is a comedy mostly in the sense that the endings of the episodes are not unhappy. The return of black comedians in black comic roles was still several years off: *The Flip Wilson Show* (NBC, 1970–74) in comedy-variety, and *Sanford and Son* (NBC, 1972–77), starring Red Foxx, in the sitcom.

The comic traditions of poor white southerners were more easily absorbed by the mass media. *The Grand Ole Opry* (ABC, 1955–56) provides a living example. The Opry began in 1925 as a live show that was broadcast over a local Nashville radio station, and it has since expanded to include a theme-park, hotel, and resort complex and a national cable-TV network. Though the original program was primarily devoted to the presentation of hillbilly music, the Opry's impresario, Judge George D. Hay, gradually added other rural American musical styles and punctuated the music with comedy spots.

In the early days of the show, Judge Hay brought in comedy acts directly from the indigenous media of the region. Jamup and Honey were a white blackface team that was plucked off the shriveling minstrel circuit. Rod and Boob, the Brasfield Brothers, were discovered by Judge Hay while they were playing in an Alabama tent show as members of Bisbee's Comedians, a troupe that toured the Bible Belt with a repertoire of comic melodramas. According to the country-music historian Jack Hurst, *The Grand Ole Opry*'s first regular weekly comedy act was a Chattanooga team known as Sarie and Sally, whose specialty was down-home gossip humor:

Sarie: Will Miss Lulu be entertaining this week?
Sally: I don't see why. She ain't never been before.

Minnie Pearl (Sarah Ophelia Colley), who would become one of the Opry's most popular comedians in the early 1940s and then a television star after World War II, coined the term "double comedy" to categorize the vaudevillelike semidramatic dialogues that were the structural bases of these radio duos. Pearl defines "double comedy" by its lack of a traditional straightman: "Like Burns and Allen, [and] Laurel and Hardy, . . . each had to be as funny as the other one or it was no good."[50]

Not surprisingly, *musician*-comedians, such as Uncle Dave Macon, Grandpa Jones, Bill Carlisle, and Stringbean Akeman were at the core of Opry comedy. Cousin Jody (James Clell Summey), though one of a kind, in some ways epitomizes the Opry comedian. With loud, ballooning striped pants that were short enough to showcase his white socks, with his flowered shirt, wide suspenders, and spectacular toothless grin beneath his turned-up felt hat, Cousin Jody, like Minnie Pearl, Charlie Weaver, or, for that matter, Harpo Marx, never appeared in public out of character. Joining the Opry in the 1930s as a member of the Crazy Tennesseans, he cracked jokes and danced to his own accompaniment on the Hawaiian guitar for the Opry until his death in 1974.

With radio penetrating every nook and cranny of the continent by the mid-1930s, a massive commercial mainstream was materializing that regional artists might hope to cross over into. WSM, the 50,000-watt "clear channel" station that broadcast *The Grand Ole Opry* all over the South made the Nashville show

36

into a regional institution. By 1939, the regional institution had become national: "For thirty minutes every Saturday night the National Broadcasting Company carried a segment sponsored by Prince Albert Tobacco. The thirty-minute program, representative of the larger four-and-a-half-hour show, featured a top performer supported by other acts, including comedians such as Lazy Jim Day or Minnie Pearl."[51] Opry touring units, whose musicians and comics were familiar throughout the states reached by WSM, played gigs around the South, offering a trademark entity under the banner of the Grand Ole Opry. This brought a measure of quality control to the world of rural hoedowns, barn dances, and tent shows. By the early 1940s, under the sponsorship of Camel cigarettes, Opry tours were expanded throughout the United States to meet the demands of a national audience.

Content, of course, shifted with the center of the ever-expanding audience. Instrumental numbers, which had dominated the early Opry, gave way to the preponderance of vocals; the genesis of country pop had begun.[52] Monologues were now interspersed with the familiar double comedy. Comedians such as Whitey ("The Duke of Paducah") Ford, Red Foley, and Minnie Pearl had become national radio stars, making "country and western" a style that was easily recognizable to all, even "city and eastern" folks. Tennessee Ernie Ford became network television's first country-and-western comedy star, hosting a network variety show on NBC from 1956 to 1961. By the sixties, TV shows such as *The Beverly Hillbillies* (CBS, 1962–71) and *Green Acres* (CBS, 1965–71) had reprocessed basic country gags into top-rated prime-time sitcoms. *Hee Haw*, which premiered in 1969 on CBS, became country comedy's greatest national success. Borrowing the hyperactive pace and structure of *Rowan and Martin's Laugh-In*, a major NBC comedy hit of the previous season, *Hee Haw* simply plugged in country content to the formal mechanisms of the urban-oriented *Laugh-In*. "The Cocktail Party," a weekly feature of *Laugh-In* in which a group of comedians dancing the Watusi at a party told each other one-liners, was transmuted into a barn dance. "The Joke Wall," which had *Laugh-In* comedians popping out of doors and windows, was transplanted to a cornfield with comedians popping out of the stalks. Comics such as Archie

Campbell, Stringbean Akeman, and Grandpa Jones, after long careers as Opry stars, achieved national followings. Though *Hee Haw* finished sixteenth in the prime-time Nielsen ratings in 1970–71, CBS dropped the show in its celebrated purge of "rural" comedy. The show's producers, however, kept it in production, and through syndication, *Hee Haw* became the longest-running comedy show of any kind in television history. Today, the Opry's cable outlet TNN (The Nashville Network) telecasts internationally via satellite in color and stereo from Opryland, U.S.A., providing a range of country programming packaged in the mass-culture lingua franca of familiar "mainstream" TV formats. TNN series have included *I-40 Paradise*, a country sitcom; *Fandango*, a country game show; *Nashville Now*, a ninety-minute country talk-variety show à la *The Tonight Show*; and *Video Country*, a country music-video show.

If Nashville comedy provided the spectacle of country folks sitting in an urban theater (Ryman Auditorium) and later a suburban drive-in theme park (Opryland), listening to a fellow "rube" joke in their own idiom, Catskill Mountain comedy was its mirror image. Here, city folks came to the country to listen to a fast-talking urban hustler make self-conscious fun of their particular "outgroup" subculture. The emergence of the urban style that would eventually achieve centrality in American comedy in the television age owes much to a species of cheap entertainment that was peculiar to the working-class Jewish summer resorts of Upstate New York and northeastern Pennsylvania.

In his excruciatingly nostalgic memoir, *The Borscht Belt*, Joey Adams identifies the origins of the modern stand-up comedian in the *toomler*, a kind of combination social director/trickster figure who flourished in the Catskills from the 1920s until the advent of cheap air travel anachronized the commercial vitality of large-scale tourism in the region: "His job it was to keep the guests from getting bored with card playing, dieting, or viewing nature. He had to compensate for the leaky faucets and/or leaky customers. If the sink overflowed in Bungalow Six, the word went out: 'Get the Toomler.' A Toomler who lived in was a better investment than a plumber by the hour. . . . The name Toomler comes from one who makes tumult. A 'tumult maker,' alias 'tumulter.'[53]

Telling dirty stories to the men around the poker table, flirting with the women out by the pool, romancing the homely with a dance and a squeeze, showing off some sleight of hand and bragging to the kids, the *toomler* was a comic performer not permitted the luxury of distinguishing his life from his art. The jokes and songs performed on the stage of the hotel casino merely constituted one aspect of the job. Handball playing, sexual reputation, and a wiseass comeback to any line a guest could throw at him were of no less importance. In *The Professor of Desire*, Philip Roth describes the *toomler* of Kepesh's Hungarian Royale, a Catskill Mountains hotel:

> Herbie Bratasky, social director, bandleader, crooner, comic, and m.c. of my family's mountainside resort. When he is not trussed up in the elasticized muscleman's swim trunks which he dons to conduct rhumba lessons by the side of the pool, he is dressed to kill, generally in his two-tone crimson and cream-colored 'loafer' jacket and the wide canary-yellow trousers that taper down to enchain him just above his white, perforated sharpie's shoes. A fresh slice of Black Jack gum is at the ready in his pocket while another is being savored, with slow-motion sassiness.[54]

Bratasky, "a second Danny Kaye," a "Jewish Cugat," boasts to the young narrator of the novel that "I could be in Ripley's," while showing off at a urinal. The *toomler*'s most important physical attribute, however, was his tongue. Sid Caesar, Red Buttons, Lenny Bruce, Jackie Mason, Jerry Lewis, Buddy Hackett, Shecky Green, and many members of what would become the Jewish old guard paid *toomler* dues in The Mountains before making their way into the mainstream of Hollywood film, network broadcast, and gambling casino entertainment.

The aggressive, hyperactive, *shpritzing* style demanded of entertainers by urban immigrant working-class vacationers did not suit every Jewish entertainer who got a start in the hotels and bungalow colonies of the Catskills and Poconos. The situation for some was analogous to the dilemma of black artists who were forced to play stereotyped roles on the minstrel stage in order to work. Bert Williams was perhaps the greatest of the black minstrel comedians. In 1907, Albert Ross, a professor at

Western University, wrote a letter to Williams, criticizing his stage caricatures as a bad example for black youth. In his reply, Williams admitted that he knew he was "getting the worst of it" by performing these characters in front of white people, but what else could he do?[55] (He defended his work by pointing to the fact that black people were among his most ardent fans.) Similarly, there were those in the Borscht Belt who viewed themselves as artists being forced by social and economic circumstance to vulgarize their talents. Moss Hart, who began his career as a Catskills hustler, expresses markedly unnostalgic sentiments about the *toomler*'s life in his autobiography, *Act One*: "Social directing provided me with a lifelong disdain and a lasting horror of people in the mass seeking pleasure and release in packaged doses. . . . A bad-complexioned girl with thick glasses and unfortunate front teeth does nothing to kindle the fires of pity within you, but instead makes you want to kick her right in her unfortunate teeth."[56]

In Herman Wouk's 1955 novel *Marjorie Morningstar*, the character Noel Airman expresses similar feelings. In the film adaptation, released in 1958, Gene Kelly plays the role of Airman, a hotel "theater director" who is determined to free his artistic talents from the narrow commercialism and downscale mentality of resort hotel culture. Not long after the film's premiere, Leslie Fiedler wrote, "In the form of Noel Airman, Wouk has isolated all that is skeptical, anti-Philistine and indifferent to bourgeois values in the Jewish American tradition; and Airman he has made his villain. With him he identifies everything that stands between the Jew and social acceptance, the novelist and popularity; with Marjorie he identifies all that makes the Jew acceptable and the Jewish novelist a best-seller."[57] Indeed, far from glorifying the ghetto muse of the Borscht Belt, the story builds the impression that Airman's potential as an artist and a human being will be measured by his ability to transcend the shlocky, abrasive subculture of the immigrant lower classes and enter into a more subdued, quasi-genteel, world of second-generation assimilation. Wouk treats the ghetto as a precious but dying past, with an emphasis on the dying. We see this most graphically illustrated in the character of Marjorie's Uncle Samson-Aaron, an aging ne'er-do-well, played in the film by Ed Wynn. Working as a dishwasher at the hotel, he comes out of the kitchen to perform a vaudeville pantomime for the crowd. Samson-Aaron's act, like the Diaspora itself, contains flashes of artistic brilliance but precipitates a fatal heart attack.

Noel Airman's name contains the elements of his crisis. He is born Saul Ehrmann, the son of a New York judge; better Jewish middle-class credentials are hardly imaginable. However, Noel is unable to appreciate the discreet charms of the bourgeoisie. Rejecting the roles of both ghetto clown and assimilated midcult entertainer, he drops the names Saul ("King of the Jews") and Ehrmann ("honored man") in favor of Noel Airman. Airman is a literal translation of *Luftmensch*, a Yiddish term for an uncompromising artist, intellectual, or similar unfortunate who must survive without visible means of support (that is, one who must make a living out of thin air). His self-bestowed "Christian name," on the other hand, suggests his view of himself as the Messiah (also, ironically, "King of the Jews"), but mockingly points to Noel Coward, the epitome of "high-class" WASP entertainment. As drawn by Wouk, Noel is correct in looking for a way out of the confines of the ghetto Catskills hotel. He is vilified, however, for the path he chooses: he gets his chance on Broadway, but asks too much of democratic culture with his artsy-fartsy material. His play flops and he winds up a hopeless failure. Marjorie, meanwhile, makes the right decision when she forsakes Noel for a brutally straitlaced lawyer, a Jew in the gray flannel suit of middle-class obeisance. Witnessing the sunset of Yiddish-dominated immigrant culture in the fifties, Wouk has little positive to say about either it or about those with dreams of transferring its energies to the making of great works in the Western tradition. Instead, he makes a case for measured assimilation into anonymous middlebrow respectability. As much as his own novels, *My Fair Lady* serves as a good example of the art that Wouk is advocating. Adapted from a modern British classic (with origins in Hellenic mythology) by a jewish writer and a Jewish composer, staged in fact by Moss Hart, it is precisely the kind of play that Marjorie and her "professional" husband, residents of a fancy Westchester suburb, would attend for an evening at the theater.

Moss Hart's perception of the Borscht Belt as "people in the mass" is directly opposed to Joey Adams' remembrance of "a handsome ghetto."[58] The Jewish Alps, as Adams likes to call it, was both *gemeinschaft* and *gesellschaft*, at once a warm community nourishing an integral culture and a cold commercial venture designed to extract the disposable income of an outgroup that did not have many vacation choices. This dual mythography is perhaps what made it such an excellent training ground for radio and television, media in which the comedian is required to penetrate the undifferentiated mass with an illusion of one-to-one contact. "To you people who are visiting," Henny Youngman begins a monologue, "what makes you so sure you turned off the gas back home?"

Paul Grossinger, of the Catskills hotel that bore his family name until its sale in 1986, has said that "what appeals to a middle-class Jew appeals to a middle-class Gentile."[59] If so, the converse is no less true. Today, tennis, golf, skiing, and aerobics instructors have largely replaced *toomlers* as the prime hustlers of the old Sullivan County resorts. The New York City surburbs have crept close enough to tip the balance in some areas of the Catskills from country to exurban. While speeding down the overscaled expressway lanes of New York Route 17, billboards still scream the names of Alan King, Steve and Edie, Jerry Lewis, and a host of Jackies and Lennys. But they also plead to the motorist-voters that "Casinos Mean Jobs!" The proprietors of underbooked hotels and crumbling bungalow colonies dream of Las Vegas and Atlantic City; it surely would take at least the miracle of legalized gambling to bring the Catskills back to the role it enjoyed as triple-A farm team to American major-league entertainment immediately after World War II.

Irving Howe described the 1950s as a decade during which "American culture turned toward a philo-Semitic phase."[60] Indeed, breaches appeared in the physical and psychological barricades of New York Jewish ghetto culture after 1945, and nowhere was this more readily apparent than on television.

Before the Nazi era, Jewish characters had been common in American pop entertainment. Al Jolson and his brother Harry, for example, had played "The Hebrew and the Cadet" on the vaudeville stage, and there had never been any mistaking the ethnic identity of Fanny Brice or Sophie Tucker. In 1927 the subject chosen for the box-office gamble of the first talking picture had been Jewish assimiliation; the singing of the Kol

Nidre had been among the first songs ever recorded for the "talkies," following "My Gal Sal" and "Down on the Levee" in *The Jazz Singer*. But as anti-Semitism was translated into a popular political ideology in the 1930s, Jewishness became an "issue" that the purveyors of popular entertainment felt was better left out of the popular marketplace. By 1944, Ben Hecht had witnessed "the almost complete disappearance of the Jew from American fiction, stage, and movies."[61]

After the war, the Jew returned to American popular-culture cosmology with a vengeance. Milton Berle, Sid Caesar, Groucho Marx, Red Buttons, George Burns, Jack Benny, Phil Silvers, and Georgie Jessel were among the Jewish comedians starring in their own prime-time network comedy series in the early fifties. At one extreme, Berle and Caesar peppered their work with verbal and physical Yiddishisms. Though it baffles the imagination, the ratings coolly substantiate an image of a lone TV antenna standing against the stark Nebraska prairie pulling down a snowy black-and-white image of Sid Caesar performing in a spoof of Japanese art films, written by Carl Reiner and Mel Brooks, which included characters with names such as Gantze Mishpuckeh, Gehackte Leber, and Shmateh (in Yiddish, respectively, "the whole big family," "chopped liver," and "rag").

The star of the television comedy-variety show, in his role as "emcee," emerged as a kind of electronic *toomler*, kidding the guests, introducing the sketches, and providing continuity between program and commercial. All of the early comedy-variety shows were performed in front of studio audiences; many were telecast live for the eastern-and-central network feed. The blackout sketch, an electronic approximation of the short dramatic skits of the Catskills revues, was the mainstay of the genre, but the star's opening stand-up monologue became a convention that survives to this day on the talk-variety shows of comedians such as Johnny Carson and David Letterman.

While the hosts of the comedy-variety shows were frantically asserting their Jewishness in public, the Jewish sitcom stars were considerably more subdued. George Burns and Jack Benny created sitcom vehicles in which they portrayed "themselves" celebrating Christmas and playing golf down at the country club. *The Goldbergs*, a radio crossover starring the former Yiddish stage actress Gertrude Berg, was the one sitcom that called a Jew a Jew on early TV. But even here, considerable effort was made to homogenize the drama. Though they had lived on Tremont Avenue in the Bronx for twenty years on radio, the TV Goldbergs eventually moved to Haverville, a suburb somewhere out there in Middle America. With the end of *The Goldbergs* in 1955, only families of northern European descent populated the sitcoms (with the exception, of course, of Ricky Ricardo).

Despite the good money and unprecedented exposure that television could bring, not all stand-up comedians were completely comfortable with the medium. A monologue that might serve for a national nightclub tour would be made unusable by a single appearance on a network show. This was especially problematic for comedians who wrote and performed their own material. Even more important to some, television was a medium that put severe limits on subject matter and language. The urban nightclub of the 1950s was, or at least strove to be, a missing link between day-to-day respectability and what Jack Kerouac was calling "the great American night." People came to the clubs to enjoy themselves—to drink, dance, meet other people, and keep up with the latest jazz, both musical and verbal. After a day, a week, a lifetime at the office, they expected, or even demanded, something of the exotic, the naughty, the "adult"; otherwise, why not stay home and watch TV? Young middle-managers and Ivy League aristocrats could, if but for a weekend's moment, feel a connection to the beatnik America of dark streets, open sex, militant drug use, and racial intercourse that teased them from the pages of *Esquire* and *Playboy* as they toiled in the office towers.

Television created no such liberated space. It went directly to the home of whoever turned it on—and as far as the accountants who ran it were concerned, the more who turned it on, the better. The prissiest common denominator had to be considered. The needs of the family had to be served. The aim was to be attractive, but not at any cost. Cuteness, blandness, emptiness, and boredom were all acceptable alternatives to exciting the puritan beast that lay buried beneath the go-go surface of a postwar America that seemed bound and determined to raise the City of Heaven on the shoulders of credit and technology.

In a handful of urban nightclubs, including the Bitter End (New York), Second City (Chicago), and the hungry i (San Francisco), comedians such as Lenny Bruce, Dick Gregory, Mort Sahl, and Mike Nichols and Elaine May developed a relatively didactic, politicized, sometimes even angry response to mass society, the cold war, the indignities of Jim Crow, the denial of free speech, and a hypocritical web of traditions and taboos that gratuitously valorized religion and vilified sexuality.

The Realist, Paul Krassner's "magazine of freethought criticism and satire," fell off the left edge of this comedy. Madelyn Murray, the avant-garde atheist media comedienne, provides a sample of its style in a 1960 *Realist* article: "I am against religion. I am against schools. I am against apple pies. I am against 'Americanism,' mothers, adulterated foods, nuclear fission testing, commercial television. I am against all newspapers, 99-and-44/100% of the magazines. I am against Eisenhower, Nixon, Kennedy, Lodge. I'm even against giving the country back to the Indians. Why should the poor fools be stuck with this mess?"[62] The agnostic cosmic *weltschmerz* that pervaded the "high culture" of postwar philosophy and literature stood at the margin of terminally happy popular culture, insisting upon a subjective counterpoint to the well-promoted images of upwardly mobile mortgagees happily abandoning the complexities of urban life in station wagons. "Businessmen are serious./Movie producers are serious," wrote Allen Ginsberg. "Everybody's serious but me."[63]

Meanwhile, the television played on. A message so old— "Good is rewarded; evil is punished"—from an oracle so new (and convenient) implied a historical continuity that belied the bombed-out world of the dying inner-city streets and the pockmarked suburban carscape. Television was a medium committed to happiness, and it had little use for comedians or anyone else who refused to share in the joys of material consumption. "We" were an audience, one nation under Bob Hope (and under John Wayne and Walter Cronkite in their respective genres).

While the sitcom developed in a relatively monolithic fashion in the careful hands of the Hollywood–Madison Avenue complex, two types of stand-up comedy emerged: one based on social consciousness and one based on social consensus;

a comic monologue speaking to its audience and a comic monologue speaking for its audience; Lenny Bruce, perched on a stool in a dark, smoke-filled big-city nightclub, laying down raps about U.S. police terror, and Bob Hope making remarks about Anita Ekberg's breasts in front of thousands of screaming sailors somewhere on the Pacific rim. The naming of Bruce or Hope as an American hero was, and remains, a personally revealing act, an implicit indicator of a thousand political opinions and cultural stances. These polar phenomena of American stand-up—the hipster and the toastmaster—form the extreme boundaries of American popular comedy, while the sitcom came to occupy the oceanic middle.

Notes

1. Vladimir Nabokov, *Lolita* (Greenwich, Conn.: Fawcett Crest, 1958), p. 18.
2. See Hans Magnus Enzensberger, *The Consciousness Industry* (New York: Seabury, 1974).
3. Waldo Frank, "Seriousness and Dada," *1924*, 3 (1924).
4. As quoted in Sherman Paul, *Edmund Wilson: A Study of Literary Vocation in Our Time* (Urbana: University of Illinois, 1965), p. 59.
5. See Dwight Macdonald, "A Theory of Mass Culture," *Diogenes*, 3 (1953), pp. 1–17; reprinted in *Mass Culture: The Popular Arts in America*, ed. Bernard Rosenberg and David Manning White (New York: Free Press, 1957), pp. 59–73.
6. For detailed historical and critical accounts of this phenomenon, see Marshall McLuhan, *The Gutenberg Galaxy* (Toronto: University of Toronto, 1962), or Ian Watt, *The Rise of the Novel* (Berkeley: University of California, 1957).
7. Alexander Pope, "Epistle to Dr. Arbuthnot" (1735), 1. 304.
8. Pope, *The Dunciad* (1728), IV, 11. 21–24, in Williams, p. 356.
9. Peter Conrad, *Television: The Medium and Its Manners* (Boston: Routledge and Kegan Paul, 1982) p. 1.
10. Cited in J. Hoberman, "Love and Death in the American Supermarketplace," *Voice Literary Supplement*, November 1982, p. 12.
11. Daniel J. Czitrom, *Media and the American Mind: From Morse to McLuhan* (Chapel Hill: University of North Carolina, 1982), especially Chapters 4–6.
12. Walt Whitman, Preface to 1855 ed. of *Leaves of Grass*, ed. Malcolm Cowley (New York: Penguin, 1959), p. 5.
13. T. S. Eliot, "Notes Towards the Definition of Culture," 1948; reprinted in *Christianity and Culture* (New York: Harvest, 1968).

14. F. Scott Fitzgerald, *The Great Gatsby* (New York: Scribners, 1925), p. 24.
15. For a penetrating discussion of simultaneous urges toward celebration and despair in the American hero, see Ihab Hassan, "The Character of Post-War Fiction in America," in *Recent American Fiction*, ed. Joseph J. Waldmeir (Boston: Houghton Mifflin, 1961), pp. 215–30.
16. Nabokov, p. 133.
17. Norman Mailer, *An American Dream* (New York: Dial, 1965), p. 248.
18. Mailer, p. 251.
19. "A Good Bomb?" New York *Times*, September 30, 1984.
20. As cited in Paul Boyer, "The Cloud over Culture," *New Republic*, August 12–19, 1985, p. 28.
21. New York *Times*, September 30, 1984.
22. Robert Toll, *The Entertainment Machine* (New York: Oxford, 1982), pp. 227–228.
23. For a discussion of the similarities between the clergyman and the stand-up comedian, see Seymour Fisher and Rhoda Fisher, *Pretend the World Is Funny and Forever* (Hillsdale, N.J.: Eribaum, 1981), p. 62.
24. For a discussion of the former president's comic persona, see Stephen Whitfield, "Richard Nixon as Comic Figure," *American Quarterly*, 37:1 (Spring 1985), pp. 114–32.
25. Hal Himmelstein, *Television Myth and the American Mind* (New York: Praeger, 1985), p. 290.
26. Lawrence Mintz, "Stand-up Comedy as Cultural and Social Mediation," *American Quarterly*, 37:1 (Spring 1985), p. 71.
27. Mintz, p. 75.
28. Ibid.
29. Fisher and Fisher, p. 36.
30. Max Wilk, *The Golden Age of Television Comedy* (New York: Delacorte, 1976), p. 176–77.
31. Himmelstein, p. 89.
32. See J. Hoberman, "Ralph and Alice and Ed and Trixie," *Film Comment*, September–October 1985, pp. 62–68. In addition to his analysis, Hoberman cites Gilbert Seldes, who made similar observations about the lovelessness of the Kramden marriage in his essay, "The Gleason Case," which appeared in his critical anthology *The Public Arts* (New York: Simon and Schuster, 1956), pp. 158–64.
33. I am, of course, referring to the American sitcom. The British sitcom, for example, developed largely under the patronage of a state bureaucracy.
34. See Macdonald for further elaboration.
35. It is worth noting that certain nonnarrative entertainment forms, such as sporting events and rock concerts, have flourished as spectator-attended events in electronic mass culture.

36. J. Hoberman, "The Show Biz Messiah," *No Rose*, 1:2 (Spring 1977), p. 5.
37. Ibid.
38. Paul D. Zimmerman and Burt Goldblatt, *The Marx Brothers at the Movies* (New York: Putnam, 1968), p. 17.
39. Ibid.
40. Ibid., p. 65.
41. Ibid., p. 124.
42. Ibid., p. 103.
43. Ibid.
44. Ibid.
45. Ibid., p. 123.
46. Todd Gitlin, *Inside Prime Time* (New York: Pantheon, 1983), p. 32.
47. Robert Toll, *Blacking Up* (New York: Oxford, 1974), p. vi.
48. Ibid., p. 56.
49. Ibid., p. 55.
50. Jack Hurst, *Nashville's Grand Old Opry* (New York: Abrams, 1975), p. 165.
51. Bill C. Malone, *Country Music U.S.A.* (Austin: University of Texas, 1968), p. 195.
52. Ibid.
53. Joey Adams, with Henry Tobias, *The Borscht Belt* (New York: Bobbs-Merrill, 1959), p. 41.
54. Philip Roth, *The Professor of Desire* (New York: Bantam, 1977), p. 1.
55. Toll, pp. 257–58.
56. Cited in Stephen Kanfer, "The Buckle on the Borscht Belt," *Gentleman's Quarterly*, 55:8 (August 1985), p. 201.
57. Leslie Fiedler, "The Breakthrough: The American Jewish Novelist and the Fictional Image of the Jew," in Waldmeir, p. 102.
58. Adams, p. 3.
59. Ibid., p. 212.
60. Irving Howe, *World of Our Fathers* (New York: Simon and Schuster, 1976), p. 568.
61. Ibid., p. 567.
62. Paul Krassner, ed., *Best of "The Realist"* (Philadelphia: Running Press, 1984), p. 26.
63. Allen Ginsberg, "America," *Howl and Other Poems* (San Francisco: City Lights, 1956), p. 32.

CHAPTER 2

Waking Up to Television: A Garden in the Machine

It was about this time I conceived the bold and arduous project of arriving at moral perfection.
—Benjamin Franklin, *Autobiography*[1]

Will we stroll dreaming of the lost America of love past blue automobiles in driveways, home to our silent cottage?
—Allen Ginsberg, "A Supermarket in California"[2]

Woody Allen's *Radio Days*, a 1986 film about the forties, presents the spectacle of working-class New Yorkers using commercial radio as an oracle of urban mythology. Three generations of an economically depressed Jewish family live beneath the same roof in a crumbling Rockaway cottage, too ashamed to let their ten-year-old boy know that his father is a taxicab driver. They find glamour and adventure, however, in the chatter of nightclubbing bons vivants—radiovisions of painlessly sophisticated men in smoking jackets and women in full-length dressing gowns sitting in front of eggs Benedict and sterling coffee services, filling the airwaves with lighthearted stories about "Broadway last night." Allen's otherwise hapless family sits by the radio in underwear listening to a thirty-piece orchestra play for the beautiful people at the Starlight Roof of the Waldorf-Astoria. "Society," for the unnamed family of *Radio Days*, was still an elite institution, something for the wellborn, the talented, or the lucky—a penthouse above the teeming masses of urban peasants, visitable only in dreams. Many were called; few were chosen.

It would be absurd to try to update Allen's story to the TV days that followed. By the fifties, the penthouse (and the city in general) had been largely discredited in the mass media as the Olympus of upward mobility. The manners of the tuxedo-and-evening-gown high-life crowd could never be obtained during a fan's lifetime. The top-hat America of Fred Astaire Paramount musicals—an American dream born of the twenties stock market boom that had mutated into working-class thorazine during the Depression—was robbed of its potency by the erection of the interstate highway system. A freestanding house and a personal automobile offered quicker, if somewhat more modest, status gratification. Elegance, once a state of grace that the cleanest of the unwashed might identify with, was revealed as antidemocratic snobbery. Television—especially the sitcom—valorized suburbia as democracy's utopia realized, a place where the white middling classes could live in racial serenity, raising children in an engineered environment that contained and regulated the twin dangers of culture and nature. The American geniuses of Jefferson and Hamilton had at last found each other, producing coast-to-coast tracts of relatively egalitarian single-unit dwellings obtainable at favorable mortgage rates. The media campaign for this burgeoning way of life included the black-and-white nuclear-family sitcoms that proliferated on television during the late fifties and early sixties.

Contrary to popular memory, the networks did not instantly embrace the suburb as the promised land that would give meaning to the sufferings of the Depression and World War II. The very first television sitcom, in fact, had a distinctively prewar Hollywood screwball movie flavor. *Mary Kay and Johnny* (Dumont, 1947–48; NBC, 1948–49, 1949–50; CBS, 1949) took place in the high-society environs of a Cole Porter song: Johnny was a banker (order), and Mary Kay, his "zany" wife (chaos)—a silk-pajamas comedy. *My Little Margie* (CBS, 1952, 1953; NBC, 1952, 1953–55) reached perhaps the epitome of urban elegance, such as it was in the sitcom. The Albrights were fixed in a luxury high-rise, attended to in their comings and goings by doormen and elevator operators. The suave widower Vernon (Charles Farrell) was a stockbroker, while his "zany" adult daughter Margie (Gale Storm) provided the irrational "female" principle, from which comic situations were bound to spring. The supporting characters were familiar urban types: Mr. Honeywell, Vernon's unforgiving white-mustachioed Wall Street tycoon boss; Mrs. Odetts, the happy-go-lucky Upper East Side dowager, always eager to help the young Margie with her latest scheme; Freddie, Margie's no-account playboy suitor.

But gradually, as the closed-access highways snaked radially from the hubs, suburbia established itself as the sitcom's genus locus. *The Goldbergs*, having lived in the Bronx on radio and television for over a quarter of a century, moved to suburbo-mythic Haverville (Village of the Haves?) in 1954. With the immigrant Jewish family now living in a real house, just like Ozzie and Harriet, the show sacrificed its signature image: Molly Goldberg (Gertrude Berg) would never again be seen leaning out the kitchen window of a tenement apartment shouting, "Yoo-hoo, Mrs. Bloom," to her favorite upstairs *yenta*. As urban identity faded, ethnic identity waned; even the title of the series was eventually changed from *The Goldbergs* to *Molly*. In 1957, Lucy and Ricky abandoned their East Side apartment for a house beyond the city limits. In a quaint bit of period innocence—the suburbs themselves had not yet become cities—Lucy's argument for buying a house in Westport, Connecticut is that the move will allow Little Ricky to grow up "in the country."[3] Though programs such as *The Danny Thomas Show*, *Family Affair*, and *The Jeffersons* would manage to keep the Manhattan luxury apartment on the sitcom map through the decades, family action, beginning in the mid-1950s, had clearly moved out of town. The sitcomic middle class would not make a decisive return to urban settings until the MTM and Norman Lear shows of the seventies.

The popularity of *Father Knows Best*, *Leave It to Beaver*, *The Donna Reed Show*, and other nuclear family sitcoms produced during this suburban ecstasy period has endured by syndication and been given new life by cable and UHF proliferation. Cable services such as the Christian Broadcasting Network, Turner Broadcasting, and Nickelodeon have repackaged these programs and brought them to national market as worthy morality tales (CBN), nostalgia (TBS), and high camp (Nick-at-Nite). Throughout the eighties, for example, all three of the series mentioned above have been shown at least twice a day on national cable, as well as on numerous independent stations in local markets across the country.

Public affection for these sitcoms can easily be attributed to a romantic folkish yearning on the part of the audience for a return to a stable, divorce-free, two-parent household in which father ventures out into the world to hunt for a paycheck while mother stays at home enforcing physical and spiritual cleanliness. Drugless and antierotic (though never asexual, for explicit courtship instructions abound), this suburb of dreams is devoid of dangerous strangers, public transportation, economic fluctuation, and other anxiety-producing phenomena associated with the urban world. The prizes of technology—cars, refrigerators, a bottomless tub of hot water—have been paid for on the installment plan with nothing more than money. At the same time, the rural world of dirty physical labor—of mud, of stench, of vulnerability to the elements—has been utterly transcended. If the legacy of the city to the suburb is technology, the legacy of the land to the suburb is more metaphysical: the individually tended but uniformly trimmed lawns of the curving tree-lined streets bespeak the values of a homogeneous folk community, where a common moral will, forged of a shared sense of blood and honor, ensures a peaceful and prosperous destiny.

Father Knows Best (CBS, 1954–1955, 1958–60; NBC, 1955–58) survives in syndication as the sum and substance of these benevolent Aryan melodramas. Set in a fictive Springfield —more Illinois than Massachusetts or Missouri, but all of these and more—the sitcom drew upon the masscult back yard traditions of Henry Aldrich, Jack Armstrong, and Andy Hardy to transport the viewer to a kind of Eisenhower Walden where adolescence and moral ambiguity were ritualistically trotted out and proven to be no match for the paternal instincts of a rational whitebreadwinner. Evil was not among the problems one encountered in Springfield. The Andersons, according to TV critics Harry Castleman and Walter Podrazik, "were never greedy, stupid, or mischievous, just unlucky or unwise."[4]

Ostensibly classic American small towns, the Springfield of the Andersons, the Mayfield of the Cleavers (*Leave It to Beaver*), and the Hilldale of the Stones (*Donna Reed*) are charged symbols to the urban, ethnic, blue-collar audiences of early television. These sitcom "towns" (they are really more like

52

pure tract developments; we hardly ever see a downtown or even a village green) embody a promise of upward passage into bourgeois legitimacy that was, during this period, luring many recently solvent white American urbanites out of the city: "No man who owns his own house and lot can be a Communist," observed master suburb maker William Levitt. "He has too much to do."[5]

The domestic sitcom romanticized the suburb as an idyllic small town that was located not merely miles from the modern city but the better part of a century away as well. In *I Love Lucy*, Fred and Ethel follow the Ricardos to Westport to start a chicken farm—in 1960! To make the idealization complete, the downside of American small-town life, as described in such gripping detail by Sherwood Anderson, is utterly ignored. The shrieking lunatics of *Winesberg, Ohio* are nowhere to be seen. At the turn of the century, railroad passenger service had been instrumental in establishing the economic and cultural primacy of the big cities, thereby robbing the provincial towns of much of their talent. Sixty years later, a new technology allowed these hinterland communities to return the favor. The closed-access highway made it possible for them to become bedroom satellites that would rob the American city of much of its middle-class residential tax base.

Father Knows Best was one of the last of the popular radio sitcoms (NBC, 1949–54). It came to television at a time when the sitcom, as a genre, was in deep commercial crisis. Race and ethnicity, which had played so well as radio exotica, seemed to spell nothing but trouble for the new visual medium. *Amos 'n' Andy*, the only sitcom ever to be set in Harlem, had been the highest-rated weekly series in the history of radio, playing continuously since 1928. The TV adaptation, however, was met with increasingly passionate protests from the NAACP and other activist civil rights organizations, culminating in the show's ceremonious cancellation by CBS in 1953, after only two seasons of telecast.[6] ABC responded similarly to the resistance provoked by its popular "Negro" sitcom, *Beulah*. Urban ethnicoms such as *The Goldbergs* (Jews in New York) and *Life with Luigi* (Italians in Chicago), both radio powerhouses, went into ratings decline after some early TV success, leaving behind no spin-offs or imitators.

The WASP-com of course was already a familiar subgenre when CBS placed *Father Knows Best* on its fall schedule in 1954. *The Adventures of Ozzie and Harriet* and *The Stu Erwin Show* were two of the most popular. The inventive kicker of *Father Knows Best*, however, was that it had no kicker at all. In *Ozzie and Harriet*, the Nelsons were a show-business family who played "themselves." Ozzie had been a big-band leader; his son Rick would perform a rock-and-roll number at the end of the episode. Stu Erwin (also playing "himself") was the archetypal "bumbling father," an ungainly middle-aged high school principal in a suit and tie who was made the butt of physical sight gags (soaked with a bucket of water, door slammed in the face). But *Father Knows Best* eschewed music, slapstick, and other such nutty stuff, aiming right at the lawn-mowing heart of a Zen conformity. The television archivists Tim Brooks and Earle Marsh have written the following:

> *Father Knows Best* was the classic wholesome family situation comedy. It was set in [a] typical Midwestern community . . . where Jim Anderson was an agent for the General Insurance Company. Every evening he would come home from work, take off his sports jacket, put on his comfortable sweater, and deal with the everyday problems of a growing family. In contrast with most other family comedies of the period, in which one or the other of the parents was a blundering idiot, both Jim and his wife Margaret were portrayed as thoughtful, responsible adults. When a family crisis arose, Jim would calm the waters with a warm smile and some sensible advice.[7]

Robert Young, who had created the role of Jim Anderson on radio, owned *Father Knows Best* in partnership with the show's producer, Eugene Rodney. Perhaps not coincidentally, Young was the only radio cast member to make the jump to television. The Rodney-Young Company motto, displayed on a corporate crest at the end of each *Father Knows Best* episode, was *Ars pro multis* (Art for the Masses), a giant step toward candor from the *Ars gratia artis* (Art for Art's Sake) of Metro-Goldwyn-Mayer. A tall, hometownish leading man in the movies during the forties, Robert Young had at first played romantic parts and, with the coming of middle age, solid husbands and fathers, in over a hundred feature films. But, like many Hollywood stars of the postwar studio crack-up period (such as Donna Reed and Fred MacMurray), Young happily abandoned the erratic work schedules of movie production for the clock-punching timetable of a weekly broadcast series.

Far from an instant hit on television, *Father Knows Best* very nearly died a quick death in the ratings during its first season. Inexplicably placed in a 10 P.M. Sunday slot by CBS programmers, this definitive family show was forced to compete at that late hour against such "adult-oriented" offerings as NBC's *Loretta Young Show* (a drama anthology) and ABC's *Break the Bank* (a big-money quiz). When the show was canceled by CBS at the end of its first TV season, Robert Young and company were saved at the last minute by NBC, which opted to pick up the series and try it at 8:30 P.M. on Wednesdays, a slot more convenient to intergenerational family viewing. Thus properly positioned, the show quickly performed; a total of 203 episodes were produced during a prime-time production run lasting until 1960.

Father Knows Best is rich text, a germinating artifact of the period that many historians like to call "the American Celebration." Boldly precubist in its narrative structure, the sitcom relentlessly pursues social and political issues with a friendly, confident, authoritarian zeal that gives contemporary viewers of diverse political orientation much to think about. The Andersons' Springfield America is so white, so Anglo-Saxon, and so Protestant that even their seemingly Hispanic gardener (Natividad Vacio) goes by the name of Frank Smith! Within the family, the chain of command is equally clear; father, as the show's title indicates, retains biblical prerogative. The static character of social relations in the series is arresting. Unlike her fellow wives in such sitcom hits of the period as *I Love Lucy*, *Burns and Allen*, and *The Honeymooners*, Margaret Anderson (Jane Wyatt) never seriously contests her husband's male hegemony, not even for comic purposes.

On *I Love Lucy*, to cite the most striking example, Ricky's moral, economic, and intellectual superiority is relentlessly questioned by Lucy. Her famous, outrageous "harebrained schemes" are almost always aimed at undermining Ricky's authority. Despite her best efforts, Lucy's schemes inevitably backfire and their failures become ritual celebrations of female deference to patriarchal structure: Lucy should not enter show business because Ricky opposes the idea of his wife working; Lucy should not buy a new dress because Ricky thinks it is too expensive; Lucy should not take up painting because Ricky thinks it is a waste of time. *Father Knows Best* differs from *Lucy* in that these are lessons that Margaret Anderson does not even need to learn. While the restless, scheming top-rated redhead is more than willing to risk public humiliation in her struggle to break the black-and-white sitcom chain of being, Margaret is utterly satisfied (and often says so) with what she perceives to be her humble but noble calling in life—housewife and mother.

The episode "Margaret Wins a Medal" explores a self-reflexive exception that proves the rule. Jim, the earnest executive in the gray flannel suit, comes home from work, briefcase in hand. Jim, Jr., known to all as Bud (Billy Gray), in sweater and jeans, greets Dad at the door with news of his latest athletic accomplishments, displaying the medals he has won that day in a track meet: first place in the quarter-mile relay, second in the half-mile, third in the 220, fourth in the broad jump.

"That's wonderful, Bud," chimes in Margaret, who is apparently getting this news for the first time, even though she has been at home with Bud before Jim's arrival. "It's a shame that those will be thrown in the dresser drawer with all your other medals. You ought to put them in a frame or something, where people would see them."

At first Bud resists this idea, expressing a fear that people might think him a "glory guy" for making such a conspicuous display. But the other members of the family see the possibilities in Mother's selfless suggestion. Betty (Elinor Donahue) offers to contribute her plentiful tennis and debating trophies. Little sister Kathy (Lauren Chapin) promises her spelling-bee medals and the Golden Donut that she won for selling the most donuts in the Little Squaws' fund-raising drive.

"You've got a cup or something to chunk in, don't you, Dad?" asks Bud.

"What do you mean 'a cup?' I've got two golf cups and a bunch of basketball and track medals," Jim replies with mock defensiveness to his oedipal rival, "not to mention my biggest triumph—third-place ribbon in the State Bookkeeping Contest."

Everybody laughs as the family reaches a fulcrum of unity through mutual admiration and collective satisfaction. At this point, however, a gradual acceleration of conflict begins. When Bud suggests building a trophy case and putting it smack in the middle of the living room, Margaret, a modern housewife, replies, "Oh no! I don't want any old homemade furniture in my living room." Jim immediately defers to his woman on this domestic matter, authoritatively announcing that the trophy case will be placed in the basement. This settled, Bud begins action on the family project by taking a written inventory of the trophies to be displayed in the case:

Bud: OK, Mom, how many medals have you won?
Margaret: Who me? I haven't won any medals.
Bud: You haven't?
Kathy: Not even one medal?
Betty: You must have won something.
Margaret: Oh, don't look so sad. I'm perfectly happy cooking
            the meals to keep all you champions hale and
            hearty—and [glancing at her watch] I'd better go
            do that or you won't have enough strength to
            carry all your medals down to the trophy room.
            [She exits.]
Bud: Poor mom. It must be awful not having any talent.

Overhearing this last remark at the kitchen door, Margaret is, at once, bemused by her children's arrogance and self-conscious about the implications of their sympathy. She expresses anxiety to her next-door neighbor Myrtle Davis over coffee in the kitchen the following morning, confiding that she wishes she could win one medal of some kind, just to dispel her children's ridiculous, but annoying, image of her as a pathetic nonachiever.

"What are you good at?" asks Myrtle.

"You've hit the nub of the problem. There's nothing. I can't ski jump or high dive. I can't hurl the shot put. I can't even work a yoyo," Margaret admits.

Myrtle tells Margaret that there is a fly-casting contest for women down at the park every year and that her husband often urges her to compete, because "none of the women are very good" and it would be easy to win. She arranges for Margaret to take lessons from Cliff (played by Cliff Wyatt, a perennial National Flyfishing Champion during the fifties). A blatant beginner, Margaret pledges her "determination and hard work" to the taciturn Cliff. An Anderson, Margaret quickly becomes championship material, reaffirming the redemptive power of pure will. However, on the eve of the competition, she falls down and sprains her arm. Even this seemingly random happenstance is given a moral dimension. The accident takes place as Margaret is running up the steps of Myrtle's front porch to express her confidence and exhilaration at the imminent competition. A good case can be made here for housewife hubris.

When Betty, Bud, and Kathy learn what has happened, they feel more sorry for Mother than ever. But Father, who has understood all along that Margaret is one of life's winners and that she is above the superficial rewards of trophies and medals, comes up with an idea to cure the twin problems of the children's misplaced values and Margaret's disappointment: he has the family stage a mock episode of *This Is Your Life* in which each of the Andersons awards Mother a prize.

Betty, the oldest, begins. She recalls "lean years when Mother used to make creamed tuna and convince us it was chicken." She tells the story of falling in a mud puddle on the way to her first costume party at age nine. "Mother didn't bat an eyelash," but instead improvised a new costume on the spur of the moment—for which Betty won first prize. Welling with emotion as she realizes that the prize she won actually belongs to Mother, Betty presents Margaret with a frying pan that has the words "MOST VALUABLE MOTHER" painted on the bottom.

Bud tells the story of how Mother delivered the newspapers on his paper route during "the big rainstorm." He presents her with a shaving mug (this comically emblemizes the clumsiness of young males in matters of social grace, such as gift-giving) that reads, "Boy's Best Friend." Kathy proudly describes a PTA bake sale during which her teacher, in front of the whole class, commented on how dependable Kathy's mother was and "how much better the world would be if there were more people like her." Kathy awards Margaret a blue ribbon for "Being Mother I'm Most Proud of." Jim, who doesn't need to trivialize Margaret's overall contribution to the family with any one particular anecdote, gives her a fishing rod and reel, demonstrating his full understanding of her achievement. Cliff, a surprise guest, enters the living room and presents Margaret with a box of fishing flies "For Best Pupil."

This episode, an emphatic, good-humored reaffirmation of traditional gender role models, won the 1958–59 Emmy Award for "best direction of a single program of a comedy series" for series director Peter Tewksbury.[8] "Margaret Wins a Medal" is a bit unusual in the overall context of the series in that it seems to conjure the specter of role restlessness on the part of one of the parents. But even in this instance, dissatisfaction with middle-class gender destiny is shown to be a red herring. The narrative gradually reveals that what we have witnessed is not the result of Margaret's dissatisfaction with the anonymity of wifehood or motherhood, but rather a consequence of the children's immature values. Resolution of the conflict is achieved as the children learn an important lesson about the true meaning of "winning" in life. Medals and trophies are fine, but modern homemakers (that is, modern women) are motivated by something more complex—love and the sense of duty that grows from it.

More typically, episodes are directly structured around the problems of Betty, Bud, and Kathy, three American citizens-in-training. Betty Anderson, the firstborn, is among the most thoroughly obnoxious characters ever created for situation comedy, easily surpassing such latter-day sitcom repulsives as *Mary Tyler Moore*'s Ted Baxter or *WKRP in Cincinnati*'s Herb Tarlek. Impossibly high strung, Betty, whom Father likes to call "Princess," is apt at any moment to come running into the house whining in tears because some boy at school has called her "plain." In the episode titled "Whistle Bait," she goes absolutely to pieces when a new girl, a "beauty queen," transfers to her school, stealing the feminine limelight from her. An immature version of Margaret, she is obsessed with status and personal power, having yet to learn the "womanly" satisfactions of self-sacrifice. By the same token, Bud is an unripened Jim, a bit too concerned with his car, his athletic

59

prowess, and other crude symbols of masculinity. The implicitly prepubescent Kathy is pointedly androgynous during the first several years of the series, vacillating between "tomboyish" imitations of her father and brother and "feminine" imitations of her mother and sister. In the later episodes, however, as she begins to physically mature, she makes decisive role choices. The tomboy image is put to rest in the final season in the episode "Kathy Becomes a Girl," in which the entire family takes part in her metamorphosis from a baseball-playing polymorph into a young American lady, à la Betty.

In an episode that might as well have been titled "Betty Meets the Lesbians," Betty is nominated to become Flower Queen of the annual Spring Flower Festival at Springfield Junior College.[9] She is, needless to say, enthralled by the possibility of this recognition of her femininity, bragging to the family about how she was chosen over fifty other girls for the honor of the nomination.

"Does that mean that they think that *you* are one of the prettiest girls in that college?" asks Bud derisively.

"Well, I guess it amounts to that," she replies with mock pained humility.

Several days before the Flower Queen Pageant, Elvia Horshen, captain of the girls' track team, pays Betty an unexpected visit. Elvia, with close-cropped hair, truck-driver grammar, and a viselike handshake, is a grotesque period caricature of a homosexual woman. She entreats the glamorous Betty to pose for pictures with the girls' track team, so that this hapless bunch ("Face it, we're not exactly the prettiest girls at school") can get some publicity in the local newspaper during the Flower Festival. Her ego aloft on the wings of her nomination, Betty effects great noblesse oblige, agreeing to help out the needy oddball girl athletes. However, when she learns that both other candidates for Flower Queen have already turned Elvia down and that, furthermore, she must pose for newspaper pictures in an "awful" (that is, "unfeminine") track uniform, Betty despairs of her decision. In typical style, she throws a tantrum, pounding the living room couch with her fists, shouting "Stupid me, stupid Betty," convinced that presenting such an unladylike image in public will destroy her chances in the Flower Queen election.

Unable to find an honorable way out, Betty fulfills her commitment in true Anderson style. The action cuts to the photo session: Betty curling up into a classic Greek discus thrower's stance; Betty crossing the finish line. Unhappy, but performing dutifully, Betty is pushed over the brink of distress by the razzing she gets from Gloria, the fastest runner on the team, who, like Elvia, has short hair and talks like a tough guy.

When Betty asks if the session will end soon, Gloria snaps, "What's a matter? Your dainty little feet tired?" Though Elvia commands her to "knock it off," Gloria scornfully persists. Betty's prissy complaint about the bagginess of the track uniform provokes Gloria to sharper sarcasm: "If we'd a known you was coming, we'd have whipped up a gold bathing suit for you."

The photographer then asks Betty and Gloria to pose for a starting-line shot. But when the gun goes off, their mutual animosity causes them to race for real. "Okay, cream puff, you asked for it," Gloria hisses. Lo and behold, an incensed Betty, though she has never raced competitively in her life, defeats the cocky school champion in a one hundred-yard dash. The effect of this discovery of yet another of her talents is, however, a mixed bag for Betty. Struck by Betty's "natural . . . grace and stamina," Elvia begs her to compete in the big track meet against Alden, despite the fact that it will take place just hours before the Flower Queen contest: "Let's face it, you're our only chance for a little bit of glory. The girls' track team isn't much, but it represents your school and every girl on it will be tearing her heart to win tomorrow. All the girls want is a chance to win. With you in the 100-yard dash, we've got that chance. You can give us a chance to win."

Characteristically brought to the brink of tears, Betty is torn between achieving the personal, "feminine" satisfaction of being elected Flower Queen and the call to civic duty by the school team. "Why fight it?" she finally sighs, agreeing to help Elvia and the pathetic, overlooked, unpopular, but hardworking women athletes. But just as Betty is resigned to the painful loss of a chance at individual glory, Father comes to the rescue. Convinced that personal satisfaction and community spirit can never be in true conflict, Jim devises a plan by which the girls on the team will spirit Betty back to the gym on a golf cart after the race, undress her, clean her up, and prepare her for the beauty pageant. Everyone, even Margaret, doubts the viability of the scheme, claiming that it would take "at least three hours" for any woman to get into formal attire. Needless to say, Betty wins the hundred-yard dash and, with the help of her teammates, is prepped, primed, and elected college Flower Queen in less than ten minutes. Not only does Betty's victory in the race win the track meet for Springfield, but her victory in the pageant allows the deviant women of the track team to feel that they have gained, through their contribution, a bit of acceptable feminine reward for themselves. Betty benefits by learning that the greatest personal achievements are made in concert with group aims and values.

If Betty too often overvalues status and gentility, the Anderson male child, Bud, errs in the opposite direction. Unselfconsciously entering the house covered with the axle grease of his beloved jalopy, he plays earthy wiseguy foil to the pretentious Betty. He is often guilty of sins of enthusiasm, but his sometimes irresponsible behavior is trivialized as the healthy impulsiveness of a precocious bourgeois boy. Adolescent foibles aside, when the chips are down, Bud demonstrates that he is destined to genetically replicate the solid-citizenry of his father. In one episode, he interviews Mr. Herman W. Bernard, an international trucking magnate (with headquarters in Springfield) for the school newspaper. Learning that this self-made millionaire is a high school dropout, Bud decides to quit school, go to San Francisco, and ship out to the Far East on a steamer, a bold antifamily fantasy containing beatnik implications. Margaret urges Jim to put his foot down immediately. However, they did not call this show *Father Knows Best* for nothing. Jim, having been a boy himself, is aware that parental pressure might only make the taboo more attractive. He *advises* his son to finish school and go to college, but agrees, now that Bud is over the legal school age of sixteen, that the decision is his. Jim comforts Margaret by expressing his confidence that Bud will come to his senses and make the right decision.

Bud is so unprepared for the "real world" that he leaves home the next morning without even eating a good breakfast. Taking nothing but the shirt on his back with him—not even money—he goes to Mr. Bernard's office to ask for a job on a company ship. While sitting in the waiting room, however, he begins to drool as the secretary eats a sandwich at her desk. Apparently having seen young boys from "good" families try this silly stuff before, the secretary tells Bud that the boss won't give a job to a boy who hasn't finished school. Mr. Bernard's greatest regret, she informs Bud and the viewer, is that he never got an education. She offers Bud an orange, which he gladly accepts as he runs out the door to return home. Not only is Jim's faith in his son (and himself) redeemed, but the objective correctness of Jim's point of view is reified by the self-made millionaire's explicit echoing of it.

In "Bud Joins the Carnival," the scion of the House of Anderson once again makes the mistake of flirting with a male role model other than Father. This time he becomes infatuated with Bert, a carnival barker whose motto is "Never give a sucker an even break" (a philosophy that Jim, an insurance salesman, claims to abhor). Bud is impressed by the way the conman fleeces the pigeons, and he resolves to run off and join the carnival. Bert gives Bud a job at a sideshow, but when Bud goes to collect his pay the next day, the carnival has already left town. Crestfallen, Bud once again returns home to the Anderson way of life. As in the going-to-sea episode, the correctness of Jim's approach to life is objectified: a small package has been left on the doorstep. It contains a two-dollar watch that Bud had admired at the carnival and a note from Bert warning Bud not to "hang around with guys like me."

The lessons of *Father Knows Best* are never dramatized as revelations. They are more in the spirit of smiling reminders, aimed at well-fed, rational, civilized citizens, of the universal and eternal truths that already dwell in a Christian soul tempered by American egalitarianism. So stable and safe and favored by God are Jim and Margaret Anderson, so confident are they of who they are and from what options they might choose, that for them child rearing has become an activity akin to gardening—indoor gardening at that. If the seedlings are planted and watered properly, if appropriate temperature is maintained, if a sharp watch is kept for minor distresses, then DNA encoding will do the rest.

This orderly optimistic image of family life in America did not escape the attentions of the U.S. government. In 1959 the

Treasury Department underwrote the production of a special episode of *Father Knows Best* titled "Twenty-Four Hours in Tyrant Land." Anticipating the ABC miniseries *Amerika* by almost three decades, the half-hour narrative depicts Springfield under Communist rule: utopia turned dystopia. Never broadcast, 16mm prints of the film were screened for school, church, and civic groups across the country, free of charge, as part of a U.S. Savings Bonds (formerly War Bonds) drive.[10]

But a viewer need not see "Twenty Four Hours in Tyrant Land" to find evidence of the cold war's impact on Springfield, U.S.A. Even among the regularly televised episodes, the state of permanent war manages to make itself felt. In "Betty and the Jet Pilot," for example, Bud finds a fighter pilot's helmet on the not-so-mean streets of Springfield. Good citizens to say the least, the Andersons jump in the family vehicle and rush over to a local Air Force base to return this bit of government issue, which, they learn, was inadvertently dropped by the pilot while bailing out over Springfield. Overcome with gratitude, the brass arranges for Bud to go for a ride in one of their latest jets; viewers are treated to reassuring file footage. Betty, meanwhile, falls in love with the Steve Canyon-like pilot (and vice versa). In what can best be described as a typical single-episode sitcom romance, the two go on a picnic, overcome initial shyness, and decide to get married. They call off the wedding, however, when the would-be groom is transferred to a Strategic Air Command base in Alaska. There is just too much danger out there; he might never come back. Betty understands. A beautiful and talented girl like her can find a husband and get married any old time. She swallows her disappointment, accepting the protection of the free world as happiness enough.

The clear and present danger of a hostile attack by a foreign power acts as a kind of framing device around the otherwise idyllic video portrait of Middle American family life. Television historian Erik Barnouw has written extensively on the effects of McCarthyism on TV content. He notes that "in 1954, and increasingly in 1955, sponsors and their ad agencies began to add drastic revisions and to take control of script problems."[11] This kind of politically motivated meddling weakened and ultimately destroyed live serious drama series such as *Playhouse 90*

64

and *Studio One*. By the same token, it strengthened the generic hand of the sitcom, whose structurally guaranteed "happy ending" tended to celebrate the status quo of a capitalistic consumption-oriented society that was well worth dying for.

In *Television and the Red Menace: The Video Road to Vietnam*, J. Fred MacDonald cites *Father Knows Best* as one of the fifties TV series that portrayed the United States as "a fat, contented place," threatened by the rest of the world, which was "wretched and unsettled."[12] Placing the suburban domesticom in the context of a prime-time schedule that was top-heavy in the late fifties with explicit military and spy adventure shows, MacDonald writes, "As well as being malnourished and on the verge of turmoil, the world beyond the United States was pictured as treacherous and terrifying. Enemy spies seemed to be everywhere, working to inhibit individual freedom and disrupt peace."[13]

The success of *Father Knows Best* in the ratings, coupled with its natural immunity from McCarthyite criticism, established the show's suburbo-pastoral sitcom gestalt as industry wisdom for almost a decade. Close ideological fellow travelers included such hits as *The Donna Reed Show* (variation: emphasis on wife's point of view); *Leave It to Beaver* (variation: emphasis on relationships between two brothers); and *My Three Sons* (variation: household without women). Hal Himmelstein has characterized these sitcoms as "Cold War comedies of reassurance," describing their cosmic territory as "the suburban middle landscape."[14]

Social critics acknowledged the power of the image. "There is a familiar America," wrote Michael Harrington in 1962. "It is . . . advertised on television. . . . It has the highest mass standard of living the world has ever known."[15] Harrington titled his exposé of poverty, racism, and corruption in the U.S. during the fifties *The Other America*. His use of the word "other" implies the existence of a "first" America, a cheerfully painted facade America of smiling suburban families. That America might easily be understood as the one portrayed in *Father Knows Best* and other sitcoms of its type. But despite the politically loaded picture painted by these popular shows, they provoked virtually no direct commentary from culture critics (even mass-culture critics) during their halcyon days in prime time.

This is not to say that the ideological underpinnings of these shows failed to capture the attention of some writers during the "silent" decade. Allen Ginsberg, for example, was expressing a very different vision of American postbomb family life, even as *Father Knows Best* was making its climb up the Nielsens. In "Howl" (1956), "the best minds" of Ginsberg's generation "accuse the radio of hypnotism" as they "sit listening to the crack of doom on the hydrogen jukebox." The poet likens the emerging permanent-war, mass-mediated consumer society to Moloch, the ancient heathen deity who demanded the sacrifice of human children:

> Moloch who entered my soul early! Moloch in whom I am
> a consciousness without a body! Moloch who frightened me
> out of my natural ecstasy![16]

Single-home zoning notwithstanding, there is the compelling image in Ginsberg's poem of an America so deeply committed to war and materialism that the pastoral folk community of Springfield is revealed as a ludicrous breeding ground for the young meat who will be fed into its wars and rat races and inhuman conformities. Far from a princess shown in the process of unfolding into a queen who will one day preside over her own split-level castle, Betty Anderson can be seen in such a context as a spoiled neurasthenic prig who has been stripped of her organic erotic heritage by a system that values competition above sorority. Bud, who wears tight, revealing T-shirts and jeans, will one day "mature" and cover himself with the suit-and-tie uniform that Jim wears, even while "relaxing" at home. The Neal Cassady that dwells within Bud—his love of girls, his love of cars, his dreams of knowing the low and vulgar sides of the world—are shown to be childhood diseases, like the measles or the mumps, conditions that will pass as his cultural immunities to eros are developed. Once her dangerous breasts appear, little Kathy will no doubt walk in high heels behind Betty, just as Betty follows lockstep behind Margaret.

> Moloch! Moloch! Robot apartments! invisible suburbs!
> skeleton treasuries! blind capitals! demonic industries!

spectral nations! invincible madhouses! granite cocks! monstrous bombs!

Ginsberg mourns the passing of the America of Walt Whitman, the America of "Visions! omens! hallucinations! miracles! ec-stasies!" That erotically idyllic "lost America of love" has "gone down the American river."[17] The sitcom has triumphed: Huck Finn is dead, long live Tom Sawyer!

Jack Kerouac suffers a more complex relationship with the imperial suburbia of the 1950s than does the messianic Gins-berg. Kerouac's novels, most of which were released during the production run of *Father Knows Best*, are generally filed in collective cultural memory banks such as *Time*, CNN, and *USA Today* as unabashed celebrations of bohemianism, icons of dropoutism to be mentioned each year on the anniversary of the writer's death and then returned to storage disk. When carefully read, however, these novels betray a profound ambiguity con-cerning the relative merits of suburban family life and alterna-tive modes of existence. In *On the Road*, Sal Paradise wanders the tenements and prairies of the continent with Whitmanian abandon, but dutifully returns to the white-picket-fence home of his aunt in New Jersey every time he feels "the pull of my own life calling me back."[18] The concluding image of the novel finds Sal's onetime "road" idol, Dean Moriarty, reduced to a pathetic, shivering hitchhiker standing on a midtown Manhattan street corner, while Sal rides off in a limousine to Carnegie Hall, his fiancée in tow. In *The Subterraneans*, Leo Percepied is torn between a life in San Francisco with his lover Mardou Fox, the black sex goddess of North Beach, and a life in his mother's comfortable home in the Peninsula suburbs. Mardou answers Leo's deepest erotic yearnings, but his love for her is plagued by her "dirty room, the unwashed sheets."[19] Unable to let go of what he calls his "white ambition,"[20] Leo leaves Mardou—and San Francisco—for mother and suburb, where he can concentrate on his work and the advancement of his career. When the chips are down, Leo, like Sal Paradise and Bud Anderson, just goes home.

Though Kerouac's novels usually take place in an anti-Springfield America that vibrates with erotic response, rec-reational drug use, and forms of human devotion and cruelty

that are still largely unknown in prime-time television, there
is a kind of sitcom dream deep in the heart of his heroes that
promises them suburban sanctuary if they can just find a way
through the not-made-for-TV urban night. It is worth noting that
when *On the Road* was finally published, following seven years
of painful rejection, Kerouac took his own shot at masscult
legitimacy, perhaps envisioning more of a white-picket-fence
future for himself. The writer appeared on several turn-of-the-
decade television programs, including *The Steve Allen Show* and
William F. Buckley's *Firing Line*. His friend John Clellon Holmes
commented years later that Kerouac "wrote that astonishing
series of books in a short period of time in total obscurity. Fame
came, and he was supposed to go on talk shows where he was
treated like Marlon Brando. He was treated as a curiosity, not as
a serious man; this inevitably does something to an artist."[21]

Indeed, a kinescope of the *Steve Allen* episode reveals Jack
Kerouac as anything but a commodity salable on American
television. In his 1959 appearance on the Sunday night comedy-
variety hour, he is nervous and perplexed, clearly out of place
physically, emotionally, and intellectually. Allen conducts the
interview while sitting at a piano musing over some suitably
nutty jazz improvisations, interpreting Kerouac's answers with
whimsical-cosmical chords and runs. Introducing his guest
as "the embodiment" of a "social movement called 'Beat Generation,'" he admits to Kerouac, "I've got a couple of square
questions for you, Jack."[22] Kerouac's responses to Allen consist of a series of brooding, laconic monosyllables and facial
expressions that force the harried host to carry the interview
on his own show-business shoulders:

Allen: How long did it take you to write *On the Road*?
Kerouac: Three weeks.
Allen: Three weeks? That's amazing. How long were you
actually 'on the road?'
Kerouac: Seven years.
Allen: Hmmm . . . I was once on the road for three weeks
and it took me seven years to write about it.

Kerouac then gives a vague, mysterious, mock-dutiful smile,
and the camera quickly abandons a close-up.

Viewed thirty years after the fact, Kerouac's *Steve Allen* appearance survives its historical moment as both a rare period artifact and a failed marketing experiment. The confusion and dislocation that dominates the black-and-white exchange is broken just once:

Allen: How would you define the word "beat"?
Kerouac: Well . . . sympathetic.[23]

A composer and critic himself, Steve Allen's appreciation of jazz—as a temperament as well as a music—occasionally revealed itself beneath his masscult professional drag. He was all but alone among the TV impresarios of the fifties in making some attempt to shine a network spotlight on artists whose visions otherwise kept them at the margins of the entertainment-industrial complex. Another of his notably controversial, off-beat guests was Lenny Bruce, who, though orignally a show-biz professional himself, was by 1959 just as much out of place in prime time as Jack Kerouac. A nightclub comic who had formed his character on the playing fields of the Borscht Belt, Bruce had tried several times during the fifties to find a way into television, despite his growing reputation as a "blue" comedian. He was, however, too enamored of personal vision, too much of a "street Jew," and, finally, too stoned to get there.

A look at Bruce's appearance on *The Steve Allen Show* of April 5, 1959, reveals much about the evolving character of prime time at the turn of the decade. Steve's guests that night were the Three Stooges, Lenny Bruce, and a couple of singers, along with the show's regular troupe of comedians: Louis Nye, Tom Poston, and Don Knotts. Sponsored in full by Du Pont chemical company ("Better Things for Better Living . . ."), the comedy-variety hour drew much of its energy from the lighthearted identity crisis of its host.

A man whose eclectic resumé included writing jazz criticism for *Downbeat* magazine and jumping into a vat of Jell-O on *The Tonight Show*, Steve Allen cut a prismatic figure on fifties television. Following the instincts of a democratic advocate of pluralistic diversity, he delighted in patrolling the broad American demilitarized zone that divides "art" from "enter-tainment" in his search for television material. But if the booking of a Lenny Bruce onto his network TV show was an attempt at cultural cross-fertilization, the presentation of such a guest also saddled Allen with certain awkward problems and responsibilities. As host of the prime-time comedy-variety hour, he was obliged to provide his audience with a sense of Bruce's position on the familiar show-biz continuum.

Though few viewers had ever been to a nightclub to see Lenny Bruce perform, most knew by way of media report that he was a "sick comedian." The use of this term has all but disappeared from show-business jargon today, but in the 1950s "sick comedian" was a potent, double-edged appellation. On the one hand, it meant that the comedian told "off-color" jokes about "tasteless" subjects.[24] But "sick" also implied a kind of sophistication and intelligence in subject matter that distinguished such comedians from the burlesque comics who had been telling potty jokes and anatomical one-liners since the dawn of modern show business. Mort Sahl's penchant for topical political badinage had gained him the "sick" tag; Shelley Berman and Bob Newhart were "sick" because they talked about psychoanalysis and made reference to historical phenomena. The sickness of sick comedians could either be seen as their own sick insistence on exploiting vulgarity, despite their obvious intelligence, or as a reference to their insistence on exploring the sick aspects of society in an urbane, articulate way. It was clearly Allen's strategy to emphasize the latter interpretation. At the very top of his opening monologue, Allen tells the audience, "The question before the house tonight is, Will the audience who tuned in to see the Three Stooges know what Lenny Bruce is talking about, or versy-vicey? Heh, heh, heh."[25]

Like Kerouac, Bruce is treated with a kind of mysterious sanctified respect that turns him into a curiosity even among the curiosities of show business. His controversialness is immediately—in the very first words of the show—acknowledged and co-opted by Allen, repackaged into a commodity which, now ready for market, can be sold to the audience. As with Kerouac, that commodity is Genius: "Will the audience . . . know what Lenny Bruce is talking about?" But while the "genius" label can be merely annoying to a novelist, it is absolute death to a stand-up comedian. Bruce's cool is blown before he even appears on camera. The comic possibilities of Lenny Bruce suddenly un-leashed on a TV show between a commercial for Du Pont and an appearance by the Three Stooges are sacrificed to television's paranoid, lowest-common-denominator legacy. Ironically, the "least objectionability" principle is upheld even as it is seemingly subverted by the presentation of an outspoken advocate of racial desegregation, First Amendment rights, and sexual freedom.

Later on in the show, as the introduction to Bruce's actual stand-up appearance, Allen offers further co-optive apologia:

> We get a great deal of mail from our viewers commenting on our sketches. Whether you realize it or not, there is no joke or sketch, particularly of a satirical sort, that will not offend somebody . . . you know, a cowboy or a drunk or someone.—Now we'll probably get mail from cowboys or drunks. Heh, heh, heh.—I tell you how we are going to face that problem: we have decided that once a month we will book a comedian who will offend everybody and then we'll get it all over with—a man who will disturb many social groups watching right now because his satirical comments refer to things not ordinarily discussed on television. That way, the NBC mail department will know in advance that the complaints are coming in. They'll hire three extra girls and get the stamped answers ready: "We're very sorry. We didn't mean it." You know, that kind of thing. And so the whole thing will be handled with neatness and dispatch. So, ladies and gentlemen, here is the very shocking comedian, the most shocking comedian of our time, a young man who is skyrocketing to fame . . . Lenny Bruce.[26]

Bright-eyed and bushy-tailed, an eager Lenny Bruce jumps out from the wings in a stylish suit, looking every bit the clean-cut young 1950s entertainer who is getting a shot on a network TV show. "Here I am, the skyrocket," he cracks. His performance, however, as anyone who has seen or heard him work in another medium will likely tell you, is a painful exercise in compromise, suggesting vulgarization rather than the vulgarity he was so famous for.

Immediately acknowledging his reputation as "offensive," the comedian offers a list of "things that offend *me*." It includes

71

"Governor [Orville] Faubus" (no laugh), "segregation" (a few titters), and "shows that exploit homosexuality, narcotics, and prostitution under the guise of helping these societal problems" (no laugh).[27] Things lighten up a bit when Bruce goes into an imitation of a child getting high sniffing airplane glue, an idea merely amusing to a 1959 audience unable to take it seriously as a reality-based phenomenon that will soon make The News.

Unable to curse, discuss sex in graphic detail, or lapse into what the comedian characterized as his "hip and Yiddish idiom,"[28] his performance is bland and disjointed. The viewer can sense the way in which the monologue has been reconstructed by committee in a series of meetings and countermeetings with producers and censors. The civil rights jokes are short one-liners. There is but one topical "Jew joke" ("Will Elizabeth Taylor become bar mitzvahed?"); otherwise no Yiddish is used. Most importantly, with the monolithic time constraint of commercial air staring him in the face, the comedian is unable to probe and mumble his way toward clarity, the process by which he often came to his most powerful imagery. The routine ends with Steve coming out to give piano accompaniment to Lenny's singing-talking of "All Alone," a sentimental number that the comedian punctuates with seriocomic beatnik-flavored poetry:

> I don't want a chick who can quote Kerouac and walk with poise,
> I just want to hear my old lady say, "Get up and fix the bathroom. It's still making noise."[29]

Fade to black. Judging from the frequency and the level of enthusiasm of the laughs he got, the comedian received more applause than he deserved. The studio audience had not found Bruce particularly funny, but it had been convinced by hype that it had seen a "heavy" act on the cutting edge of official taboo. Prompted by the "applause" sign, the audience demonstrated appropriate appreciation.

The Three Stooges, who followed Bruce, carried charged cultural baggage of their own before the camera. Survivors from the age of vaudeville—the biblical era of modern show business—the Stooges, by the 1950s, could do not wrong in the high art of low comedy, even though they seemed more than willing to test the limits of their own credentials. Suffering through their utterly pathetic post–Curley Howard, post–Shemp Howard, post-Joe Besser period, they somehow, after thirty-five years of doing short bits, managed to show up for a gig without anything resembling a script.[30] The aging Moe just stormed out onstage and started slapping and gouging the dumbfounded Joe Dorita, who, for reasons unexplained, was wearing an Arabian sultan's costume. Pretty soon Larry entered the picture, took a few smacks in the head, and fell down; the act had been performed. The Stooges had apparently become so self-reflexive a cultural institution (probably owing to the ubiquitous TV release of their 200 Columbia short subjects during the fifties) that they had transcended the necessity for narrative continuity. They simply came out before the cameras and *were* the Three Stooges.

The studio audience showed that it knew it had been given a rare opportunity to see "classic comedians," saints of vaudeville. The Stooges' routine may have *seemed* confused, insipid, banal, and even downright stupid, but that was only because the boys were such remarkable greasepaint primitives that their clown art defied comprehension by the corrupt mind of the TV era. In any case, Lenny Bruce, the hottest ticket in the hip nightclub circuit, had, in effect, opened for the Three Stooges and made them look good.

Bruce, it should be noted, was not a complete stranger to commercial television when he agreed to do *The Steve Allen Show* in 1959. He had performed on several network shows during the fifties, including Johnny Carson's CBS variety hour and *The Robert Q. Lewis Show*. As early as 1951, he had appeared as a "find" on the top-rated *Arthur Godfrey's Talent Scouts*. His mother, Sally Bruce, appeared with him on the show as the "talent scout" who had discovered the comedian:

Godfrey: What kind of comedy does [Lenny] do?
Sally Bruce: Oh, impersonations . . . mimicry . . .
Godfrey: Oh, wonderful!

Thus introduced to the American public, Bruce walked out in front of network cameras for the first time and said, "Good evening, everyone. It's great to see that television is coming in so strong in vaudeville."

A mystifying observation today, the basis for Bruce's remark is better understood in historical context. Vaudeville had all but died in the late twenties at the hands of talking pictures, although in some places it shared the bill with films up to about 1950. Ironically, the memory and spirit of the old variety theater had been kept alive in public consciousness largely by movie musicals—including (irony of ironies) *The Jazz Singer*, the first commercial talkie. In the late forties, however, the growth of television seemed to signal a technological resuscitation of the vaudeville show. Milton Berle, Burns and Allen, Jack Benny, and other survivors of the vaudeville era, none of whom had experienced much success in the movies, were achieving new heights of stardom doing vaudeville bits for home consumption. As early as 1948, the William Morris Agency, anxious to book acts on *Texaco Star Theater* proclaimed, in a two-page ad in *Variety* "Vaudeville Is Back . . . Wanted—Variety artists from all corners of the globe."[31]

In a shrinking market for live entertainment (the stand-up "concert" had yet to be invented), a television dominated by comedy-variety, TV's approximation of vaudeville, held out the best hope for a young comedian who might otherwise be destined for "the toilets," as Bruce characterized most of the night spots of the era.[32] As we have seen, however, "TV vaudeville" was not to be. By the end of the decade, comedy-variety, far from determining the character of prime time, was gradually disappearing from view. Beginning in the sixties, whole generations of stand-up comedians—Morey Amsterdam, Don Rickles, Robin Williams—would have to seek sitcom vehicles at the risk of otherwise being shut out of prime time. Moreover, not all who tried to make the transition from TV vaudeville to comic drama (the sitcom) were able to accomplish it gracefully. Rickles' long string of sitcom failures, for example, can be traced to the difficulties in containing his compulsive, performance-oriented persona into a proscenium framework that would allow for both the spontaneity of the insult and the integrity of the fourth-wall illusion. Lenny Bruce, though radically different from Rickles in style, faced similarly enormous problems in this respect.

Imagine a Lenny Bruce sitcom. A suit and tie, a house on Elm Street, a wifette and kids, and a script written in the blood of a Standards and Practices Department executive could hardly have withstood the fission of Bruce's "white Negro" slang and free-flowing Yiddishisms:

Wife: What would you like for dinner tonight dear?
Lenny: I'm a carnivore and I don't care what animal has to get *shlepped* around to satisfy that carnivore urge, man. How about pot roast? Let's *fress* pot roast. Your pot roast really cooks, baby.
Wife: Junior wrecked the car today, dear.
Lenny: Oo, if that kid wasn't such a *shtarker*, I'd give him a *zetz* in the *kishkas*.

No Robert Young, Bruce's one actual chance at his own television program came in 1958. Metromedia toyed with the idea of trying the comedian as the host of a syndicated Monday-through-Friday desk-and-sofa talk show that would aim for a share of the late-night audience that Jack Paar had to himself as the host of NBC's *Tonight Show*. Bruce's biographer, Albert Goldman, wrote:

Lenny was delighted [at the chance] to get on the tube, but was worried about the shift from his usual raunchy material to the white-on-white stuff demanded by television. He decided that he needed a taster, an arbiter of gentility: an intelligent and reliable person who would curb his worst excesses and spark him to TV concepts. So he called up Kenny Hume, the drummer who had been his pal . . . and asked him if he would like to come out to Palm Springs for a week, while they struggled to get the pilot project into shape. But the big script conference out in the desert turned into a straight dope orgy that lasted three days and left both men right where they started—without the semblance of an idea for the New York series.[33]

In his 1961 Carnegie Hall concert, Bruce seems to have decisively recognized his essential incompatibility with network television. He identifies three problems that disqualify him from partaking in the prime-time bonanza. "My language," he admits to the audience, "is completely larded with hip idiom and Yiddish idiom." He compares doing stand-up on television to playing a nightclub where everyone keeps asking everyone else, "What does *shmuck* mean?" The second problem is generational. His act, he tells the midnight Carnegie Hall audience, seems to appeal only to people between the ages of twenty and forty. With an audience restricted to under-forty adults, he claims, he could "take on fifty Berles . . . and eight Bob Newharts." His market analysis may have been prescient. Had Bruce survived into the target-market cable era, he indeed might have found a niche for himself on television as the perfect HBO comedian. In 1961, however, television was still strictly a mass medium—and that meant giant head counts with little regard for age, gender, income, or any of the other demographic factors that dominate television programming today. His third problem, and perhaps the most insurmountable in terms of commercial television, was a personal performance problem: "As soon as it becomes repetitive to me, I can't cook with it."

All of these points soon became moot. The comedian's arrests in the early sixties on obscenity and, later, narcotics charges effectively blacklisted him from any further television appearances. Albert Goldman, writing in *Commentary* in 1963, notes the changes that took place in Bruce as he drifted further and further away from the possibilities of television and other forms of mainstream show-business success:

> Whereas in the past Bruce would walk briskly out on the floor, good-looking, impeccably groomed, wearing a chic Italian suit, now he comes on stiff-legged and stooped, wearing shabby clothes, his face a pale mask of dissipation. Having discarded the civilized mask that people wear in public to protect themselves, Bruce comes before his audience as a mythic figure—beat, accused junkie, "underground" man—who has suffered in acting out his own forbidden desires.[34]

Having descended beneath the aesthetic and legal limits of Gleason's Poor Soul and Skelton's Freddie the Freeloader into a plausible manifestation of the underside of American culture, Bruce gradually disengaged his art from show business. Goldman observed that "Bruce . . . always tries to *reduce* the barrier between the stage and reality. He has never wanted to appear as an entertainer doing an act, but rather as himself."[35] The same, of course, could be said of many comedians—Jonathan Winters, Don Rickles, Jerry Lewis. The difference, however, was the explicit and explosive anticommercial "self" that Bruce had to bring to the stage. He could not, like Steve Allen, smile gracefully for the network cameras on command.

With comedy-variety dying and unable to revive itself with the fresh energies of any outside (or "underground") sources, there was no formal rejoinder on network television to *Father Knows Best*'s white-on-white comedy of bourgeois gentility. It and the other suburban domesticoms defined the "normal" point of view from which the world was viewed on American television. The Andersons were a model family living a model life in a model environment—if not in sociological reality, certainly in the mythic reality of situation comedy. Any given sitcom could be measured by its distance from the suburban center established in *Father Knows Best*.

Rural life, though paid sentimental lip service, had deteriorated in situation comedy from its noble role in America's past into a kind of class condition for those too simple to live the normal (that is, suburban) way. This idea is explicitly promoted in the *Father Knows Best* episode "Jim, the Farmer," in which Jim becomes fed up with modern life in Springfield and decides to get back to his—and America's—agrarian roots by moving to a farm. By the end of the episode, he's back in the insurance business, having realized that a return to such a lifestyle for a capable twentieth-century citizen such as himself is impossible; it is just too selfish.

The Real McCoys (ABC, 1957–62; CBS, 1962–63) was the only sitcom during the fifties (or since) that concerns the life of a working farm family.[36] The McCoys were emigrants from West Virginia to California. Typical episodes of the series concern young Hassy suffering the embarrassment of having to make her own dress for a school dance or Little Luke being teased at school for his hillbilly origins. The desire of the children to become real suburban Californians clashes with the homespun values of Grandpa McCoy (Walter Brennan). Though Grandpa's values are treated with great respect, the inevitability of the suburban future is taken for granted.

The Beverly Hillbillies also concerns a backwoods family that has made the move to California. When oil is struck on their subsistence Ozark farm, the Clampetts are thrust from sub-McCoy rural poverty to hyperbolic urban wealth, thus leaping over the dead center of suburban reality. In the Ozarks, the Clampetts had lacked electricity and indoor plumbing; in the city they suddenly have a thirty-five-room mansion in Beverly Hills and 26 million in the bank. Their collective lack of familiarity with what Himmelstein calls "the suburban middle landscape," however, endows Jed, Granny, Jethro, and Elly May with farcical, almost surrealistic comic license. They are liminal figures who have never experienced the conditions of normal life in the suburbs. Most of the jokes concern their naïveté of suburban mores and appliances.

The American city, which had been home to nuclear families in the early days of television, was increasingly depicted as the habitat of emphatically exotic persons grouped in abnormal living arrangements. A curious subgenre of domestic comedy was built around the principle of synthesizing suburbanesque Anderson-like family situations into urban bachelor households. In shows such as *The Bob Cummings Show*, *Bachelor Father*, and *Family Affair*, an unmarried uncle is thrust into the role of parent to orphaned blood-related children. In each case the sudden parent is a youngish middle-aged urban professional bon vivant, a playboy who dutifully accepts family responsibility out of a sense of decency and love. But what photographer Bob Collins and attorney Bentley Gregg (both of Los Angeles) and architect Bill Davis (New York) will learn from their parenting experiences is that raising kids will in no way cramp their bachelor lifestyles. Rearing children is shown to be not only compatible with a "swinging" life, but in some ways indispensable to it. These were shows in which father knew best, but in which he could also go on dates. In a strange and subtle way, they predicted or perhaps even helped to precipitate the historical age of single-parent households that was just around the corner.

The Bob Cummings Show (NBC, 1955, 1957–59; CBS, 1955–57; syndicated as *Love That Bob*) is about as far away on the sitcom spectrum as a fifties TV viewer might get from *Father Knows Best*. In dress and gesture, Bob Collins (Bob Cummings) strikes the contemporary viewer as a gay sunbelt computer programmer. But Bob—sporting a perfect tan through his short-sleeve, open-neck leisure shirt—was the early sitcom's premier ladies' man. A Hollywood fashion photographer, he lived life in the fifties fast lane. Like other sitcom surrogate fathers, Bob found no conflict between enjoying the comforts of family life and reaping the rewards of heavy dating. Bob, in fact, had the best situation of all. While *Bachelor Father*'s Uncle Bentley (John Forsythe) had to employ a house servant, Peter (Sammee Tong), to cook, clean, and philosophize for him, and *Family Affair*'s Uncle Bill (Brian Keith) had to import the insufferable gentleman's gentleman Mr. French (Sebastian Cabot) to whip his Upper East Side bachelor pad into dating shape after a day of madcap mischief with Sissy and the twins, Uncle Bob is so slick that he gets his domestic tranquillity for free, sharing a Los Angeles house with his widowed sister, Margaret MacDonald (Rosemary DeCamp), and her teenage son, Chuck (Dwayne Hickman).

As a Los Angeles photographer, Bob works with his share of Hollywood's most glamorous women. He comes on strong, taking extra care to physically position the girls for just the right shot. For their part, the "bombshell" models can do naught but respond to his animal magnetism. Shultzy (Ann B. Davis), Bob's secretary, who unfortunately has received no greater gift from God than a nice personality, seriously longs for the boss, but to no avail. She voyeuristically peeks through the little window that divides the outer office from the studio where "the Make-out King" is at work. (Davis would reprise her role as eunuch servant to another generation of TV viewers a decade later as Alice the Maid on *The Brady Bunch*.) Meanwhile, back at home, Margaret, still loyal to the midwestern homespun values of her childhood, worries about the influence of Bob's bad bachelor habits on the impressionable Chuck.

In one episode, the legendary football player Elroy ("Crazy Legs") Hirsch (playing himself) brings his Youth Crusade to the neighborhood. Margaret sees in Crazy Legs an alternative hero for Chuck, whose stated goal in life is to reach the level of debauchery set by his father figure, Uncle Bob. Margaret convinces Crazy Legs to pretend that he is Chuck's long lost Uncle Roy. Crazy Legs does one-arm pull-ups (no stuntman needed) and then proceeds to beat the arrogant Uncle Bob at every sport known to California manhood. Chuck thus discovers the rewards of clean living and vows to follow the righteous path. But Chuck's lapse into rectitude is only a temporary manifestation that cannot outlast the end of a given episode. He worships Uncle Bob, studying his every "move" and asking for tips on "technique." He even invites his friends over to let them have a look at Uncle Bob's latest girlfriend. Bob protests, but his pride is obvious. What's a romantic guy to do?

The urban universe of the show is utterly lacking in the democratic fairness that structures life in Springfield. The models, including Ingrid Goude, Miss Sweden of 1956, who played herself, are uniformly beautiful, dumb—and happy. The plain women, Bob's sister and his secretary, are intelligent and capable, but in marked contrast to Margaret Anderson, they are unfulfilled and frustrated with their stations in life. Perhaps no character provides greater living evidence of the unfairness of somatic destiny than Pamela Livingston (Nancy Kulp). Pamela, usually dressed in her bird-watching uniform, is an expert ornithologist, can quote Shakespeare at will, and is an all-around Renaissance person in contrast to the voluptuous bubble-brains who otherwise inhabit Bob's photography studio. Like any "normal" woman, she cannot resist Bob's innate charms. But Bob, Chuck, and all the male characters wince at the very sight of her and are not bashful about making cruel comments concerning her appearance. Unlike Elvia Horshen and the other "plain" girls on the Springfield track team, Pamela is offered no reward at all for her virtues.

Paul Henning, the Missouri-born creator-producer of the Cummings program, would eventually take many of these same themes—most notably the conflict between Middle American virtue and Los Angeles decadence—and develop them further in his next show (and greatest hit), *The Beverly Hillbillies*.[37] The Clampetts, like the Collinses, are typical of sitcom families living in large cities during this period: no one in the family is married. The city is not a proper place for normal married families. The only urban marriage portrayed in the series is that of the greedy banker, Milburn Drysdale and his snobbish wife,

Margaret; their union is singularly cold and loveless, very unlike the blissful state enjoyed by Jim and Margaret Anderson, Ward and June Cleaver, and other suburban couples.

By the end of the 1950s, all the "normal" families had moved to the suburbs. The city was a place where one might find an eccentric bachelor like Jack Benny or a "working girl" (i.e., spinster) such as Susie McNamera of *Private Secretary*. The city was a place where one might find childless couples like Ralph and Alice Kramden (*The Honeymooners*), Gunther and Lucille Toody (*Car 54, Where Are You?*), or Cosmo and Henrietta Topper (*Topper*). In a nation that liked to think of itself as composed of one gigantic middle class with tiny pockets of millionairedom and poverty at either end, the sitcom city was a place where one might find the high-rise rich (*Family Affair*) and the working poor (*The Many Loves of Dobie Gillis*). The city was even a place—perhaps most appropriately a place—where one could find families of monsters such as *The Addams Family* and *The Munsters*. However, the city was not the place where a viewer could expect to find a white, all-American middle-class traditional nuclear family in which father knew best—and everyone else knew that he knew it.

Notes

1. Benjamin Franklin, *Autobiography and Other Writings*, ed. Russel B. Nye (Boston: Houghton Mifflin, 1958), p. 75.
2. Allen Ginsberg, "A Supermarket in California," *Howl and Other Poems* (San Francisco: City Lights, 1956), p. 24.
3. At an academic conference titled "Suburbia Reexamined," Peter O. Muller of the University of Miami pointed out that "recent changes of the American metropolis have transformed [the suburb] . . . into the burgeoning outer city that is well on its way to urban dominance in every region of the United States. . . . In the 1980s, the outer city is no longer 'sub' to the 'urb.'" See Philip S. Gutis, New York *Times*, June 15, 1987.
4. Harry Castleman and Walter Podrazik, *Watching TV: Four Decades of American Television* (New York: McGraw-Hill, 1982), p. 119.
5. As quoted in Kenneth T. Jackson, *Crabgrass Frontier: The Suburbanization of the United States* (New York: Oxford, 1985), p. 231.
6. See Thomas Cripps, "*Amos 'n' Andy* and the Debate over American Racial Integration," in *American History/American Television*, ed. John E. O'Connor (New York: Ungar, 1983), pp. 33–54.

7. Tim Brooks and Earle Marsh, *The Complete Directory to Prime Time Network TV Shows*, 3rd ed. (New York: Ballantine, 1985), p. 274.
8. Ibid., p. 994.
9. According to Joel Eisner and David Krinsky, *Television Comedy Series* (Winston-Salem: McFarland, 1984), p. 267, the episode's actual title is "Betty Track Star."
10. Attempts to view a print of "Twenty-four Hours in Tyrant Land" have proved futile.
11. Erik Barnouw, *Tube of Plenty* (New York: Oxford, 1975), p. 163–64.
12. Fred MacDonald, *Television and the Red Menace: The Video Road to Vietnam* (New York: Praeger, 1985), p. 109.
13. Ibid., p. 111.
14. Hal Himmelstein, *Television Myth and the American Mind* (New York: Praeger, 1984), pp. 84–97.
15. Michael Harrington, *The Other America* (New York: Macmillan, 1962), p. 1.
16. Allen Ginsberg, "Howl," p. 17.
17. Ibid., p. 18.
18. Jack Kerouac, *On the Road* (New York: Viking, 1957), p. 83.
19. Kerouac, *The Subterraneans* (New York: Grove, 1958), p. 59.
20. Ibid., p. 62.
21. Arthur Knight and Kit Knight, *The Beat Journey*. Offered as a book under this title, *The Beat Journey* comprises volume 8 of *The Unspeakable Visions of the Individual*, p. 165.
22. John Antonelli, director, *Kerouac* (videotape documentary), 1984.
23. Ibid.
24. To keep the degree of Bruce's notoriety—and notoriousness—to a 1959 audience in perspective, it should be noted that the comedian's first arrests for narcotics and obscenity would not occur until 1961. Several further arrests on these charges would lead him into financial bankruptcy by 1965; in 1966 he died of an apparent heroin overdose.
25. *The Steve Allen Show*, NBC, April 5, 1959.
26. Ibid.
27. A script for Bruce's appearance on the *Allen Show* is reprinted in *The Almost Unpublished Lenny Bruce*, ed. Kitty Bruce (Philadelphia: Running Press, 1984), pp. 31–34. The script does not include the one-liners on Governor Faubus and segregation, nor do the words "homosexuality, narcotics and prostitution" appear in the text. Bruce most likely inserted these without consulting the network. Nothing in the monologue, however, was bleeped out.
28. Lenny Bruce, *Carnegie Hall Concert* (record album).
29. *The Almost Unpublished Lenny Bruce*, p. 34.
30. See Moe Howard, *Moe Howard and the 3 Stooges* (Secaucus, N.J.: Citadel Press, 1979). In this autobiography, Moe recalls that by the late fifties things had gotten so bad for the Stooges that the manager of a Holiday Inn in Bakersfield, California, closed their show after the first night of a two-night engagement.

31. Castleman and Podrazik, p. 36.
32. Lenny Bruce, *Live at Carnegie Hall*.
33. Albert Goldman, *Ladies and Gentlemen–Lenny Bruce!!* (New York: Random House, 1971), p. 223.
34. Albert Goldman, "The Comedy of Lenny Bruce," *Commentary*, 36:4 (1963), p. 317.
35. Ibid., p. 316.
36. I am purposely not counting *Green Acres* as a depiction of a farm family.
37. Henning would have Nancy Kulp reprise her Pamela Livingston character in *The Beverly Hillbillies* as Miss Jane Hathaway, the pathetic, sex-starved Vassar graduate who chases the dumb Jethro—and every other passing bachelor—without success.

CHAPTER 3

The Making of the Sitcom, 1961

I was driving my car downtown from New Rochelle, wondering what grounds do I stand on that no one else stands on? I thought I am an actor and writer who worked on the Sid Caesar shows.

—Carl Reiner[1]

I don't want to be an artist; I'm a good writer.

—"Rob Petrie"[2]

Any discussion of the American transmogrification of *la condition humaine* into consumer lifestyle could do worse than to begin with an examination of *The Dick Van Dyke Show*. In terms of the evolution of prime time, the show's portrayal of suburban life in the Northeast Corridor bridges the gap between the idealized We Like Ike nuclear family home-ownership epics of the fifties (*Father Knows Best, The Stu Erwin Show, Leave It to Beaver*) and the stagflation-era designer social comedies of the seventies, such as the Norman Lear and MTM productions. Since completing its five-year CBS production run in 1966, *Dick Van Dyke* has proven itself to be what the syndication industry likes to call an "evergreen," having achieved continuous play in many important markets, both in the United States and around the non-Communist world. Moreover, it is perhaps the only emphatically New Frontier sitcom ever produced by television—a domestic video wall painting of those politically ebullient thousand days.

In the early sixties, television was coming into its own as an oracle supplying narrative continuity to even the most preposterous of situations. John F. Kennedy, the handsome instant New World aristocrat, and Nikita Khrushchev, the pithy proletarianized Old World peasant, were an iconic diplomatic dynamic duo, the likes of which has not since presided over the lives of the viewing audience. Both superpower button men were well made for television, carrying mythic baggage laden with elements of action-adventure, romance, and comedy. Here were the living precipitates of a century of Western politics: representing capitalism, a prince of an immigrant Boston dynasty with roots in urban ward-heeling and Prohibition; and in the corner to the left, a pauper who had lent a hand in the overthrow of the Romanovs, fought the Nazis in Kiev, denounced the cult of the personality before the Twentieth Party Congress, and lived to tell the tales with relish.

Neither head of state was camera shy. World-class adventurers who were not reluctant to exploit their triumphant, even grandiose personalities, each in his own way savored the unprecedented opportunities afforded by television for intimate mass exposure. The dashing young senator from Massachusetts appeared as Edward R. Murrow's guest star on *Person to Person*, accepting compliments from his future U.S. Information Agency director on the charm of his Boston apartment, the graciousness of his New York wife, and (though the term had yet to leap forth from psychology textbooks into television discourse) his entire "lifestyle."[3] Khrushchev, in New York to attend the opening of the fifteenth session of the United Nations General Assembly, went uptown, the world press in tow, to take a lunch with Fidel Castro at the Hotel Theresa in Harlem. With dozens of international leaders present—Eisenhower, Nehru, Nkrumah, Tito, to name just a few—he stole the show at the United Nations by taking off his shoe and banging it on the desk in spontaneous protest of capitalist-imperialist propaganda (a breach of parliamentary procedure for which the Soviets would be slapped with a $10,000 fine by Secretary-General Dag Hammarskjöld).[4]

The News had only recently become important enough to rate a daily coast-to-coast half hour at suppertime and the two superpower leaders stood behind events—Harvard and the Ukraine, touch football and tractors, proto–Mr. Goodbar and bald, fat grandpa—as the compellingly colorful players in what had mushroomed into the postmodern multimedia contest of world affairs. They battled. They compromised. They closed missile gaps. They engaged in cultural exchange. They sought "peaceful coexistence." Their dueling images offered a bonus of heightened intensity to those viewers brave enough or mad enough to notice the stakes.

Ironically, this colorful cold-war programming met with early and abrupt cancellation. *The Dick Van Dyke Show* was barely into its third season in prime time when Kennedy was murdered under circumstances still not fully clear to the public; less than a year later Khrushchev was unceremoniously issued a one-way ticket to Palookagrad by a Central Committee not amused to see Lenin's heir struggling with the West to gain entry into Disneyland. "JFK" and "K," as New York *Daily News* headlines had once so familiarly called this unlikely pair of hundred-megaton godfathers, gradually achieved the distance of "slain President John F. Kennedy" and "former Soviet Premier Nikita Khrushchev," fading from daily electric screen life into the sanctity of history books. By the end of the decade, the magic had faded to the grim political five o'clock shadows of Nixon and Brezhnev.

Carl Reiner, the *The Dick Van Dyke Show*'s creator, was still hard at work on his as yet unsold sitcom even as the hatless Kennedy was swearing allegiance to the U.S. Constitution on Earl Warren's Bible, an event carried simultaneously by all three networks. A survivor of the "golden age" of live TV comedy-variety, Reiner had worked for Sid Caesar as both on-screen second banana and uncredited staff writer during most of the 1950s. Reiner's new show, his first effort at series authorship, was a timely swan song for the dying genre in which he—and others, including Woody Allen, Neil Simon, and Larry Gelbart—had made their professional marks. In this and several ways *The Dick Van Dyke Show* is a revealing use of network television as a medium of personal expression; its autobiographical depth rivals that of Gleason's *Honeymooners*.

A native of the Bronx (Evander Childs '38), Carl Reiner was not an unfamiliar face in America during the pioneer years of network telecasts. His prime-time acting credits can be traced back as far as 1948, when he played the role of a comic photographer in ABC's *The Fashion Story*, an obscure experimental sitcom set each week in the context of a fashion show (an idea that would lie dormant for over thirty-five years before turning up again as an eighties action-adventure concept in such series as *Cover Up* and *Miami Vice*). He became best known, however, for his sketch performances as a regular member of Caesar's comedy-variety repertory troupes on *Your Show of Shows* (NBC, 1950–54), *Caesar's Hour* (NBC, 1954–57), and *Sid Caesar Invites You* (ABC, 1958).

Like Caesar, Reiner was a second-generation upwardly mobile Westchester homeowner with a consciousness minted in a Jewish New York City Depression childhood.[5] Members of what Jimmy Breslin would one day call "the bridge and tunnel crowd," both artists had crossed the river to take up their show-business vocations in the fabled midtown Manhattan culture complex. In *A Walker in the City*, Alfred Kazin explores the psychosocial distance between neighborhood life in the boroughs of New York and cosmopolitan engagement in Manhattan. But Carl Reiner, Neil Simon, Mel Brooks, Selma Diamond, and the other hungry young writers who had come to early television from the Bronx and Brooklyn triangularized this mythic geography to a third point, a place, perhaps, of less interest to the Irving Howe crowd—the affluent bedroom town on the parkway several exits beyond the last stop of the subway. The ongoing blackout sketches that Caesar performed with Imogene Coca (and later Nanette Fabray), Howard Morris, and Reiner—minidomesticoms with titles such as "The Hickenloopers" and "The Commuters"—exploited the self-amused peccadilloes of emerging alrightnik culture in post–World War II America: dented fenders, forgotten anniversaries, wives with charge accounts, impossible in-laws, the darned plumbing, and so on. If there could be no poetry after Auschwitz, there could at least be New Rochelle.[6]

Though comedy-variety stars such as Caesar, Milton Berle, Martha Raye, Jack Carter, and Jackie Gleason are often credited with having sold many American families their first TV sets during the wonder years of video, the comedy-variety show was already withering on the vine as the fifties drew to a close. As early as 1957–58, not a single example of such programming could be found in Nielsen's Top Ten, even as the Western (enjoying what proved to be its own brief moment in the sun) placed five programs in the charmed circle that season. With the television audience now roughly equivalent to the population at large, the economic stakes of prime-time telecast had suddenly risen steeply and no top was in sight. The ad agencies became increasingly anxious to assert quality control over the TV product. Spontaneity and uniqueness of occasion and performance—precisely those qualities that were potentially most satisfying in a comedy-variety show—came to be viewed as liabilities. Seed money was attracted by the rationalized system of film production. In terms of comedy, that meant the sitcom.

The mighty fell quickly: the 1957–58 season was the first of the decade to open without Sid Caesar on the prime-time schedule. Let go by NBC, the desperate star went hat in hand to ABC and made a deal with the last-place network for a new, live Sunday night show—a stubborn attempt to retain the purity of the genre within the limits of a half hour (*Your Show of Shows* had run ninety minutes in prime time). Furthermore, the revival would reunite Caesar in comedy blackout sketch performance with Imogene Coca, his original costar from *Your Show of Shows*, whose own career had also suffered in the comedy-variety crash.[7] With as much fanfare as ABC could muster, *Sid Caesar Invites You* premiered as a midseason replacement in January 1958; it was canceled, however, after only thirteen weeks, unable to outpoint the anthology dramas of *General Electric Theater with Ronald Reagan* in the 9 P.M. time slot.

Milton Berle—"Mr. Television"—who had signed a thirty-year contract with NBC in 1951, found himself earning his keep as host of *Jackpot Bowling* for the network in 1960. His 1974 autobiography contains bitter reflections on the death of the genre that had helped make both Berle and TV household items: "Seven solid years of live television when it was really live, seven years of going seven days a week trying to make each week's show better, bigger, and funnier than the week before—and for what? To end up axed, out. . . . I was really working my way down to the depths."[8]

Berle was not the only comedy-variety Brahmin headed for a game-show mike. Jackie Gleason, whose comedy-variety hour was cut in half by CBS in 1957–58 and then canceled altogether at the end of the season, left television completely to try his hand at Hollywood movies for the next several years. When the "Great One" attempted a grand return to CBS prime time in 1961, it was as the emcee of *You're in the Picture*, a game show, which in spectacular Gleason style flopped after a single telecast. Similarly, Ernie Kovacs, who had hosted game shows for Dumont before achieving critical acclaim as commercial television's greatest comedy-variety artist, found himself back in the moderator's chair as host of *Take a Good Look* (ABC, 1959–61).

Even an injection of promising new talent could not revive the genre. Bob Newhart's comedy album *The Button-Down Mind of Bob Newhart* had made him the hottest young stand-up in America in 1960. Described by the New York *Times* that summer as a "rising young comedian who specializes in satire,"[9] Newhart was essentially a monologist who preferred sitting on a stool with an imaginary telephone in his hand (in the style of Shelley Berman or Mort Sahl) to running around on a vaudeville set with a seltzer bottle. The comedian had won network interest by stealing the 1959 *Emmy Awards Show* with his takeoff on an officious TV director going through a dry run of Khrushchev's arrival in the United States. CBS approached Newhart first, hoping to bolster its weak Thursday evening schedule with a fresh face. The network, however, dropped out at the last minute. Its reasoning offers a glimpse at how low confidence had fallen in comedy-variety. Lee Rich, who had been engineering the CBS deal for Benton and Bowles, explained, "Considering the time period we had lined up for the show [it would have faced *The Untouchables* and *You Bet Your Life with Groucho Marx*], we reconsidered and decided not to take the risk."[10]

NBC, the network that had traditionally been most closely associated with comedy-variety, took a more optimistic view. Perhaps, it was thought, this type of program could rebound in the hands of a relatively sophisticated humorist who might attract a new viewership. But *The Bob Newhart Show*, premiering in the fall of 1961, went nowhere. It was quietly canceled at the end of its first season, losing out in the ratings to representational dramas (*Naked City* and *The U.S. Steel Hour*) on the other two networks. Newhart disappeared from national television, only to reemerge twenty years later as a sitcom star. With the failure of the Newhart show, the handwriting was on the wall for comedy-variety. Except for a few hangers-on—most notably Red Skelton—the presentational showcases enjoyed by the pioneer comedians had pretty much become a thing of the past. The few hours of comedy-variety left in prime-time passed into the painfully mellow hands of singers such as Andy Williams and Perry Como.

By the turn of the decade, the prime-time network game show seemed to be the last refuge for a comedian who wished to work on national television without donning the mask of a sitcom character. The model for success in this now extinct genre was clearly Groucho Marx's *You Bet Your Life*. Though billed as a quiz show, the program was a thinly disguised talking-heads vehicle for the comedian's talents as a witty raconteur, a talk show that eschewed the pretense of being one. In terms of production control, *You Bet Your Life* was filmed in sixty-minute sessions and then edited down to thirty-minute episodes, affording a greater degree of quality control than could be exercised over live comedy-variety.[11] Though Groucho was apparently at liberty to go after the incredible collection of Southern California wild life that took the stage as quiz-show contestants on *You Bet Your Life*, any remarks that violated network, agency, or sponsor sensibility could be put to rest on the cutting-room floor, just as in a sitcom. Groucho had synthesized the talk show and the quiz show, much as Jack Benny had synthesized the sitcom and the comedy-variety show. *You Bet Your Life* had been a consistent ratings winner for NBC television since 1950, when it had crossed over from network radio.

In the fall of 1958, thirty-five-year-old Carl Reiner had read the situation accurately and was ready to make a career move. Like Berle, Gleason, and Kovacs, he turned first to the prime-time game show, replacing Monty Hall as the host of a CBS series, *Keep Talking*: "The players. . .were divided into two teams of three each. The emcee gave each player a different secret phrase, which the player was then required to incorporate into a story. After the phrase had been used the emcee would stop the story and ask the other team what the phrase was."[12] The show was one of several attempts to rehabilitate the scandal-tainted quiz-show genre as a celebrity parlor game which was so much fun to watch that the audience would fail to notice that no cash prizes were on the line. Regulars

90

included Elaine May, Joey Bishop, Peggy Cass, Paul Winchell, and Morey Amsterdam. In less than a year, however, Reiner was himself replaced by the rapidly ascending Merv Griffin.

That same year, Reiner also completed *Enter Laughing*, a nostalgic autobiographical coming-of-age-in-the-city novel. David Kokolowitz, Reiner's innocent, idealistic first-person narrator, is an apprentice sewing-machine repairman living with his parents in a Bronx apartment. The action focuses on his effort to transform himself into Don Coleman, sophisticated Manhattanite and Broadway actor. Early in the story, after a seemingly disastrous audition, the hapless though politically prescient Kokolowitz comments, "As I left the Lyric Theater, I felt that my chances of [getting the part] were as slim as my chance of becoming the first non-Protestant President of the United States."[13] The novel was adapted for the Broadway stage by Joseph Stein in 1963 and Reiner himself directed a 1967 film version.

But Reiner's cash project in the period immediately following the demise of TV comedy-variety was a situation comedy that he had been developing under the working title of "Head of the Family." Whereas *Enter Laughing* had been a memoir of Bronx adolescence dissolving into Manhattan worldliness, Reiner would build the fictive order of the new sitcom from his experience as a Manhattan artist seeking to establish adult mainstream assimilated domesticity in New Rochelle. The autobiographical roots of the work were clear: the author had cast himself in the lead role of Rob Petrie, head staff writer for a live New York comedy-variety show titled (at that point) "The Alan Sturdy Show."[14] The name "Sturdy" was an anglicized compromise of the Yiddish word *shtarker* ("big bruiser"), a reference to the six-foot, two-inch Sid Caesar, a man who, in Mel Brooks's words, "was considered a giant among Jews." Rob would be married to a former dancer who had given up her career as an artist to be his wife; Reiner was in fact married to a former painter. The Petries would have a son; the Reiners had a son (Rob Reiner, who grew up to play Meathead in *All in the Family*). The Petries would live at 448 Bonnie Meadow Road in New Rochelle; the Reiners lived at number 48. The narrative line, like the sitcom auteur, would commute between the mythic poles of downtown show biz and winding-lane family life. "It was actually what my wife and I were doing," recalls Reiner.[15]

The comic relationship of stage and hearth was, of course, nothing new in American culture. It provided, for example, the narrative framework that tied together the song-and-dance numbers of the Judy Garland–Mickey Rooney musicals directed by Busby Berkeley in the thirties and forties. In terms of television situation comedy, the "show-biz family" had always been a strong subgenre. Burns and Allen refused to distinguish between home and theater; their home was a theater. Danny Thomas and Desi Arnaz had masked themselves as Danny Williams and Ricky Ricardo, professional nightclub entertainers, which, in fact, both had been before transforming themselves into sitcom stars. Chief, perhaps, among the advantages of building a storyline on this premise was that it allowed presentational forms of entertainment—singing, dancing, even stand-up comedy—to be worked into the episodes of otherwise representational programs: a Cuban number for Ricky, a ballad for Danny, a few yarns for George.

In *The Adventures of Ozzie and Harriet* show biz and middle-class family life were revealed as emphatically compatible. Ozzie Nelson's duties as a bandleader made so few demands upon him that he was left free virtually twenty-four hours a day to play golf, improve the house, and otherwise cultivate himself as a source of ethical inspiration for his wife and children. His son Rick's budding career as a rock-and-roll singer was encouraged as a positive opportunity for both Rick and the family, even though rock and roll in the 1950s still had a long way to go before achieving the status of American family music. As portrayed by the Nelsons in *Ozzie and Harriet*, there was indeed no business like show business.

In *I Love Lucy*, however, the relationship is not quite so congenial. Lucy was frankly jealous of Ricky's show-biz career. The Ricardos lived in the East Sixties in a residential neighborhood that was close enough to the midtown entertainment world so that Lucy could get over to the Tropicana quickly. However, the nightclub is territory verboten to wife Lucy by her bandleader husband. She plots and schemes to find a way out of her drab routine domestic life and into one of Ricky's "shows." With her friends the Mertzes, retired vaudevillians who own the apartment building and who themselves yearn for the roar of the greasepaint, Lucy is often stuck at home for most of an episode, emerging only in the climactic segment to sneak onto the stage of the Tropicana for the grand finale. Even though she is funny—to both the on-screen nightclub audience and the television viewer—her attempt to cross over from neighborhood (urban provincial) life into the cosmopolitan world of show business is revealed as both ridiculous and futile. She is funny, but incompetence is the source of her humor. The audience, which watches television and knows professional entertainment when it sees it, laughs at Lucy Ricardo, not with her: she sings in an opera sketch with a horrendous voice. She dances in a bebop routine with a crazed jitterbug who throws her all over the stage like a sack of potatoes. She gets stage fright and forgets her lines. As the episode ends she is, in quick order, reminded of her rightful place, forgiven by her exasperated but loving husband, and sent back to Little Ricky and the roast.

In "Head of the Family," however, Reiner would tap his own memory to strive for a new autobiographically based realism that would eschew the fantastic extremes of the Nelsons and the Ricardos. "I was examining my life and putting it down on paper," Reiner claims. He was trying to create "the first situation comedy where you saw where the man worked *before* he walked in and said, 'Hi, honey, I'm home!'"[16] The fact that the place where the man worked happened to be a network television production company seemed perfectly normal to Reiner, who had spent over a decade doing just that. The paradigms of Reiner's life—ethnicity and assimilation, urbanity and suburbanity, presentationalism and representationalism—would be the mythic resources from which the show would be refined.

Reiner's dedication to "Head of the Family" led him past the conventional wisdom that guides TV show creators: instead of completing just a pilot script, he went ahead and—with no money or guarantee of any kind—wrote scripts for thirteen series episodes. "This would be a nucleus, a bible, for anybody who would help write it after that. It would guard against supposition; everything would be spelled out."[17] Clearly, the author was envisioning more than syndication residuals.

Harry Kalcheim, Reiner's agent, took the material to Peter Lawford, the "Rat Pack" film actor who was then attempting to establish himself as a television producer. Lawford was the husband of Patricia Kennedy, the sister of Senator John F. Kennedy, who was at that moment neck deep in his race for the U.S. presidency. Joseph P. Kennedy, the patriarch of the clan, was keeping close watch over all activities of family members during this crucial period. He demanded to read the sitcom script before sanctioning Kennedy involvement. "Everything the Kennedy money went into had to be approved by him," recalls Reiner.[18] After a weekend of careful study at the family's Hyannis Port retreat, the elder Kennedy gave the venture a resounding thumbs-up. He was so enthusiastic about "Head of the Family" that he not only granted the go-ahead to Lawford, but agreed to personally finance the production of the pilot.

Kennedy, of course, was no stranger to the mass-entertainment industry, having been deeply involved in Hollywood during the interwar years. He had owned FBO, a major distributing company, and for a time he had even served as chairman of the board of the Keith-Albee-Orpheum theater chain. Kennedy had also had his share of experience playing the angel. In 1925 he had personally backed his intimate friend Gloria Swanson in the ill-fated *Queen Kelly*, a nonstudio production directed by the difficult Erich von Stroheim. Though costs ran in excess of $1 million (mostly out of Kennedy's pocket), the film was never released in the United States.[19]

On July 19, 1960, the pilot episode of "Head of the Family" appeared on *Comedy Spot*, a "Failure Theatre" summer replacement anthology series that CBS was using to showcase would-be sitcoms.[20] On the strength of Reiner's reputation, the New York *Times* placed a star next to its listing of the show, denoting "a program of unusual interest" (the network competition consisted of *Arthur Murray's Dance Party* and *Colt .45*). The dramatis personae, especially Rob's colleagues at the office, had a decidedly New York flavor: Rob Petrie (Carl Reiner), Laura Petrie (Barbara Britton), Ritchie (Gary Morgan), Sally Rogers (Sylvia Miles), Buddy Sorrell (Morty Gunty), and Alan Sturdy (Jack Wakefield).

In *Watching TV*, a season-by-season history of American television, Harry Castleman and Walter Podrazik describe the "Head of the Family" pilot: "Petrie and his wife Laura had to convince their son Ritchie that his father's job was as interesting and important as those of the other kids' fathers. To prove his point, Rob brought Ritchie to the office to see firsthand how valuable he was. . . . The format seemed workable, the cast adequate, and the writing mildly clever."[21]

Though there was some sponsor interest, the series was not picked up by CBS. For one thing, situation comedy seemed to be in eclipse in 1960. Only one new sitcom had premiered during the 1959–60 season, *Love and Marriage*, which starred William Demarest as an aging music publisher who hated rock and roll and had little patience for his hipper-than-thou son-in-law and partner. NBC canceled it almost immediately. Westerns were the hot properties as the election of 1960 rolled around, with *Gunsmoke*, *Wagon Train*, and *Have Gun, Will Travel* finishing win, place, and show in the Nielsen Top Ten for two consecutive seasons. Reiner fully believed that "Head of the Family" had died a quiet death in a bad sitcom market.

Kalcheim, however, was not so sure. In September 1960 he persuaded Reiner to meet with another of his clients, Sheldon Leonard. Though a fellow New York Jew, Leonard had followed a different path into show business. A theater graduate of Syracuse University, Leonard first found a career in B movies in the forties as a stock Runyonesque gangster heavy, but then jumped to the production end in the television era, where he achieved phenomenal success. In 1953 he had joined Danny Thomas' production company as executive producer of *Make Room for Daddy* (later retitled *The Danny Thomas Show*) and the show had been running ever since. More recently, he had sold a new sitcom to CBS, *The Andy Griffith Show*, which was set for a fall 1960 premier.

The Reiner-Leonard relationship was that of student to mentor. Leonard tutored Reiner in the fine points of cranking out situation comedy (as opposed to comedy-variety), giving him license to roam the Thomas production facilities and observe the day-to-day operations of making a narrative TV series. Asked for his opinion on the all-but-moribund "Head of the Family" pilot, Leonard remembers being "torn between a desire to be helpfully honest and a desire to be tactful. . . . The only thing I could say was 'Carl, you're not right for what you wrote for yourself!' I believe that if recast, the show would have every chance of making it. Do you mind if I try to rewrap the package?"[22] After some initial reluctance, Reiner accepted this judgment and Leonard was hired to direct a new pilot.

The short list of candidates to replace Reiner in the role of Rob Petrie consisted of two thirty-five-year-old nationally familiar (but not yet star) performers, both midwesterners by birth: Johnny Carson and Dick Van Dyke. The Iowa-born, Nebraska-bred Carson had been a television personality since 1951, when he had hosted *Carson's Cellar*, a local Los Angeles satire program in which the comedian riffed on the day's headlines, much as he would in his *Tonight Show* monologues years later. The show drew the attention of several West Coast comedy giants, including Red Skelton and Groucho Marx, both of whom willingly appeared as unpaid guests to help out the young comedian. In 1953, Skelton gave Carson his big break, hiring him to write the stand-up monologues with which he opened his weekly CBS show in less than two years, the network decided to try Carson in a comedy-variety hour of his own. Johnny, however, proved not ready for prime time. The only TV series ever actually titled *The Johnny Carson Show* was dumped at the end of its first season. As Reiner and Leonard began their search for a new Rob Petrie, Carson was biding his time, building an "F Score" with the daytime audience as host of the game show *Who Do You Trust?* (formerly *Do You Trust Your Wife?*), on ABC.[23]

Dick Van Dyke seemed, on paper, the underdog in the competition. A native of West Plains, Missouri, he had started out in the forties by opening his own advertising agency in Danville, Illinois. Moving over to the performance end of the business, he gradually built a prime-time resumé that offers an eclectic panorama of 1950s television: a summer as host of *CBS Cartoon Theater starring Heckle and Jeckle*; a season as a regular on Mike Stokey's *Pantomime Quiz*; a dramatic role opposite George C. Scott on *The U.S. Steel Hour*; two guest spots as a hillbilly private on *The Phil Silvers Show*; and a brief stint as comic relief on *The Andy Williams Show*. TV stardom, however, eluded Van Dyke. Unable to find a suitable format in television for his considerable talents as a physical comedian, he turned his efforts away from the medium in 1959 and scored a tremendous smash on Broadway in the musical comedy *Bye Bye, Birdie*.

Leonard, however, strongly favored the gangly, pratfalling Van Dyke to the mesomorphic, wisecracking Carson, despite Johnny's greater public recognition factor. He had envisioned Rob Petrie as the kind of guy who is not "too glamorous to be sharing your living room with,"[24] and following this logic, Carson's relative fame worked against him; the newer the face, the better, as far as Leonard was concerned. He had also imagined Rob as someone who "doesn't want to get up in front of an audience, but who can perform in a room at a party."[25] In this respect, Van Dyke's proven abilities in musical comedy offered distinct advantages for the presentation of nonnarrative performance art in what amounted to a backstage sitcom. While Carson could do stand-up, some yeoman's party magic, and a bit of ventriloquism, Van Dyke could sing, dance, do pantomime, and play broad slapstick. Leonard sent Reiner to New York to see *Bye Bye, Birdie*, and the issue was settled. Van Dyke received permission from his Broadway producer for time off to go to the West Coast and shoot the pilot.

As Sheldon Leonard had predicted, the cast change proved to be the key to getting the series on the air. But the significance of recasting Rob Petrie from a Bronx-born Jew to a heartland gentile surely could not have been lost on an author who had so self-consciously set out to produce an autobiographical work. Carl Reiner had never worn his Jewishness on his sleeve. He had in fact played the ethnically nondescript "interviewer" of Sid Caesar's "German Professor" on many occasions. The low-key (assimilated?) nature of his style can be seen perhaps most plainly when Reiner performs with the hyperactive Mel Brooks. On *The 2000-Year-Old Man* record albums (which contain not only the title cuts, but a wide variety of sketches) Reiner characteristically plays the "American" straightman to Mel Brooks' howling ghetto *mishuganeh*.

By what logic had Leonard come to the conclusion that "if recast, the show would have every chance of making it?" After ten years in front of the camera, Reiner's competence as a television performer could not have been the issue. Was there an unspoken agenda to the change in personnel? It has been suggested that Berle and Caesar in particular had proved "too Jewish" for the vastly expanded television audience of 1960. Was Leonard's new plan to sell "Head of the Family" based on the WASPing of Rob Petrie?

As the series unfolded it was obvious that Rob's background had been thoroughly reimagined to reflect the life of the actor who now played the role. In flashback episodes, we learn that the comedy writer is a native of Danville, Illinois;[26] that he met Laura, a dancer with a USO troupe, while serving in the army; that Rob and Laura lived as newlyweds in Joplin, Missouri, before moving to New York. Whereas in "Head of the Family," the Rob character had played a Carl Reiner to the Buddy character's Mel Brooks, in *The Dick Van Dyke Show*, the relationship was removed one more level: Rob played the Middle American to Buddy's Jewish New Yorker.

The transformations in ethnic cosmology brought about by Van Dyke's assumption of the lead role is a subject that has apparently never been broached in print. In *The Dick Van Dyke Show: Anatomy of a Classic*, the only book ever devoted to the program, Ginny Weissman and Coyne Sanders go into otherwise exhaustive detail about the mechanics of recasting the series, but completely ignore the issue of ethnicity. There is no mention at all of it in an interview that Reiner and Leonard gave to *Television Quarterly* in 1963, at the height of the show's popularity.[27] The newspaper and magazine reviewers of the day were similarly silent on the subject.

Leonard, with his excellent sitcom track record, had little trouble in placing the revamped show on the CBS prime-time schedule. In the early sixties, advertising agencies tended to control blocks of time on network television and had great leverage in making program decisions. Using his liaison with the Benton and Bowles agency (which handled the sponsor accounts for both *Danny Thomas* and *Andy Griffith*), Leonard obtained an assurance from Procter and Gamble that the retailing giant "would back any pilot I chose."[28] A company, Calvada Productions (Carl Reiner, Sheldon Leonard, Dick Van Dyke, Danny Thomas), was formed to produce the show, with each partner to receive a percentage of the profits. Thomas, who provided much of the financing for the new pilot out of his own pocket, was to receive the lion's share.

As for the name of the program, it was generally agreed that "Head of the Family" would be abandoned so as not to confuse the series with the Kennedy-backed pilot of the previous summer. Several titles that referred to Rob's dual management functions in the office and at home were considered. "Double Trouble" was adopted as a working title at one point, but was dropped in favor of "All in a Day's Work." In the end, however, Leonard reverted to form. *The Danny Thomas Show* and *The Andy Griffith Show* had both done quite well for him and the new sitcom was christened *The Dick Van Dyke Show*.

Like the television industry itself, Reiner (under the tutelage of Sheldon Leonard) had made the transition from the black-out sketch vaudeville of live East Coast comedy-variety to the prerecorded, studio-edited filmed drama of West Coast situation comedy. He was one of the very few who did this successfully. Caesar, Berle, Coca, and other golden-age stars attempted periodic comebacks, but to no avail. Imogene Coca's *Grindl* (NBC, 1963–64) was a particularly ambitious sitcom in which Coca, playing the title role of a housemaid, was afforded generous opportunities to perform pantomime bits and other types of high-tone physical shtick. Unfortunately *Grindl* was programmed against *The Ed Sullivan Show* during a season that included appearances by half the groups in the British invasion—the Beatles and the Rolling Stones among them—and it never had a chance.

While the fifties comedy-variety performers frantically tried to retool for the brave new prime time that Madison Avenue was inventing for the sixties, the best golden-age writers abandoned the medium, using their TV resumés to gain entrance into the relatively genteel circles of popular theater and cinema. After penning several "Sergeant Bilko" scripts for his friend Nat Hiken's *Phil Silvers Show*, Neil Simon headed for Broadway and became the most widely produced playwright of the century—some say of history. Woody Allen and Mel Brooks dabbled in stand-up performance, but soon began new careers as movie directors and, eventually, producers. Each of the three won a national audience by focusing his lower-middle-class Brooklyn Jewish sensibility on a different social circle:

Simon created a theater of consumer realism that made him a comic plaintiff voice for New York middle-class *arrivistes*. Allen, with his *shiksas* and poetesses, became the bard of the uptown condominium cosmopolitans. Brooks, apparently knowing no shame, continued to cultivate the scatological excesses of the schoolyard.

Ironically, Reiner—who had been both performer and writer during the comedy-variety era—accomplished his feat of network survival by creating a nostalgic West Coast sitcom about the life of a New York comedy-variety writer. In the bargain, he was forced to reinvent his Bronx persona in the image of a tall, skinny gentile who had grown up next to the Mark Twain National Forest in Howell County, Missouri. Leonard, the bicoastal mastermind of this transmutation, apparently mixing up his midwestern states, once referred to Van Dyke as "an Indiana Baptist."[29]

The Dick Van Dyke Show pilot went into production on a soundstage at the Desilu Cahuenga complex in January 1961. The "three-camera system," which Desi Arnaz had originated for *I Love Lucy*, was used. This system synthesized film, theater, and video techniques so that a live audience, in effect, attended the filming of a short movie that was shot with three stationary cameras and then cut in an editing room. In April, CBS chose to pick up the series without a preseason airing of the pilot; full-scale episode production began on June 20. Reiner's original writing staff consisted of the team of Jerry Belson and Garry Marshall; in subsequent seasons another team, Bill Persky and Sam Denoff, was added, along with several contributing free-lancers. The half-hour, black-and-white show premiered that fall in the Tuesday 8 P.M. slot, hammocked between *Marshall Dillon* (reruns of the old half-hour *Gunsmoke*) and *The Many Loves of Dobie Gillis*. The competition was *Bachelor Father* on ABC and the second half of *Laramie* on NBC.

Each episode of *The Dick Van Dyke Show* opens in a fashion that makes it recognizable as a turn-of-the-decade nuclear-family sitcom: an instrumental musical theme plays on the soundtrack as the members of the family gather together in the house. The signature scene of *Dick Van Dyke*, however, distinguishes itself in several ways. Most fifties suburban domesticoms opened with brief but potent establishing shots of the exterior of the family home. These sut·urbopastoral house portraits emphatically underscore the family's unbearably secure upper-middle-class status. No such shot, however, is offered of the Petrie house. Their class status must be gleaned instead from the more subtle connotations of interior decoration: their contemporary sectional sofa; their quasimodern *objets d'art*; their breakfast counter; their elaborate but unused woodstore fireplace. In this way, the Petrie living room transcends the traditional sitcom standard of family comfort, introducing notions of personal taste. The signature sequence then departs even further from fifties sitcom custom: instead of just dad, mom, and offspring, the picture is extended beyond blood members to include Rob's office co-workers, Buddy and Sally—a Jew and an unmarried career woman.

Rob enters the living room (his and yours) through the front door, emerging from behind the superimposed series title, as it is vocally announced. The white-collar dignity of his suit and tie is immediately betrayed by a slapstick pratfall over the ottoman. (Later, this was self-reflexively revised so that Rob enters and *avoids* tripping over the ottoman.)[30] He is greeted and surrounded, first by Laura and Ritchie, who approach Rob from the viewer's right, and then by Buddy and Sally, who follow from the left. The show-business world, as symbolized by the pratfall (or nonpratfall) and the joke writers, is resolved into the domestic world of wife, child, and spacious but warm living room. All constitute one big happy family—only forty-five minutes from Broadway. Though Rob is a "real character," in the midwestern sense of that phrase, his soul is "out here" in the New Rochelle house, among the prosperous eight-cylinder families—and not "down there" among the Others of Manhattan.

There is a kind of curious narrative anomaly embedded in this opening. What, a regular viewer might ask, are Buddy and Sally, city-dwelling Others, members of minorities, doing in the idyllic Middle American house? They seem somehow to be waiting for Rob to come home from the office. The typewriter sitting on the coffee table (foreground, viewer's left) suggests that a work session is about to take place, but this is something that never happens in the course of the 158 episodes. The scene might as easily have been shot at the office, with Laura and Ritchie dressed for a visit. The use of the living room, however, establishes the show's cosmic priorities: family, blood, and home constitute both the alpha and the omega of Rob's consciousness; city, art, and commerce, while important, are, in the final analysis, only transitory experience. Though the series will spend more time at the office than other family sitcoms, it proclaims itself no less a family sitcom than *Donna Reed* or *Danny Thomas* by reaffirming the primacy of family life.

Much like the New Frontier, the show viewed in reruns a quarter century later waxes and wanes as a series of promises and compromises. Fresh and unconventional styles are used to package familiar morals in what evolves as an upbeat saga of a bright, fast-track couple playing by the rules and making it. The power—and the possibilities of power—all belong to a youngish middle-aged white male hero, an unpretentious college graduate of liberal sensibility who makes good money in a creative position with a Madison Avenue industry. A modern guy riding the wave of late-twentieth-century technocracy, Rob outranks the older, more experienced writers on *The Alan Brady Show* staff by virtue of his college diploma. Luckily, his political outlook is just as up-to-date. "Head writer" is only a title to Rob; he is careful to treat Buddy and Sally as equals and valued collaborators at all times. Perhaps he is satisfied to simply make more money than they do.

Laura (Mary Tyler Moore) is Rob's sitcomic Jackie, a talented beauty who has given up any number of possibilities in life to pilot the family station wagon. With their pointedly youthful good looks, with their emphatically *moderne* suburban detached single-family dwelling, with a respect for art and Kultur that is topped only by a love of show business and what it can do for you, the Petries were perhaps the last sitcom couple who could simultaneously take for granted their unnamed (and, on television unnamable) white, middle-class, heterosexual advantage and still manage to exhibit a kind of quasi-sophistication and personal warmth that imply sympathy for civil rights and possibly even advocacy of welfare-state measures.

The politically progressive feel of the show is due in part to the inclusion of black actors as extras in crowd scenes at public places and private events, such as museums and parties. Reiner was by no means the first sitcom producer to attempt to integrate his cast. Nat Hiken had always included one or more black soldiers in Sergeant Bilko's platoon on *The Phil Silvers Show* (CBS, 1955–59) and several black officers in the police squad of *Car 54, Where Are You?* (NBC, 1961–63). *Car 54*, premiering the same season as *The Dick Van Dyke Show*, was perhaps the most integrated series that had ever appeared on network television. Regulars included Officer Anderson (Nipsey Russell) and Officer Wallace (Frederick O'Neal) and many episodes of the series, which took place in the Bronx, featured black extras and walk-ons. But *Dick Van Dyke*, unlike the Hiken shows, was about suburban family life and even token integration stood out as extraordinary.

In "A Show of Hands," Rob and Laura are to go to a banquet to accept an award for Alan Brady from the Committee on Interracial Unity. Before leaving the house, however, they accidentally dye their hands indelibly black while helping Ritchie make a costume. Embarrassed, they wear white gloves, but take them off when they are reminded by their hosts that truth is the only path to human understanding and therefore world harmony. In "That's My Boy??," Rob recounts the birth of Ritchie in flashback. A series of events influences Rob to believe that the hospital has given them the wrong baby, switching Ritchie Petrie of Room 206 with Richie Peters of Room 208. Rob calls the Peters family and tells them what he thinks has happened. Punchline? The Peters walk in—and they are black. Though blacks are otherwise never seen on sixties sitcoms as guest stars, Godfrey Cambridge appeared on *The Dick Van Dyke Show* as secret agent Harry Bond in "The Man from My Uncle," a 1966 spy-spoof episode.

Could Rob or Laura have voted for Nixon in 1960 or Goldwater in 1964? Could Carl Reiner have voted for them? (The Petries and the Reiners might well have parted ways, however, in 1952 and 1956.)

While an identifiable if tepid political statement is implicit in Reiner's casual integration of middle-class blacks into the series mise-en-scène, Reiner is more explicit on other, perhaps less controversial themes. One of the recurring leitmotifs in *Dick Van Dyke* is a kind of status-based tension between art and mass entertainment. Artists who work in relatively low-return media—painters, poets, independent filmmakers—are almost always treated skeptically. At the same time, the pursuit of money by the commercial artist is tied to common sense, love of family, and humane social values, all of which are embodied in Rob, who is utterly valorized. *Artistes* who show up on *The Dick Van Dyke Show* can expect rough treatment.

In "I'm No Henry Walden," Rob is mysteriously invited to a charity cocktail party where all the other guests are poets, playwrights, novelists, critics, and assorted literati given to avant-garde hyperbole. Everycouple Rob and Laura are completely out of place. The "serious" writers turn out to be nothing but a bunch of intolerable snobs who can't even get Rob's name straight, no matter how many times he introduces himself. When he mentions that he is a TV writer, they are aghast, one of the guests exclaiming, "Why I don't even own a television machine." Doris Packer, who was typed as one of the great sitcom snobs for her stunning performance as Chatsworth Osborne, Jr.'s mother in *Dobie Gillis*, plays the party's hostess, Mrs. Huntington. She introduces the "Petrovs" to Yale Samsden (Carl Reiner), "one of our budding British anti-existentialists." Reiner, with a goatee and a virtually incomprehensible Oxbridge accent, launches into a crazed exegesis on "the state of American culture in our times." Phrases such as "plethora of the mundane" and "atrophy of the brain" emerge from his otherwise brilliantly incoherent rantings. "Verisimilitude," Yale warns in a backhanded swipe at the sitcom, "must be stamped out."

Henry Walden, as the name suggests, is a "true" poet conjured from America's nineteenth-century literary heritage. He is brought by Reiner to *The Dick Van Dyke Show* much as Kennedy had produced Robert Frost for his inauguration. The snowy-haired Walden, who has not been seen for most of the episode, appears at the end to right the wrongs that have been done to Rob. Unlike his snotty friends, he is a Whitmanian appreciator of mass culture, an unabashed fan of *The Alan Brady Show*. He even proves his sincerity by reciting the complete career resumés of Buddy and Sally. (Interestingly, we learn that Buddy, like Morey Amsterdam, had once had his own comedy-variety show and that Sally had been a gag writer for Milton Berle.) The real reason he invited Rob to the party was to ask him to collaborate on a TV documentary on the history of American humor from the Revolutionary War to the present. When Rob protests that he knows nothing about American history, Walden assures him, "Don't worry, I know all about that stuff. I need someone who knows television."

The episode ends with the same group of snobs from the party gathered at Mrs. Huntington's Park Avenue apartment to watch the documentary on a "television machine" that has been placed in the living room just for the occasion. Henry Walden reads the writers' credits aloud at the end of the broadcast and the literati are forced by the revered poet to recognize Rob's talent—and the "validity" of television as an art. Poor Henry Walden, however, must remain with the entourage of pseudointellectuals; he is dependent on their patronage. Rob, on the other hand, is lucky to be "no Henry Walden" but a self-sufficient breadwinner with a beautiful wife who can choose his own friends.

In "Draw Me a Pear" (a risqué pun on "pair"), Rob and Laura take art classes from a devious female painter who praises Rob's work in an attempt to seduce him. Laura sees through the ruse from the start, but wishing to appear modern, she tells her husband to do "whatever makes you happy, darling." The seductress-in-smock invites Rob into the city for "private lessons" at her Greenwich Village studio. After giving him a phony line about "freeing himself from his inhibitions," she makes her move. Instructing Rob to feel her face with one hand while sketching it with the other, she fondles Rob's fingers with her mouth, an extraordinarily frank bit for an early sixties sitcom. Perhaps more extraordinary, the sexually aggressive home wrecker is not made to seem either excessively evil or pathetic. Her personality flaw is revealed as deviousness, not hypersexuality. The conclusion, however, is strictly fifties: Rob tells Laura in the coda, "It's a good thing I'm such a good boy." (A variation on this episode can be seen in "Teacher's Petrie," in which Laura's creative writing teacher betrays similarly lecherous designs on her.)

Perhaps the most sarcastic dig at noncorporate artists takes place in "October Eve," in which Reiner once again caricatures the *artiste*, this time playing the role of Serge Carpetna, a Russian painter—complete with goatee, beret, and insufferable ego. Many years ago, Laura had commissioned Carpetna, then an unknown, to do a painting of her for $50. Though she had posed for him fully clothed, the artist had taken license to paint her as a nude. Enraged, Laura attempted to destroy the canvas by throwing black paint on it. But Carpetna, we learn, has restored the painting. It shows up in a swank New York gallery with a $5,000 price tag attached to it.

In a flashback sequence, Laura tells the story of the painting to Rob, apologizing for having kept it a secret from him for all these years. We see Laura's reaction as she gazes at Carpetna's image of her nude body for the first time. Though her outrage is presented as the only reasonable attitude in such a situation, the arrogant artist shows no understanding for her middle-class morality. In a stereotypical display, he calls her a "peasant" and tells her to "go back to New Rochelle, land of peasants."

Realizing that Laura owns the painting by virtue of the $50 she paid for it long ago, Rob decides to go down to the city to confront the artist in his Greenwich Village studio. The maestro is hard at work on a new masterpiece—with squirt guns. When Carpetna learns the reason for Rob's visit, he throws a tantrum, threatening to knock Rob in the head before allowing him to destroy his work of art. Revealing sensitivity and fairness, however, even as he seeks to protect his own interests, Rob offers Carpetna a deal: the Petries will forgo their ownership of the painting if they can pick the buyer. The "happy" ending has the artist selling his painting to a reclusive South American millionaire who will place it in his Brazilian mountaintop retreat. As if this is not enough, an extra potshot is added after the climax. Carpetna does a new painting of Laura, which he promises will not be a nude. Keeping his word, he creates a Marcel Duchamp-like "portrait" in which no one can even find Laura. The *artiste*, unlike the TV writer and most people, simply cannot comprehend the "normal" human preference for simple representationalism. Carpetna would no doubt agree with Yale Samsden that "verisimilitude must be stamped out."

The caricaturing of artists (as well as intellectuals) is a convention of the pre-1970s sitcom that is by no means limited to *The Dick Van Dyke Show*. Male artists are usually portrayed as either effeminate or lecherous; female artists, as either sexually maladjusted or just downright daffy. But the fact that Rob himself is a writer gives a certain edge to Reiner's obsession. There is a plea for identification with Rob's relatively down-to-earth attitude. The audience is asked to accept the TV writer as one of the bourgeois crowd. Rob is a writer the way Jerry Helper (Jerry Paris), his next-door neighbor, is a dentist. There are no callings in New Rochelle, just professions. Each man democratically pays off his auto loan with the same green money. Ironically, the signature credits sequence concludes each week with the superimposition of an episode title across the Petrie living room, a flourish that in sitcom terms suggests no small artistic pretension. Who does Reiner think he is, Quinn Martin?[31]

With the seemingly divided world of the commuter given continuity and coherence by Rob's ability to maintain a single consciousness at both ends of his daily trip on the New Haven Railroad, the notion of the artist as marginal person is disputed. The avant-gardists down in the city of art are provocative, but they are too self-important to be the cognoscenti of a democracy. Let them jump off the deep end, as is their right; Rob, the American poet, seeks the center. It is left up to him, the man with the mortgage, to be the divine literatus of posturban society. Rob—the male, the breadwinner, the homeowner, the artist, the manager, the Middle American—is the hub of all of the drama's dynamic human relationships.

The lack of emphasis on parenting problems in *The Dick Van Dyke Show* was another factor that helped create the penumbra of sophistication that still surrounds the series twenty-five years later. Compared to children on other Sheldon Leonard shows—*Danny Thomas* and *Andy Griffith*—Ritchie Petrie is the sitcom's answer to the neglected child. As is the case with *I Love Lucy*, the plots tend to focus on adult problems, often excluding the couple's son completely. When Little Ricky does appear in an *I Love Lucy* episode, however, he is often trotted out in grand style, wearing miniature Xavier Cugat outfits, playing the bongos, and joining dad in a chorus of "Babalu." Ritchie (Larry Mathews) rarely if ever gets such attention. He is occasionally used as a font of cute remarks, but his personality and his consciousness remain largely unexplored. His problems are presented only to the extent that they allow the viewer to see how Rob and Laura react to them. Besides being obedient and painfully well adjusted (or perhaps because of these things) he is pretty much of a nebbish. The screaming apple-of-my-eyeism that so thoroughly dominated the genre during this period was absent from the show.

Robert S. Alley has argued that the classic domesticoms of the fifties, which are often ridiculed today as ideological fossils of a conformist conservative era, actually contain many highly relevant—and in some cases quite liberal—political and social messages, especially in the area of parent-child relations.[32] For example, sitcom children are never spanked or physically punished. Instead, they are reasoned with in a calm but firm manner as prescribed by Dr. Spock, who, according to Laura in one episode, "is a genius [and] knows everything."[33] Parents who practice this progressive method will be rewarded with a Beaver or a Wally. Parents who do not can expect an Eddie Haskell or a Lumpy Rutherford.

The child-rearing philosophy of the Petries is perhaps best illustrated in the episode "Girls Will Be Boys," in which Ritchie is repeatedly harassed and beaten up by a female classmate, Priscilla Darwell, at school. Having been taught by his parents never to hit a girl under any circumstances, he refuses to retaliate, choosing instead to suffer the pain of emasculation. Under his mother's concerned and sympathetic questioning, he breaks down and reveals his shame. Rob goes to see the girl's father, but Priscilla, in perfect little party dress, looking like Patty McCormack in *The Bad Seed*, politely denies having ever hit Ritchie and, as far as Mr. Darwell is concerned, the matter is settled. Rob, whose sense of fair play transcends his paternal pride, is equally impressed by the performance and is perfectly willing to believe that his son is the liar—until an impeccable eyewitness (Jerry and Millie's son Freddie) bears Ritchie out. The attacks continue, and this time Laura goes to see Mrs. Darwell. She turns out to be an even worse parent than her husband. She refuses to believe that her little girl is even capable of such behavior and suggests that Laura try giving Ritchie some sweets to get him to tell the truth. Dumbfounded and enraged at such parental irresponsibility, Rob and Laura give Ritchie permission to defend himself.

Tension builds as Rob and Laura wait for Ritchie to get back from school; Rob has come home from work early that day just to be there. Comic harmony is breathlessly restored as the twenty-two-minute drama winds to its conclusion. We learn that Ritchie was too embarrassed to tell his parents that all the little girl ever wanted from him was a kiss. Refusing to hit a girl despite parental permission, he gives in and kisses her, ending the attacks. As in "October Eve," a bit of overkill is added after the climax: Priscilla tells Ritchie's classmates about the kiss and some boys tease Ritchie and start a fight with him. He promptly beats up all three of them. Hearing the story, Rob is devilishly delighted; he sees both his virility and his values redeemed in such good, old-fashioned male horseplay.

As the show's increasing ratings gained credibility for him at CBS, Reiner gradually became freer to leave behind parent-child situations and give more attention to the Rob-Laura and Rob-office plots he favored. By the fifth season, Ritchie had all but disappeared from the show, and quite frankly, not much was lost. In general, Reiner proved to be far more interesting and original at the office than in the home.

Morey Amsterdam and Rose Marie play the roles of comedy writers Buddy Sorrell and Sally Rogers strictly by The Method. Both had been stars of radio and early TV who made phoenixlike comebacks on the *Van Dyke* show. Amsterdam was born in Chicago in 1914. A cello-playing prodigy, he gained admission to college before the age of fifteen but chose to devote himself to show business, achieving national stature as a popular comedy-variety figure in the late forties and early fifties. He was known for his theme song, "Yuk-a-Puk," which he played on the cello as punctuation for the one-liners of his stand-up routine (a style of presentation made perhaps more famous by Henny Youngman and his violin). Along with Youngman, Jack Carter, Milton Berle, and several others, Amsterdam had been one of a rotating circle of comedians who had hosted *The Texaco Star Theater* before Berle won the job for himself in 1948. He had his own show, *The Morey Amsterdam Show*, on CBS and then Dumont in the late forties; its supporting cast included pre-Norton Art Carney and pre-*Valley of the Dolls* Jacqueline Susann, whose husband, Irving Mansfield, was the show's producer. In 1950, Amsterdam returned to NBC as the

Monday and Wednesday host of *Broadway Open House*, the first late-night network talk-variety show, an ancestor of *The Tonight Show*. Once again, however, he was passed over for an NBC top spot when the network gave the show to Jerry Lester on a Monday-through-Friday basis. As comedy-variety went into its tailspin in the latter part of the decade, Morey Amsterdam began what seemed to be a descent into game-show oblivion, appearing as a regular on no less than five prime-time network games, including *Keep Talking*, which Reiner had briefly hosted.

"Baby" Rose Marie, as she had been known when she began her career singing on network radio at the age of three, was a frequent guest on comedy-variety programs. She had been a regular on *The Ina Ray Hutton Show* (NBC, 1956), a short-lived summer replacement series that retains the distinction of having been the only program in prime-time history to have had an all-female cast, featuring Ina Ray and Her All-Girl Band. The show's subtitle was "No Men Allowed" and, indeed, not a single man ever appeared on camera during its ten-week run on Wednesday evenings. Rose Marie's game-show credits included *Pantomime Quiz*, a long-running charades vehicle that had also featured Dick Van Dyke for a time. More recently, she had tried her hand at sitcom work, playing the role of Bertha the Secretary on *My Sister Eileen* (CBS, 1960–61).

Buddy and Sally, though toned down considerably by the constraints of genre, medium, and period, evocatively conjure visions of Mel Brooks and Selma Diamond in a Max Liebman writers' room. Known as "the human joke machine," Buddy is the acknowledged master of the one-liner—the wiseguy comic from the streets of neighborhood New York. The stuffy and officious Mel Cooley (Richard Deacon), Alan Brady's bald producer and brother-in-law, is the natural butt of Buddy's obsessive schoolyard rank-out prowess. Buddy's Jewishness is for the most part implicit, though it is freely acknowledged upon occasion. In "The Ugliest Dog in the World," Rob brings a street mutt to the office and Buddy feeds it a corned beef sandwich. When Rob tries to give the dog some milk, Buddy protests:

Buddy: That ain't kosher. For him it's cream soda or nothing.

110

Sally: Rob, he's trying to kill that dog.
Rob: No, he's trying to convert him.

In "There's No Sale Like Wholesale," Buddy uses what F. Scott Fitzgerald had once called "gonnexions" to get Rob and Laura a fur coat at a wholesale price. The most "Jewish" episode of all, however, is "Buddy Sorrell—Man and Boy," in which the middle-aged comedy writer corrects an injustice of his poverty-stricken Brooklyn youth by finally taking bar mitzvah lessons. In the last few minutes, the bar mitzvah itself is presented (in English), complete with synagogue, congregation, and a yarmulke-clad Dick Van Dyke. The rabbi even refers to Buddy by his Jewish name: Moshe Selig Sorrell. Occurring as it does in the final months of the series production run, the episode seems like a whimsical revisiting of some of the autobiographical material that Reiner had been forced to abandon to put the sitcom on the air back in 1961. Amsterdam's organic *toomler* delivery makes him the surviving vessel of Jewishness in the otherwise mainstreamed narrative. "I *am* Buddy," he once told an interviewer.[34]

By contrast, Sally Rogers shows no hint of ethnicity. The archetypal sitcom career woman of the pre–Mary Richards era, her significance radiates strictly from gender. Sally's lack of a husband hangs over her like a dark cloud, adding an element of pathos that is lacking in any of the other characters. Rob and Laura frequently fix her up with blind dates, but her aggressive "unfeminine" style makes her unfit for each of these potential mates. Her one steady boyfriend is Herman Glimsher (Bill Idelson), a pathetic mama's boy whose widowed mother takes full advantage of his oedipal problems.

The "Sally episodes" take on a familiar pattern. In "Like a Sister," she misjudges the affections of guest star Vic Damone, who plays a singer named Vic Vallone. In "Jilting the Jilter," comedian Fred White (Guy Marks) tries to marry Sally as a cheap source of gags for his stand-up nightclub routine. In another episode, Rob's brother, Stacy (Jerry Van Dyke), comes for a visit and dates Sally in order to get over his shyness so he can propose to the woman he really wants to marry. In "Dear Sally Rogers," Sally appears on a network talk show and shamelessly solicits marriage proposals by mail. It is not unusual for a Sally episode to end with a tear in her eye; she has a cat named Mr. Henderson.

There is something inescapably off-center about the sitcom relationship of Buddy and Sally. Appearing together frequently at social functions, they might easily be mistaken for husband and wife. It is easy to speculate, however, on why Reiner and Leonard chose not to marry them. For one thing, Sally is not Jewish. Mixed marriages, then as now, were not considered sitcom fare.[35] On the other hand, if Sally was written as a Jewish character, a Jewish majority on *The Alan Brady Show* writing staff would violate another type of marketing wisdom. With Sally a single woman, Reiner retained the comic prerogatives of Sally's self-effacing spinster jokes as well as a dependable plotting device that accounted for more than a half dozen episodes.

Buddy's wife, Pickles (Joan Shawlee; later Barbara Perry), though often mentioned as the butt of his one-liners, is rarely seen on screen. Yet, the fact that Buddy has a wife obviates speculation about his sexuality. Sally, by contrast, is the female eunuch, unfulfilled and philosophical about her lot in life. She is typical of the pre-1970s sitcom career woman in this way. In *Our Miss Brooks* (CBS, 1952–56), Eve Arden is an English teacher who spends most of her time at Madison High futilely trying to gain the romantic attentions of Mr. Boynton, a colleague in the Biology Department. Ann Sothern carried this archetype into two series: *Private Secretary* (CBS, 1953–57) and *The Ann Sothern Show* (CBS, 1958–61). The structural supposition of both programs was that she worked for a living in lieu of marriage, which was valorized as the principal or "real" goal of any woman. In the latter show, she plays an assistant hotel manager who is passed over for promotion in favor of an outside man. The new boss is played by none other than Don Porter, the same actor who had played Sothern's boss in the earlier series. Most of the episodes are built on her attempts to "snare" the man who has taken the job that was rightfully hers.

Sally is slightly better off than the Eve Arden and Ann Sothern characters in that her career is meaningful to her, but she is still very much the victim of male domination. Though officially a full member of *The Alan Brady Show*'s writing staff, she does all the typing while Buddy lies on the couch and Rob paces the center of the room. In the two-part episode "The

Pen Is Mightier than the Mouth"/"My Part-time Wife," Sally makes an appearance on *The Stevie Parsons Show* (*Steve* Allen, Jack *Paar*, Johnny *Carson*). She is a big hit on the late-night talk show and takes an indefinite leave from her job to become one of Stevie's regulars. Rob and Buddy find themselves unable to function without Sally around to keep the office in order and do the typing. Sally, however, gives up her big chance to become a star by purposely getting into an argument with Stevie Parsons when he makes a crack about *The Alan Brady Show* on the air. She dutifully returns to her place at the typewriter in the office, learning the old sitcom lesson that a solid place in a warm gemeinschaft is worth more than anything the flashy gesellschaft can ever offer—a lesson still frequently taught in the genre.

The show's three regular women characters offer a constellation of sitcomic female figures. Laura is offered as the heroic center point of identification. Beautiful and capable, talented and motivated, she has found a comfortable and rewarding place in the world. If she is defined by her husband, at least it can be said that she has made the most enviable "catch" of the men in the series. Alan Brady is wealthy and a star, but he is arrogant and egotistical. Buddy may be funny, perhaps even funnier than Rob, but he is socially adolescent and physically endomorphic. Mel, as producer of the show, technically outranks Rob, but he is a fawning sycophant who has made his way in the world by nepotism. Next-door neighbor Jerry Helper is a successful dentist—a professional—but he is bland and ordinary. Rob stands out as the perfect blend of the domestic (loyal, loving, caring) and the artistic (funny, handsome, creative). That Laura gave up her career as a dancer is less important than the fact that she could have been a dancer, had she wanted to be anything other than Rob's wife and the mother of his children.

Her commitment to her choice is made clearest in "To Tell or Not to Tell." The episode begins with a typical *Dick Van Dyke* party scene at the Petrie home. The well dressed, middle-class, racially integrated guests are entertained first by Buddy and Sally, who do one of their Catskills song-and-dance comedy routines, and then by Rob, who does a few pantomime impressions. Next, however, we are treated to a rare performance by

Laura, who, in capri pants, does some post–Martha Graham gallivanting around the living room to the accompaniment of bongo drums on the phonograph. Mel is so impressed by Laura's work that he asks her to fill in for an injured dancer on *The Alan Brady Show*. Buddy warns Rob not to let Laura do it: "You'll be eating frozen dinners." But Rob is too progressive to take authoritarian measures and so decides to let Laura make her own decision: "I think I know what my wife wants." The episode concludes with Laura's being offered a job as a regular dancer on the weekly network TV show.

"I always wondered if I could make it again as a dancer," Laura tells Rob, "but I don't want to be a dancer, I want to be your wife." She then adds a complaint about the aches and pains of dancing, but this is only an ameliorating gesture that serves as minimal ironic counterpoint to Laura's heavy-handed denial of ego. Laura's decision is very much in the official spirit of the times. As Theodore Sorensen has written, "Providing a normal life for her children and peaceful home for her husband was only one of Jacqueline Kennedy's contributions to the Kennedy era, but she regarded it as her most important. 'It doesn't matter what else you do,' she said, 'if you don't do that part well, you fail. . . . That really is the role which means the most to me, the one that comes first.' "[36]

Millie Helper (Ann Morgan Guilbert) helps define Laura as a "modern" woman by offering the contrast of a familiarly zany sitcom hausfrau. Millie's talents in life are strictly domestic. She is hyperemotional and unable to function outside her prescribed role. When any chance for individual attention or distinction is thrust upon her, she is unable to accept it, as in "Coast to Coast Big Mouth," an episode in which Millie is picked out of the audience to be a contestant on a game show, but falls to pieces with stage fright and gives her opportunity away to Laura. Millie functions as a sidekick, a kind of sounding board for Laura, allowing her to verbalize her feelings about Rob. She is a second banana lacking the dignity, however, of an Ethel Mertz, who at least gets to be Lucy's partner in middle-class deviance. Ann Morgan Guilbert handles the role with great skill, calling attention to Laura's calm, reasonable, and relatively cosmopolitan tone with her own mah-jongg game shrillness. Is Millie a recent émigré from the Bronx? Once again the marketing concerns of the medium seem to be masking a parochial subtext.

If Millie is a house mouse, Sally is a bull in a china shop. Too assertive, too aggressive, too willing to use her "unfeminine" powers, Sally is the career woman whom Laura wisely chose not to be. She suffers much more for her excess than Millie suffers for her passivity. The only men who can accept her are her coworkers; they know how to harness her sexually ambiguous eccentricities for productive purposes. Some of the single men Sally encounters are emasculated by her verbal powers; others can only see her as a source of the valued commodity of humor. None can accept her as a woman. Both Sally and Millie are static and incomplete compared to Laura. The balance of female sitcom power would not shift decisively toward career women until the 1970s.

The critic John Cawelti has written that the development of a popular genre occurs as various authors synthesize the genre's familiar characteristics ("conventions") with innovative characteristics that freshen, surprise, and recontextualize ("inventions").[37] *The Dick Van Dyke Show* lends itself to this kind of schematic view of generic evolution quite well. Perhaps more than any sitcom that preceded it, the series incorporated an eclectic variety of elements from the sitcom canon while adding significant innovations in plot content and structure. The homogenous suburban family at home is familiar; the heterogeneous extended family at the office is new. The broad, physical comedy of Van Dyke is right out of *I Love Lucy*; the sophisticated early sixties dialogue is unique.

Symmetrical, premodernist morality-tale plotting may be built right into the formal constraints of situation comedy, but Reiner and the half dozen writers he collaborated with over the course of the show—Sam Denoff and Bill Persky, Ben Joelson and Art Baer, David Adler, Lee Erwin—at least had the virtue of being self-conscious about their didacticism. The commitment to achieving a modicum of racial integration and ethnic representation distinguishes the sitcom from other early sixties prime-time hits such as *The Beverly Hillbillies* and *The Flintstones*. A viewer who doubts the relative "hipness" of *The Dick Van Dyke Show* might remember that *Hazel* (NBC, 1961–65; CBS, 1965–66) was exactly contemporaneous with it.

Dick Van Dyke, it should be noted, had not been an instant hit. Facing a strong Western (*Laramie*) and a sitcom featuring teenagers (*Bachelor Father*), the show struggled in its original 8 P.M. Tuesday night time slot, not winning Nielsen numbers among the preadult viewers who dominate that period. Wisely, Sheldon Leonard and Danny Thomas lobbied the network tenaciously and the show was moved at midseason to a later slot, 9:30, on Wednesdays. This did the trick. Having finishing fifty-fourth during its first season, the show catapulted into the Nielsen Top Ten the following year, finishing ninth in 1962–63, third in 1963–64, seventh in 1964–65, and sixteenth in its final season.

It is worth noting that the cancellation of *The Dick Van Dyke Show* was never ordered by CBS, but rather by Carl Reiner. Having watched too many of his old colleagues from the comedy-variety days overstay their welcome on network television, Reiner, with the approval of the cast, decided to bow out gracefully while still on top. The exact timing of this rare sitcom suicide (future examples would include *The Mary Tyler Moore Show* and *M*A*S*H*) was most likely tied to a CBS policy decision to go over to an "all-color" prime-time schedule in 1966–67. *The Dick Van Dyke Show* had been shot in black and white and the expense of gearing up for such a radical technological production change could not be justified for a limited run.

The decision to voluntarily end the show rather than wait for the inevitable but otherwise unpredictable network ax gave Reiner the opportunity to create a macrocosmic climax to the five-year, seventy nine-hour narrative. In "The Last Chapter," Rob reveals to Laura that he has finished an autobiographical novel that he has been working on for the last five years. Laura sits down to read it, providing a flashback framework for a series of sentimental "greatest hits" scenes recapitulating the show's etiology: the marriage of Rob and Laura, the birth of Ritchie, and so on. The episode and the series reach completion as all the members of the cast—Buddy, Sally, Mel, Alan, and Ritchie (possibly a double; he speaks no lines and is seen only in profile)—join Rob and Laura in the Petrie living room:

Rob (to Laura):   You want to hear a bit of good news? I heard from the publisher today. . . . He *hates* it. He said it reminds him of about fifty other books.

Buddy (ecstatic):	One editor said it stunk.
Laura:	Then why is everyone so happy?
Rob:	Because Alan read it and he loved it.
Alan:	What do I know from style?
Rob:	Alan wants to produce it as a television series . . .Alan is going to play me.
Sally:	The three of us are going to write it. Leonard Delshod is going to produce it.

(Close-up of Rob and Laura embracing and kissing.)

Reiner's bone to pick with the genteel traditional arts remains a primary theme to the bitter end. It doesn't matter that editors and other such pretentious creatures reject Rob's work. Alan likes the book, and though he knows nothing about "art," whatever that is, he will make a sitcom out of it and that means fame and fortune, success and redemption. Such are the consolations for the unappreciated writers who make the millions smile.

Perhaps more impressively, Reiner achieves elliptical closure for the series in this final episode. The narrative had commenced six years previously as an autobiographical work, with Carl Reiner playing Rob. The role was then taken over by Dick Van Dyke, who became Rob in the eyes of the world; Carl Reiner, meanwhile, became Alan Brady. Rob/Dick Van Dyke then writes an autobiography, which Alan decides to produce as a television series. In the new series, Alan/Carl Reiner will play the part of Rob/Dick Van Dyke, who, in turn, will write the show. Or, as Weissman and Sanders put it, "*The Dick Van Dyke Show* was complete, indeed 'coming around full circle': Carl Reiner (as Alan Brady) would portray Rob Petrie—in essence, himself—in a television situation comedy, as Reiner had done in *Head of the Family* years before, which then became *The Dick Van Dyke Show*."[38] In any case, Reiner has a last laugh, exiting as the Rob he had originally wanted to be.

Despite the commercial success of *The Dick Van Dyke Show*, it inspired no spin-offs or even any obvious imitators. Instead, shows such as Paul Henning's *The Beverly Hillbillies* and William Asher's *Bewitched* (and their spin-offs and imitators) came to dominate the sitcom throughout the sixties. This is not surprising. As the sixties hit civil rights and Vietnam in high gear,

117

the very concept of sophistication was suddenly up for grabs and the networks sought to retain as high a degree of least-objectionability in this polarized atmosphere as possible. The sitcom, a representational art committed to harmony and consensus, found refuge in visions of America's premetropolitan past and fantasies of witches, genies, and nannies who could do the vacuuming by magic. The legacy of *The Dick Van Dyke Show* would not be redeemed until the 1970s, when shows such as *All in the Family*, *M*A*S*H*, and especially *The Mary Tyler Moore Show* would revise and revive the genre as a historically based comedy of American manners.

Notes

1. As quoted in Ginny Weissman and Coyne Steven Sanders, *The Dick Van Dyke Show* (New York: St. Martin's, 1983), p. 1.
2. "Draw Me A Pair," *The Dick Van Dyke Show* (CBS, October 20, 1965).
3. See Daniel Czitrom and David Marc, "The Elements of Lifestyle," *Atlantic Monthly*, May 1985, pp. 16–20.
4. See Roy Medvedev, *Khrushchev*, trans. Brian Pearce (New York: Anchor, 1983), pp. 153–55.
5. Caesar was born several miles away from Reiner in inner-city Yonkers.
6. For a dimmer view of Jewish suburban flight, see Philip Roth, *Goodbye, Columbus and Five Short Stories* (Boston: Houghton Mifflin, 1959), especially "Eli, the Fanatic" and "Goodbye, Columbus."
7. *The Imogene Coca Show* (NBC, 1954–55) was a pathetic casualty of the conflict between comedy-variety and situation comedy. The show premiered as a kind of autobiographical sitcom modeled after *The Jack Benny Program*. After two weeks it was changed into a comedy-variety showcase composed of blackout sketches, stand-up routines, and Broadway-style production numbers. Three months later, it reverted to a sitcom format. The show was not renewed for a second season.
8. Milton Berle, with Haskel Frankel, *Milton Berle: An Autobiography* (New York: Delacorte, 1974), p. 3.
9. Val Adams, "Newhart to Star in CBS-TV Show," New York *Times*, July 11, 1960.
10. Ibid., July 13, 1960.
11. Tim Brooks and Earl Marsh, *The Complete Directory to Prime Time Network TV Shows*, 3rd ed. (New York: Ballantine, 1985), p. 937.
12. Ibid., p. 446.

13. Carl Reiner, *Enter Laughing* (New York: Simon and Schuster, 1958), p. 5.
14. According to show-business legend, "Sturdy" became "Brady" after Morey Amsterdam observed that "Alan Sturdy" could be mistaken for "Alan's dirty." See Weissman and Sanders, p. 2.
15. Ibid.
16. Ibid.
17. Ibid.
18. Ibid., p. 5.
19. See Garry Wills, *The Kennedy Imprisonment* (Boston: Atlantic Monthly, 1982), pp. 66–67.
20. The term "Failure Theatre" was used by Robert Klein on *Late Night with David Letterman* to describe programs like *Comedy Spot* (NBC, July 24, 1986).
21. Harry Castleman and Walter Podrazik, *Watching Television: Four Decades of American Television* (New York: McGraw-Hill, 1982), p. 150.
22. Weissman and Sanders, pp. 5–6.
23. F Score or "Familiarity" Score, is computed by the Performer Q company of Port Washington, New York. Each year the company does an extensive survey that attempts to rate the public's familiarity with TV performers (actors, game-show hosts, athletes, anchormen, etc.) by asking a sample group to identify pictures. These scores are then used by the networks and production companies in casting decisions.
24. Ibid., p. 6.
25. Ibid.
26. The sitcom is inconsistent on the point of Rob's hometown. In one episode, an old high school girlfriend from Danville shows up looking for an audition with Alan Brady. In another episode, Rob's parents come from Danville to visit. But in yet another episode, a male school friend (played by Jack Carter) appears and the two reminisce about their childhood in Westville, which seems like a composite of West Plains, Missouri (where Van Dyke grew up), and Danville, Illinois (where he moved as a young man to seek his fortune).
27. "Comedy on Television: A Dialogue," *Television Quarterly*, Summer 1963, pp. 93–103.
28. Weissman and Sanders, p. 17.
29. Ibid., p. 58.
30. A third opening, used only during the first half of the first season, differs completely from these: we see abstract still photographs of the cast members with the theme music playing.
31. Martin was the highly successful producer of such action series as *Barnaby Jones*, *The F.B.I.*, *The Streets of San Francisco*, and *Cannon*. His signature was the introduction of each segment after each commercial as "Act I," "Act II," etc. There was even an "Epilogue."

32. Robert S. Alley, address, University of Iowa International Television Symposium, Iowa City, Iowa, April 25, 1985.
33. "The Last Chapter," *The Dick Van Dyke Show*, June 1, 1966.
34. Weissman and Sanders, p. 26.
35. The first notable attempt at a Jewish-Gentile sitcom marriage was *Bridget Loves Bernie* (CBS, 1972–73).
36. Theodore Sorensen, *Kennedy* (New York: Harper and Row, 1965), p. 381.
37. See John G. Cawelti, "The Concept of Formula in the Study of Popular Literature," *Journal of Popular Culture*, 3 (1969), pp. 381–90.
38. Weissman and Sanders, p. 85.

CHAPTER 4

Planet Earth to Sitcom,
Planet Earth to Sitcom

Acclimation to suburbia stimulates switches in religious affiliations.
—William H. Whyte, Jr., *The Organization Man*[1]

By 1966, American television had experienced severe genre shakeout. Comedy-variety, as discussed earlier, had suffered greatly for its eccentricities as the growing television industry sought to rationalize its product. Though a few veterans such as Jackie Gleason, Red Skelton, and Danny Kaye managed to hang on to huge aging audiences (and one significant new star, Carol Burnett, would actually carry on comedy-variety production throughout the seventies), "TV vaudeville" had already become more nostalgic than dynamic—something from the "old days," even though network television itself was less than twenty years old.

Gleason provides the grossest and saddest example of this generic burnout. In 1962, after an enforced absence of three seasons, he returned to the air with a new CBS Saturday night show, *The Jackie Gleason Show: The American Scene Magazine*. According to its star, the series would break new ground for TV comedy-variety with the weekly presentation of "topical satire."[2] The announced premise, however, soon got lost in the shuffle as the Great One, a product of McCarthy-era television still playing to his McCarthy-era fans, proved unwilling to take the risks that "topical satire" implied. He increasingly

121

relied on empty revivals of routines involving his "classic" (that is, 1950s) characters, such as Joe the Bartender and the Poor Soul.

In 1966 the *American Scene* title was dropped, along with any pretense that the show might foster a future direction for comedy-variety. Having failed to live up to his promise of innovation, but still commanding excellent ratings from a stay-at-home Saturday-night audience, Gleason took a decisive turn toward the baroque. From 1966 to 1970, though still offering his "show" in the framework of a comedy-variety hour, he attempted what can only be described as a tired and torturous revival of his greatest creation, the Honeymooners, which he had not performed in ten years. Art Carney, now sporting a "spare tire" to rival Gleason's, returned to the home screen as Ed Norton, but Audrey Meadows wisely stayed away. The difficult job of replacing Meadows fell to Sheila MacRae; her thoughtless, grinning, almost effervescent Alice Kramden added little and subtracted much.[3] The miscasting of MacRae, however, was not the only problem plaguing the new Honeymooners. The revival's sixty-minute format, inherited from the *American Scene Magazine* concept, demanded episodes that were twice the length of the classic Honeymooners episodes of 1955–56. The extra half hour created an untenable burden for the show's writers.[4] Shamelessly dreadful original musical production numbers were woven into the plots, Broadway-style, to fill up the extra time. Though full of moon-June rhymes and high-kicking chorus lines, these Kramden operettas somehow managed to evade even the pleasures of high camp. They remain the only available Honeymooners episodes—the only available Gleason material—never put into syndication.

Other programming formats, including many of the fifties' favorites, were even less fortunate than comedy-variety as the full-color era dawned on American television in the mid-1960s: (1) Not a single weekly drama anthology, live or otherwise, was to be found on any of the commercial networks.[5] (2) The Western, which had placed at least four programs in the Nielsen Top Ten every season from 1957–58 to 1961–62, had abruptly gone into what would amount to its terminal television decline; only a few old favorites, such as *Gunsmoke* and *Bonanza*, managed to hang on until the end of the decade.[6] (3) The banishment from prime time of big-money quiz shows, imposed after the *$64,000 Question* and *Twenty-one* "contestant coaching" scandals of 1959, had proved permanent. Attempts to reestablish the credibility of the genre, such as ABC's *100 Grand* (1963), proved futile.[7] (4) Though *Arthur Godfrey's Talent Scouts* had been the highest-rated show on television in the early fifties, the TV amateur show had become yet another relic of the early days. The last remaining such program, *Ted Mack's Original Amateur Hour*, was demoted from prime time to Sunday afternoons in 1959. (5) The advocacy-oriented news documentary—Edward R. Murrow's *See It Now* is perhaps the only distinguished example—disappeared completely when Murrow left CBS to become the Kennedy administration's director of the U.S. Information Agency in 1961. (6) Even professional wrestling had drifted from prime-time network glory into ignominious Saturday-afternoon syndication, where it remained until a spectacular revival in the cable era.

What few attempts the networks made at developing new types of programming in the mid-1960s bore little or no fruit. In 1964, NBC tried *That Was the Week That Was*, an American adaptation of a successful British weekly series devoted exclusively to topical satire. The show was hosted by its British star, David Frost, the pioneer comedian and performance-journalist who would achieve greater fame years later as Richard Nixon's video biographer. Unlike Gleason's tepid *American Scene Magazine*, *That Was the Week That Was*, or *TW3*, named names of politicians and took potshots at political causes and opinions. Recalling the character of the Tuesday-night thirty-minute comedy revue, Brooks and Marsh write, "The satire could be very brutal. . . . There was the 'news report' from Jackson, Mississippi, that UN paratroopers had just been dropped by Guatemalan Air Force planes to rescue Negro ministers, missionaries, and civil rights workers."[8] Ironically, while Gleason's failure at satire ended up as a fixture on CBS for no less than eight seasons, *TW3* became a victim of its satirical successes. The producers found themselves in a constant censorship crisis with NBC, which included an enforced hiatus in the weeks immediately preceding the 1964 Johnson-Goldwater election. Dismissed as more trouble than it was worth, *TW3* was not renewed for the 1965–66 season.

Similarly, youth-oriented pop-music shows such as *Hootenanny*, *Shindig*, and *Hullabaloo* came and went, unable to establish a beachhead in the prime-time lineups, despite a pop-music explosion that was transforming the radio and record industries. Though "teen music" à la Rick Nelson had proved compatible with the suburban life-stylings of *Ozzie and Harriet* in the fifties, the folk-rock wave of the mid-1960s was beginning to push even the Top Forty into increasingly didactic territory. Barry MacGuire's "Eve of Destruction" hit number one on *Billboard*'s "Hot 100" in the fall of 1965:

> The Eastern world, it is explodin'
> Violence flarin', bullets loadin'
> You're old enough to kill, but not for votin'
> And even the Jordan River has bodies floatin'
> You don't believe in war, but what's that gun you totin'?

© Words and music by Phil. F. Sloan and Steve Barri, Wingate Music Corp.

ABC Circle

With his "protest song" at the top of the charts, MacGuire was asked to be the guest star on an episode of *Hullabaloo*. Other attractions that week included the Kingsmen (with a cleaned-up cover of "Louie, Louie") and the Rolling Stones ("Get Offa My Cloud"). Though MacGuire had suddenly risen from relative obscurity to "household name" status solely on the strength of "Eve of Destruction," he was not permitted to perform the song on the show! Instead, dressed in a painfully stylish mod tuxedo, surrounded by a profusion of white-sweatered go-go dancers (one of whom introduced MacGuire by announcing, "Now our host has something new to say and it's really beautiful."), he sang an incomprehensible folk-styled love song.

The very prospect of MacGuire's appearance on *Hullabaloo* had no doubt raised more than a few paranoid eyebrows on Madison Avenue. TV and advertising executives, many of whom had cut their corporate teeth during the last big Red scare, were perhaps understandably uncomfortable with the idea of showcasing a performer whose act contained sentiments such as these:

124

Think of all the hate there is in Red China,
Then take a look around at Selma, Alabama;
You can go away for four days in space,
But when you come back, it's the same old place;
The pounding of the drums, the pride and disgrace,
Hate your next-door neighbor, but don't forget to say grace.

The answer may indeed have been blowing in the wind, but the industry shrank from the political consequences of deeming such material suitable for the airwaves. Like the satire programs, the pop-music shows can be seen as halfhearted attempts by the networks to test what the cultural traffic might allow some fifteen years after the publication of *Red Channels*.[9] These first attempts by the networks to cash in on the new popular styles of the sixties were purely formal, not matched by any willingness to take chances on appropriate content. As dutifully apple-pious as most TV programming had remained since McCarthy days, few in the industry were ready to invite closer product scrutiny by business and/or government.

As the smoke cleared at mid-decade, the big winners in the genre wars were readily apparent. Prime time was now dominated by just three programming formats, all of them narrative: the half-hour sitcom, the hour-long action-adventure drama, and the two-hour feature movie (at this point, network movie presentations were still mostly theatrical releases; the first "made-for-TV" movies began to appear in the 1964–65 season). Among this dwindling list of vital genres, situation comedy emerged as the lynchpin of network scheduling. More sitcoms finished among Nielsen's Top Twenty-five during the 1960s than all other program types combined.[10] Stand-up comedy, blackout sketches, and other presentational forms had become commercially marginal.

Television was going through this period of contraction and product rationalization at a time when other expressions of American culture were experiencing flourishes of experimentation and expansion. The novel, trying to find a raison d'être for its slow delivery in an age of instant information, was slouching its way toward New Journalism. Books such as Truman Capote's *In Cold Blood* (1965), Tom Wolfe's *Electric*

125

Kool-Aid Acid Test (1968), and Norman Mailer's *Armies of the Night* (1968) highlighted the spare pickings of television's quantitative mythopoetics with thick, erotic descriptions of personalities, ideas, and events.

The visual arts, which had by any measure been going nuts since the invention of cheap photography and possibly since the invention of the weaving loom, had been sent into cataclysmic shock by television: by its monotonous eclecticism, by its economic power, by its sheer ubiquity. Andy Warhol, whose career owed more to NBC's David Sarnoff and CBS's William Paley than to Van Gogh or Cézanne, took the very objects that the mass media had made into the visual white noise of American culture—a Brillo box, Chairman Mao, the Campbell Soup can, Marilyn Monroe—and claimed each, in isolation, as his own found work. On the radio, the supercharged eros of the electric guitar had all but destroyed the romantic, language-oriented song stylings of Tin Pan Alley. Public race segregation was in the process of being dismantled. Vietnam resisted the script of World War II. The center, for a change, would not hold.

Where was television during all of this? Describing the 1966-67 season, Castleman and Podrazik write, "The commercial networks seemed to be ignoring a wide range of controversial subjects. . . . Was the toning down of controversy deliberate? Were the networks fearful of reprisals by government and industry? Were they somehow too closely aligned to the same forces in government and industry?"[11]

The sitcom was not only the most popular of the remaining television genres in the 1960s but also the most thoroughly isolated from current events. Action-adventure shows could not help tripping over The News, because of the inherently political nature of crime-and-punishment storytelling. While the scales of American justice may have been designed to reflect universal and eternal values, the particulars of guilt and innocence have demanded constant updating to remain compelling on television. Race riots, antiwar demonstrations, and LSD trips gave phrases such as "law and order," "free speech," and "youth culture" emotional and polarizing contexts. No-nonsense cops such as *Hawaii Five-O*'s McGarrett and *Dragnet '67*'s Friday appealed to right-wing sentiments

126

in their battles with drug (including marijuana) dealers and political terrorists. Police force integration—both racial and sexual—became the subtextual essences of such series as *The Mod Squad* and *Police Woman*.

The made-for-TV movie, the only remaining prime-time format that could structurally accommodate a story with a tragic ending, also made forays into what the critics were calling "relevance." The pioneer made-for-TV features, produced by Universal for NBC, included *Fame Is the Name of the Game* (1966), which concerned investigative journalism in a big-time magazine empire, and *The Doomsday Flight* (1966), a movie about skyjacking. Many of these two-hour telefilms served as pilots to test public reaction to new weekly action-adventure concepts. Law-and-order cop shows such as *Ironside* and *Kojak* were market-tested this way.[12]

But the sitcom, the living room within the living room, the mirror of family life, the barometer of the normal thing, remained aloof from the battles outside that were raging. Drugs, sexual deviance, poverty, violent criminality, and the denial of constitutionally guaranteed rights could be shown on the mean city streets of Los Angeles or New York or Birmingham in crime shows, in movies, or on The News, but such things were not to cross the family threshold of situation comedy.

Sitcom-makers are commercial artists charged with the job of stimulating responses from the national middle. Not surprisingly, the fragmenting political climate of the sixties created peculiar problems for them. The aesthetic foundations of TV situation comedy had been built upon consensus representationalism during the fifties. The "American celebration," however, seemed to be unraveling right before the nation's eyes. NBC, CBS, and ABC were now all offering daily evening news summaries that catalogued (or, some said, precipitated) these unravelings. The divorce rate was beginning to take off. Agitation for liberalization of abortion laws was increasing. Thousands of draft-age men were leaving the country or going underground to avoid military service. The spectacular rise of marijuana-smoking from a coterie activity of hipsters, beatniks, and jazz musicians into a full-fledged bourgeois leisure-time pursuit provided a stark contrast to the relatively sober images of family life on *Father Knows Best*. Even the Petries, who had so out-hipped the Andersons, seemed pretty square compared to what a viewer might see on The News.

Indeed, The News was emerging as the chief historical reference point of television fiction, a kind of marginal metagenre that dictated the terms of reality to the imaginative drama of prime time. The "other America" of rat-infested urban ghettos, rural shacks without plumbing, workers without health insurance, single-parent welfare poverty, and homeless bums, which Michael Harrington had exposed to a shocked middle class in 1962, was, by the mid-1960s, making frequent guest appearances with Walter Cronkite on *The CBS Evening News*. The "War on Poverty" was declared by President Johnson, officially acknowledging that the home-ownership boom that had been occurring since the end of World War II had not quite solved every citizen's socioeconomic problems. At the same time, footage of organized violence began arriving daily from Southeast Asia. A war on Vietnam was not declared by President Johnson, an official refusal to acknowledge that the "peaceful containment" policies pursued since the end of World War II were failing.

While the sitcom did not portray "the other America," or the "non-war in Vietnam," the genre did respond to the philosophical relativism of the sixties by de-emphasizing the heavy-handed teaching of absolute values. *Father Knows Best*, *Leave It to Beaver*, and *The Donna Reed Show* had all gone out of production by 1963, not leaving any immediate clones. Even *The Andy Griffith Show* (CBS, 1960–68), which had started out as a father-son morality play, gradually mutated into the surrealist small-town fantasia of the post-Barney, Floyd the Barber era. In *The Dick Van Dyke Show*, Carl Reiner had perhaps inched toward a new politics of the family, but that was generally the road not taken by producers; depoliticization through escapist fantasy proved much more popular.

The term "escapism" has always been used by critics to categorize works of popular art. But during the sixties, faced with more cultural ambiguity than the genre dared handle, the sitcom went into what might be called a period of "deep escapism." If the suburbo-realist domesticoms of the fifties had strived to portray a vision of the "likely," the next generation of sitcoms, including such shows as *The Beverly*

Hillbillies and *Gilligan's Island*, seemed utterly indifferent to verisimilitude, preferring instead to explore and allegorize the turgid daydreams of American mass culture: you discover oil by accident and get $25 million; you get shipwrecked with a bunch of perfectly nice strangers on a Pacific island where there's all the food you can eat and you just hang around all day waiting to be rescued.

With U.S. troop movements to Vietnam escalating, military sitcoms constituted an extraordinary component of this surge in sitcomic fantasy: *McHale's Navy* (ABC, 1962–66) and *Hogan's Heroes* (CBS, 1965–71), covering, respectively, the Pacific and European theaters, turned World War II into a bloodless, painless, deathless male-bonding romp that seemed more like summer camp than the hell on earth that so many artists working in other media have described. As Robert Klein remarked by way of an apology for telling a Kurt Waldheim joke, "I don't often do political humor, but I get the feeling that a whole generation of kids thinks World War II was like *Hogan's Heroes*. You know, like when Colonel Klink says, 'Hogan, the Fuhrer and Goering are throwing a costume party and I have nothing to wear. Here's a pass; go over to Switzerland and rent me a good costume.'"[13] *Gomer Pyle, U.S.M.C.* (CBS, 1964–70) was particularly audacious in this respect. It presented an apparently contemporary picture of U.S. military life in which developing a caring relationship with one's sergeant was the most important challenge facing the American fighting man. The word "Vietnam" was unknown to the marines at Gomer's Camp Henderson, California, despite the fact that the show's production run coincided directly with the combat deaths of tens of thousands of American soldiers.

As fantastic as concepts such as *Gilligan's Island* and *Gomer Pyle* were, they at least paid lip service to the physical principles of the universe. This was not the case with another stratum of fantasy sitcom that featured violations of the laws of nature as its main attractions. The "magic" sitcom was the most prolific sitcom subgenre and arguably the most popular type of program on all of American television during the sixties. Magicoms aired on all three networks throughout most of the decade. The long list of sixties shows falling into this category includes *Mr. Ed* (CBS, 1961–65),[14] *Bewitched* (ABC,

1964–72), *The Munsters* (CBS, 1964–66), *The Addams Family* (ABC, 1964–66), *I Dream of Jeannie* (NBC, 1965–70), and *Green Acres* (CBS, 1965–71).

While the sitcom had seen its share of hocus-pocus in the fifties—the ghosts in *Topper*, Cleo the Talking Dog on *The People's Choice*, George Burns's omniscient TV set—a concentrated profusion of animals with human intelligence, aliens from outer space, families of monsters and supernaturally powered women who could do the dishes by sheer will, inhabited the genre during this period. Had an urge to zap America into an alternative universe been liberated by the fears, promises, and changes in consciousness that accompanied the national confrontations with war, racism, drugs, and hi-fidelity electric erotic music?

The magicom can be seen as a kind of hyperbolic extension (or sixties version) of the "zany housewife" sitcom, model first developed on *I Love Lucy*. If Lucy Ricardo had been a "zany" female force upsetting "normal" middle-class life in the 1950s, the 1960s magicoms carried *I Love Lucy's* narrative structure to absurd lengths: Samantha Stevens is an immortal, spell-casting witch living in the New York suburbs with her "normal" advertising executive husband. Jeannie, a genie who has not had an out-of-bottle experience since the Ottoman Empire, lives in Cape Canaveral with her "normal" astronaut master. Mr. Ed is a horse who talks, but only to the "normal" exurban Southern California architect who owns him and shares his stable-office. Arnold Ziffel is a pig who reads, watches television, and is being raised on *Green Acres* in a house as the son of Fred and Edith Ziffel, a "normal" Hooterville farm couple. If the popularity of these shows cannot be causally linked with the spread of recreational drug use in American culture during this period, the coincidence is at the very least a stunning conceit.

The success of *Mr. Ed*, which was originally rejected by the networks but found its way to CBS after a year of first-run syndication, opened the door for a slew of prime-time magicoms. The talking-horse concept, which itself was borrowed from the Francis the Talking Mule movies of the 1950s, was prodigiously copied and transformed. In *My Mother, the Car* (NBC, 1965–66), to name one memorable example, Jerry

Van Dyke's beloved dead mother returns to him as a 1928 Porter sedan that speaks (the voice of Ann Sothern)—but only to him—over the "rein-*car*-nated" radio.

My Favorite Martian (CBS, 1963–66) rode the early crest of the magicom wave. One day while driving around Los Angeles, Tim O'Hara (Bill Bixby) spots a one-seater UFO crash landing in the woods. Bixby—a kind of low-rent Alan Alda whose shmaltz-ridden credits would eventually include the title role in *The Courtship of Eddie's Father* and the rational essence of *The Incredible Hulk*—exhibits early signs of sensitivity as a protoyuppie bachelor and cub reporter for an L.A. daily. He takes the extraterrestrial home to his apartment, nurses it back to health, and names it Uncle Martin (Ray Walston). Symbiosis develops. Tim helps the greenhorn from another planet assimilate into the Southern California lifestyle; Uncle Martin uses his retractable organic antennae to help Tim get newspaper scoops and do the worst of the housework. Tim and Uncle Martin come, in classic sitcom style, to love each other. The show finished tenth in the Nielsen ratings its first season.

Like most magicoms, *My Favorite Martian* took particular delight in inserting special effects into ordinary middle-class settings and situations. In the early episodes, invisibility, a relatively cheap camera trick, proved particularly popular with the show's writers. In "There Is No Cure for the Martian Cold," Uncle Martin gets a cold that causes him to disappear every time he sneezes; in "Blood Is Thicker than Martian," Tim demands that the Visitor remain invisible during the visit of snoopy Cousin Harvey; in "Going, Going, Gone," a flare-up of sun spots causes Uncle Martin to lose control over his invisibility. In another type of special-effects episode, Uncle Martin gets a Martian toothache that causes him to see everything in mirror perspective. If the genre was searching for apolitical, amoral entertainment that might tiptoe across the various "gaps" of class, race, gender, and age that were dividing its audience, the generous use of technologically generated visual effects was one apparent solution.

Many of the structural features of the magic sitcom are evident in *My Favorite Martian*. Uncle Martin's wiggling index finger, which he uses to do the ironing, levitate furniture, bake, save Tim from bad guys, and so on, clearly points the way to Samantha's twitching nose and Jeannie's blinking eyes. As with *Mr. Ed*, the supernatural being masquerades as "normal" to all but his, her, or its intimate companion. Wilbur's wife, Carol, and the couple's next-door neighbors, the Addisons, believe Mr. Ed is "just a horse," though Roger Addison is suspicious that something abnormal is going on and often just misses learning the truth. Similarly, Uncle Martin's true identity is known only to Tim, though Detective Brennan suspects; in *Bewitched*, only Darrin knows that Samantha is a witch, though Gladys Kravitz suspects; in *I Dream of Jeannie*, only Colonel Nelson (Larry Hagman) knows that Jeannie (Barbara Eden) is a genie, with Major Healy (Bill Daily) as the nosy next-door neighbor. In a breakthrough, Major Healy eventually learns the truth and shares the secret, leaving Dr. Bellows (Hayden Rorke) as the suspicious outsider figure.

In all the magic shows (except *The Munsters* and *The Addams Family*, which are about entire families of innocent monsters trying to live their deviant lives among hostile, intolerant "normal" people), an unpretentious middle-class heterosexual white male is miraculously handed a roommate—animal, woman, or alien—whose magical powers turn out to be more trouble than they are worth. Out of sheer magnanimity, however, the SWM adopts the Other and tries to teach it the profound satisfactions of simple, unsupernatural, consumer-oriented bourgeois life in the U.S.A. The message is clear: Don't be fooled by the glitz and glamour of easy (that is, magic) ways of doing things. The discipline and respectability of a nine-to-five, Thank-God-It's-Friday existence are valorized as far more satisfying than the freedom to gratuitously manipulate the world to one's individual pleasure. Supernatural powers are nice, but being nice is nicer. As in *The Wizard of Oz*, "there's no place like home . . . there's no place like home." Though on the surface the Other seems capable of simplifying life with its magical powers, the heroic "normal" persona knows that achievement is only truly worthwhile if it comes as the result of self-repression; he prefers to do it the hard way.

As a spaceman tale, *My Favorite Martian* differs from fifties Hollywood movies such as *The Day the Earth Stood Still*, *Invasion of the Body Snatchers*, and *Invaders from Mars*, which had ascribed elaborate motivations for alien visits to earth: saving humanity from nuclear war, taking over human bodies and consciousnesses for physical or spiritual sustenance, or bringing humans home as pets or science experiments.[15] Though we never learn exactly what Uncle Martin was up to when his ship went down, the reason for his extended stay on earth clearly has more to do with engine trouble than with any divinely or devilishly inspired mission. Demonstrating no desire to conquer, enslave, eat, or otherwise control the inhabitants of Los Angeles, he only professes a sentimental ("human?") desire to return to the mother planet. Thwarted, however, in all efforts to repair his vehicle by the primitive state of earth technology, the alien makes the best of a bad situation by establishing close ties with the locals. He is impressed with their (our) warmth and good intentions.

In the second season of the show's run, the relatively closed world of Tim and Uncle Martin was greatly expanded as the writers searched for scripting ploys. An interspecies (non-erotic) sitcom romance develops between Tim's widowed land-lady, Mrs. Lorelei Brown (Pamela Britton), and Uncle Martin. Mrs. Brown, however, is a mature, attractive woman who makes good brownies and owns Los Angeles real estate; she is not without other suitors. Detective Bill Brennan (Alan Hewitt) is introduced into the cast as Uncle Martin's nemesis. Not only do the two become rivals for the approval of the earth woman, but Brennan, a veteran cop, intuitively knows that something is fishy about Tim's so-called Uncle Martin. What is this middle-aged man with no job and no discernible past doing living with his "nephew" in a garage apartment? There must be something he can be arrested for. Brennan was one of the first purposefully obnoxious characters to be written into a sitcom as an ongoing regular.

Despite the fact that *My Favorite Martian* enjoyed the ham-mock position between *Lassie* and the Beatles-era *Ed Sullivan Show* on the legendary CBS Sunday night schedule, the series quickly faded from the ratings glory of its premier year. Faced with falling Nielsens over the next two seasons, producer Jack Chertok pulled out all the special-effects stops: Uncle Martin turns himself into a puddle of water, which is licked up by a dog, which in turn allows Uncle Martin to take over the dog's identity; Uncle Martin uses his time machine to go back to the fifteenth century to fetch Leonardo da Vinci to help him rebuild his broken spaceship; Uncle Martin accidentally turns a squirrel into a human being.[16]

A model of introduction, maturation, and decay was thus established for the magicom, the next wave of which would include the subgenre's greatest all-time hit: William Asher's *Bewitched*. Early *Bewitched*, like early *My Favorite Martian*, is pretty much limited to a circumspect domestic world shared by intimate personae—one natural, the other supernatural. A single theme dominates these episodes: Samantha (Elizabeth Montgomery) has been forbidden by her "normal" husband Darrin (Dick York; after 1969, Dick Sargent) from practicing witchcraft. Samantha tries to be dutiful, but life in a modern American housing tract is so utterly challenging and complex that sometimes she just can't help herself. For Samantha, magic spells become like prescription drugs, forbidden but tempting "mother's little helpers" that get her through her busy day.

In the first episodes of the show, again as in *My Favorite Martian*, the special effects were generally limited to the effortless execution of domestic chores: icing cakes, washing floors, improving the lawn. Interpersonal conflict occasionally escalates to the point where Samantha or, more likely, her mother, turns Darrin into a frog or a chimpanzee. But the razzmatazz is used relatively sparingly, as if care were being taken against carrying the joke too far or telling it once too often.

As the series evolved into a spectacularly successful eight-year production run, however, this cautious balance between sitcom realism and sitcom fantasy collapsed. Time-travel was instituted, including a visit to the court of Henry VIII, a sojourn in nineteenth-century New Orleans, and two separate trips to Massachusetts Bay witch trials (one episode in Plymouth, the other in Salem). In the early *Bewitched*, only Samantha and her mother, Endora (Agnes Moorehead), were capable of magic. But as the seasons rolled on, a score of semiregular and guest witches and warlocks were added to the cast, including "senile" Aunt Clara (Marion Lorne), mischievous Uncle Arthur (Paul Lynde), wallflower Esmerelda (Alice Ghostly), and the brilliant supernatural surgeon Dr. Bombay (Bernard Fox). As if all these threats to the puritanical order that Darrin values so dearly are not enough, two children, Tabitha and Adam, both of whom possess the gift-curse of witchcraft, are added to the household.

If the straitlaced, white-collared Darrin Stevens is driven to the brink of insanity by these constant threats to his business-man's consciousness, it might be argued that he was getting what he deserved. Following a tradition of sitcom husbands that included such diverse characters as Ralph Kramden, Jim Anderson, Ricky Ricardo, and Rob Petrie, Darrin is determined that Samantha remain a contented suburban wifette, despite her extraordinary—and potentially liberating—abilities. In the sitcoms inhabited by these characters, the male—the bread-winner—ventures out into the world each day to drive a bus, sell insurance, sing "Babalu," or write a network television comedy-variety show. His wife, however, is treated as little more than a contractual housekeeper who is to be kept safely locked away at home, be that a tenement in a Brooklyn slum, an Upper East Side apartment, a ranchburger in New Rochelle, or a fine substantial house in the Springfield vortex.

The validity of this arrangement is reiterated often. When Ralph is laid off by the bus company (after he suggests a new labor-saving idea to management), Alice is forced to take a job as a secretary. Having in many episodes exclaimed, "A wife of mine will never work," the King of the Castle is driven to new depths of humiliation as Alice begins putting in evening overtime with her successful—and flirtatious—boss. When Ralph is called back to work, he does not even take the time to ask Alice to quit, but breaks in on a work session, manhandles the boss, and thus ends his wife's business career. The same story is told in more genteel terms at the Anderson household when Jim and the children complain that Margaret is giving too much time to her charitable activities and not enough to each of them. In *I Love Lucy* this point is made in what takes the form of a ritualized episode in which Ricky simply refuses, by God-given husbandly authority, to allow Lucy to attempt to break into show business. Rob Petrie is more politically sensitive in his handling of Laura, the former dancer, but he gets the same results.

Darrin Stevens, however, is the most ideologically committed sexist of them all. In episode after episode, he expects Samantha to entertain his advertising accounts at home, yet he forbids her from using her magical powers to do so. Though Sam can prepare a gourmet dinner for a dozen or a hundred guests with one short spell (usually just an heroic couplet and a twitch of the nose), Darrin demands that his wife cook, clean, and do the marketing the "old-fashioned" way—with an electric stove, a vacuum cleaner, and a station wagon—for no other reason than to satisfy his incorrigibly puritanical vision of what a marriage ought to be. Furthermore, Sam professes to agree with Darrin that what is normal is indeed proper: the status quo as platonic ideal. Writing on *Bewitched*, Isaac Asimov observed, "Here's a woman with unimaginable magical power and she uses it entirely to shore up her husband's ego, make him look good, help him keep his job, beat down his enemies. Has she no life of her own?"[17]

In "Be It Ever So Mortgaged," the second episode of the 254 that were made, much of the series' cosmos is delineated. At this point, Darrin and Samantha are newlyweds still living in the city. Returning home from work one day, Darrin announces, "I drove out of the city today to a new development to see a house. Not a rented house with someone else's furniture and someone else's carpets and drapes, but our own house, something we can own from the top to the bottom, from one end to the other. Our house! Now what do you think of that?" Samantha, who has been brought up in a decidedly nonsuburban culture, is not exactly sent into ecstatic dances by the idea. But seeing her husband's enthusiasm, she replies, "Anything that makes you happy, makes me happy."

Endora, however, is totally aghast at the prospect of her only daughter becoming a housing-tract wifette, and she implores her to reconsider. But Samantha reveals an unflappable commitment to the American dream, telling her mother, "I think we're very lucky. All young married people dream of owning their own home."

Endora then makes this impassioned plea: "That is fine for 'them,' but not for us. We're quicksilver, a fleeting shadow, a distant sound. Our home has no boundaries beyond which we cannot pass. We live in music, in a flash of color. We live on the wind, in the sparkle of a star. And you want to trade it all for a quarter of an acre of crab grass."[18]

Unmoved by her mother's eloquence—or by the poetry of the life she describes—Samantha drags Endora out to the suburbs to take a look at the house. One glance is enough: "Don't waste your time, Samantha, it's not for you." But Sam remains adamant in her desire to please Darrin. She won't even allow her mother to use magic to make the place "civilized." Refusing Endora's offer to instantly zap up a beautiful garden in full bloom, Samantha piously informs her, "We're going to do it the right way—with seeds!" Endora then offers to furnish the house, but once again Sam will have none of it: "We're going to furnish the house like ordinary people—on time!"

Darrin and Samantha Stevens are demographically similar to Rob and Laura Petrie of *The Dick Van Dyke Show*. Both are New York commuter families living in the suburbs, with the husband working at a mass-media job in midtown Manhattan. But Samantha, despite her protests to the contrary, is considerably more dislocated in this way of living than is Laura. Her new life in suburbia stands in stark contrast to her old life as a witch, something her mother is only too glad to remind her of. Indeed, Sam's decision to live such a "straight" existence often seems like the least believable aspect of *Bewitched*. A rare and extraordinary being living in a colony of conformist slugs, Samantha can develop no real ties to her "normal" neighbors.

As in *The Beverly Hillbillies*, the uncongenial normal neighbors leave much to be desired. In the nameless town where Darrin and Samantha live, the locals are represented by Gladys and Abner Kravitz, as pathetic a pair as the sitcom has ever produced. The sneaky Gladys (Alice Pearce; later Sandra Gould) is a whining Peeping Tom whose proclivity toward spying on her neighbors often leads her to secretly witness the casting of spells and the conjuring of spirits. Gladys, who takes nerve medicine, can't get anyone, especially her retired husband, Abner (George Tobias), to believe that these things are really happening. Abner Kravitz is a loveless cynic who spends most of his day reading the newspaper. Not only does he refuse to believe his wife when she tells him that Leonardo da Vinci is painting the Stevenses' house or that an elephant has miraculously appeared in the Stevenses' living room, but he doesn't even care. Doing the crossword puzzle one afternoon, he asks, "What's a five-letter word for the ultimate happiness, peace, and tranquillity?" When Gladys ignores his question and responds with her latest wild story about the Stevenses, Abner answers the question with a one-word soliloquy directed at the camera: "Death."

As older retired neighbors, Abner and Gladys Kravitz suggest a mirror image of another sitcom sidekick couple, Fred and Ethel Mertz of *I Love Lucy*. If the Mertzes are, despite Fred's outward manner, a source of warmth and support for Lucy and Ricky, the Kravitzes offer Sam and Darrin nothing resembling friendship: Abner is utterly indifferent, and Gladys goes out of her way to harass them. In *Crabgrass Frontier: The Suburbanization of the United States*, Kenneth T. Jackson notes "a tendency [in suburbia] for social life to become 'privatized,' and a reduced feeling of concern and responsibility among families for their neighbors."[19] Indeed, Samantha and Darrin spend most of their "free" time with Darrin's boss, Larry Tate, and his wife, Louise, busily engaged in work-related social entertaining. Moreover, Darrin's boss, Larry proves something less than a friend, threatening to fire him at the slightest hint that an account may be lost.

Agnes Moorehead, whose distinguished career included performances in many of Orson Welles's stage, radio, and cinema productions (see especially the Welles film adaptation of Booth Tarkington's *The Magnificent Ambersons*), was at least as great an asset to *Bewitched* as the show's special effects. Her sarcasm is limitless, as when she chides Samantha for wielding a broom when she might be off riding one. Endora simply cannot fathom the attraction of what she considers Sam's bland, run-of-the-mill life with a bland, run-of-the-mill nine-to-fiver. She says of her son-in-law, "Oh, they all look alike to me: noses to the grindstone, shoulders to the wheel, feet planted firmly on the ground. No wonder they can't fly."[20] She constantly urges Samantha to dump "Durwood" (and middle-class America), inviting her instead to share such Old World pleasures with her as lunch in Milan, a safari to Mount Kilimanjaro, or dinner and dancing on the Riviera. Not a chance. Exhibiting true sitcom love for her husband, Samantha would rather stay at home and dust or prepare a roast than visit the casino at Monte Carlo. Though the episodic plot morals emphatically valorize Darrin and Samantha's "normal" marriage against Endora's attacks, the cumulative effect of the series can be quite the opposite. Endora (and the life she represents) is daring, witty, and power- ful. She is a far more attractive personality than the wimpy, attaché-case-toting commuter-husband. Of course, given the conventions of the sitcom, Darrin's sexual prowess is never discussed; perhaps it is an unspoken text that could critically rehabilitate *Bewitched* into the realm of psychorealism.

As if to further emphasize the contradictions between the noble life of the suburban bourgeoisie and all other poss- ible (or even impossible) alternatives, Elizabeth Montgomery occasionally appears in the role of Samantha's twin cousin, Serena, a mini-skirted free-spirited "double" whose wardrobe ranges from Carnaby Street to Haight-Ashbury and back. Just as Samantha's witchcraft causes embarrassment to Darrin, Serena's "hippie" witchcraft causes embarrassment to the relatively conservative Samantha. In an episode titled "Hippie, Hippie, Hippie," Serena makes the front page of the town newspaper when she is arrested at a "love-in" (actual word used in episode). Everyone—especially Darrin—is shocked, thinking that the "weirdo" in lovebeads and sandals, chanting for peace and love, is Samantha. In the two-part episode "Cousin Serena Strikes Again," Samantha's alter ego decides that Darrin is a "turn-on" and tries to steal him away. When Darrin is too busy with one of his clients to pay attention to Serena, she zaps the client into a monkey. Darrin is surer than ever that he has made the right choice in marriage.

Serena is typical of the sitcom's treatment of "counterculture types" during the sixties. Like the so-called hippies who occa- sionally show up on *The Beverly Hillbillies* or *Gilligan's Island*, Cousin Serena is portrayed as silly and impractical, rather than malevolent or evil, thus depoliticizing the "alternative lifestyle" issue, reducing it from satire to farce. For example, in "Hippie, Hippie, Hippie," the love-in at which Serena is arrested is not a demonstration against armed forces recruitment or a chemical weapons maker; it is just a love-in. Like Lucy, Samantha, Jeannie, or *Green Acres*'s Lisa Douglas, Serena is, beneath her outlandish clothing and eccentric language, merely another chaotic "female" force. Her most frequent plot function is to disrupt "business as usual." In "The Generation Zap," she turns the daughter of one of Darrin's clients into a hippie; in another episode, she turns Darrin into a jackass just moments before Larry is due over for dinner with a client. Despite their differences in style, both Samantha and Serena—as well as all witches and perhaps all women—just can't help but cause trouble for "serious" (business)men like Darrin and Larry.

Bewitched became one of TV's all-time hits, finishing among the twelve top-rated prime-time series during its first five seasons. Again, as with *My Favorite Martian*, the writers seemed to go crazy looking for variations with the passing of the seasons. How many times could Endora or Uncle Arthur turn Darrin into a midget, make him unable to speak anything but the literal truth, or give him amnesia? Attempting to prepare a Caesar salad in one episode, the shy and bumbling cousin Esmerelda (Alice Ghostly) conjures the actual Julius into the Stevens home by mistake. Visitors to the Stevens household included not only historical personages, such as Benjamin Franklin, Napoleon, and Queen Victoria, but also such mythological figures as the Loch Ness Monster and the goddess Venus and such fictional characters as Hansel and Gretel and Prince Charming. With the birth of their daughter, Tabitha (1966), and their son, Adam (1971), we learn that witch genes are dominant in mixed-marriage offspring. Darrin, the increasingly alienated male breadwinner, must now contend with a houseful of women, children, and non–blood relatives, all of whom can turn him into a cockroach at will.

Bewitched was a curious play on the classic domesticom. Though Darrin did, at bottom line, "know best" in terms of the value system supported by the series' macrocosmic narrative, his ethical superiority did not institutionalize his power over reality, as was the case with the old domesticom dads such as Ozzie Nelson, Steve Douglas, or Ward Cleaver. Darrin can be seen as a transitional figure from the paternal omniscience and omnipotence of Jim Anderson in the fifties to the powerlessness and stupidity of Archie Bunker in the seventies. Though struggling to stay fresh during a decade that had self-consciously characterized itself as a period of change, the sitcom was not ready quite yet for the comprehensive reconfiguration of the American family that would take place under Norman Lear's tutelage (see Chapter Five). The result was a head of the household who maintained the "eternal" values of the American celebration but who was now faced with an absurd supernatural circumstance (the sixties?) that prevented him from ruling the roost with impunity.

Paul Henning's *Green Acres* is a compelling illustration of the influence of the magicom over the sitcom genre as a whole.[21] Though ostensibly the third part of Henning's Hooterville trilogy, the series burst the flimsy seams of the quasi-realism of *The Beverly Hillbillies* and *Petticoat Junction*, spilling over from ruralcom to magicom. As utterly self-reflexive as any program ever aired on network television, *Green Acres* built itself upon reversals of the popular sitcom styles and trends of its day. On the most obvious level, the show is a plain and simple narrative mirror of *The Beverly Hillbillies*: in the *Hillbillies*, poor country folk miraculously become rich and move to a mansion in the city; in *Green Acres*, rich city folk purposefully give up life on the fast track and move to the country to live in rural squalor. But the series also contains a reversal of *Bewitched*. If Samantha is a paranormal female inserted into a normal suburban setting, Oliver Douglas (Eddie Albert) is a normal male inserted into a paranormal rural setting.

Douglas, an Upper East Sider and Wall Street attorney with a deep-seated penchant for the romance of Jeffersonian democracy, decides one day to give up his law practice and penthouse apartment for the ascetic satisfactions of forty acres and a mule. His aristocratic Hungarian emigré wife, Lisa (Eva Gabor), protests, "Dahling, I love you, but give me Park Avenue!" Oliver's definition of democracy, however, does not extend to marriage and the Douglases ride off in their massive pre-energy-crisis Lincoln convertible to start anew in the fresh green breast of Hooterville, U.S.A.

Life down on the farm is not quite the Grant Wood painting that Oliver had imagined. Seeking a community of righteous yeomen, he instead finds Mr. Haney (Pat Buttram), a ruthless rural drummer who hornswoggles him into buying a ramshackle old farmhouse; Hank Kimball (Alvy Moore), a double-talking county agent whose discourses on plant and animal husbandry rival the lectures of a semiotics professor; and his neighbors Fred and Doris Ziffel (Hank Patterson and Barbara Pepper and, later, Fran Ryan), a childless couple who are raising a young pig named Arnold as if it were their son.

The major problem plaguing the Harvard-educated Oliver in his attempt to drop out of the rat race and become totally organic (this was, after all, the sixties) is that he continues to maintain modern urban man's faith in cause-and-effect logic, a template of reality that does not apply in the fertile crescent that stretches from Hooterville to Pixley and constitutes Paul Henning's sitcomic Yoknapatawpha. Determined to spread the gospel of science, Oliver reads books on "modern American agriculture" and spends his money on the items necessary to practice it. At harvest time, however, Oliver finds he must continue to live off his New York bank account while his poor "backward" neighbors get on as they always have.

Lisa, though pining for Bloomingdale's, has a relatively easier time adjusting to life in the country. When not working on her famous hotcakes, she becomes involved in the cultural life of Hooterville: in one episode, she imports a symphony conductor to the tiny rural village, and in another, she opens a state-of-the-art beauty salon in the back of Sam Drucker's General Store. Her lack of agricultural knowledge leaves her genuinely charmed when one of the chickens starts laying square eggs or when Arnold the Pig expresses romantic love for Mr. Haney's basset hound, Cynthia. Positivist Oliver, meanwhile, is driven mad by these violations of Cartesian reality.

As with other magicoms, the passage of time tended to push the lighthearted surrealism of the early episodes into the science-fiction zone. Some standout episodes include "Double Drick," in which Oliver's faulty wiring job of the farmhouse causes a ripple in the national electric power grid that blacks out New York City; "The Reincarnation of Eb," in which Lisa believes that their hired hand (Tom Lester) has died and come back as a dog; and "Oliver and the Cornstalk," in which the Jolly Green Giant pays a visit to the Douglas farm. There is nothing intrinsically "magical" in the narrative structure of *Green Acres*—no Martian, no witch, no genie, no monsters. Magic, however, was doing good business on television and it was gratuitously synthesized into the program.

As does *Bewitched*, *Green Acres* occasionally alludes—with a broad smile on its face—to the cultural gut-wrenching that America was going through during the years of the program's production. In "The Liberation Movement," Lisa gets a sudden attack of political consciousness and takes over the farm, forcing Oliver to do the housework; this was a kind of updated sixties retelling of the archetypal sitcom episode in which husbands and wives trade places (see *I Love Lucy* and *The Honeymooners*, among others). In "The Great Mayoralty Campaign," Lisa runs against Oliver when he attempts to become the mayor of Hooterville. Most notably, there is an implicit political subtext in the overall premise of the series, which is Oliver's dropping out of a privileged position in the Establishment to live off the land and the fruits of his own labor. This is brought full cycle in the prescient final episode of *Green Acres*: Hooterville secedes from the Union following a tax increase—and crowns Oliver as its first *king*. So much for Jeffersonian democracy and/or sixties idealism.

While all this implosion and distension was going on in situation comedy, the comedy-variety show seemed to be exhibiting some new signs of life. These, however, would ultimately prove to be the desperate thrashings of a dinosaur's tail rather than indications of a positive reawakening in the genre. Two programs were especially significant in the aborted late-sixties comedy-variety renaissance: *The Smothers Brothers Comedy Hour* and *Rowan and Martin's Laugh-in*. Each, in its own way, rejected the avoidance strategy of the magicom and instead risked audience polarization by seeking a degree of confrontation with The News. Despite some ratings success, neither the Smothers Brothers nor Rowan and Martin became models for prime-time development.

Tom and Dick Smothers had started out as folk singers in the fifties, playing coffee houses and colleges in the area south of San Francisco that would later become known as Silicon Valley. In 1959, they graduated to an engagement at the Purple Onion, a San Francisco outpost of the transcontinental network of "hip" downtown nightclubs where comedians such as Lenny Bruce and Dick Gregory were appearing. Their act was an old vaudeville concept, repackaged in fifties trappings. With Tom on guitar and Dick on bass fiddle, the brothers played a mixture of traditional and contemporary folk tunes, interrupting their own music to exchange comic patter, a duet variation on the delivery system made famous by Henny Youngman. Though the music qualified as "folk," the Smothers

143

Brothers owed more to the Kingston Trio than to the Weavers. "We prided ourselves," recalls Tom Smothers, "on *not* taking any political stands."[22] Their hair was short and groomed; they wore Perry Como sweaters.

The Smothers Brothers caught the eye of the California TV community in the early sixties. Their clean-cut appearance fused nicely with the "nowness" of their act. Tom and Dick could sing Woody Guthrie songs, but they were also comedians whose basic shtick was a tried-and-true "dumb guy, smart guy" vaudeville routine. The familiarity of the act's structure might serve to neutralize the politically charged aura normally attached to the very notion of folk singers. Tom and Dick were to be the George and Gracie of the folk revival, a hip but not too hip property that just possibly might appeal to younger audiences without alienating older ones or inciting political reaction. Their first national television appearance was in 1963, a performance of bits from their café routines on ABC's *Hootenanny*, a show that was being picketed at this very time for its refusal to book Pete Seeger.[23]

CBS was the only one of the three networks that had not yet tried a pop-music or satire show. Though firmly—imperially—entrenched at the top of the ratings in 1965, the network decided to take a chance on the Smothers Brothers, hoping to capture some of the increasingly important lump of eighteen to thirty-four year old viewers, who would eventually come to be called "baby boomers." As a hedge against polarization, however, CBS brought the Smothers Brothers to prime time by packaging them in a narrative format that was at the dead center of programming practice during this period: the magicom. *The Smothers Brothers Show*, a sitcom, premiered on CBS in 1965 and ran for a single season. It should not be confused with *The Smothers Brothers Comedy Hour*, the more celebrated comedy-variety series that would follow several years later.

Combining elements of such commercially proven works as *Mr. Ed* and the Frank Capra film *It's a Wonderful Life*, *The Smothers Brothers Show* translated the male-bonding metaphor of *My Favorite Martian* from science fiction to religious allegory: Tommy played an apprentice angel sent down to earth to watch over his brother, Dick, a white bachelor publishing executive living in an apartment in the city. The plot was strictly assembly-line: Tom, the supernatural Other, uses his powers to solve problems, but invariably creates even thornier problems for his normal host in the doing.

The proscenium performed its ameliorative magic. The Smothers Brothers were effectively kept away from their musical instruments and from the spontaneity of their stand-up act. But the containment of the Smothers Brothers in a representational narrative framework proved to be too claustrophobic. The series was a flop, pure and simple, both in the ratings and in the eyes of its stars. Reviewing *The Smothers Brothers Show* for *TV Guide*, Cleveland Amory chided it as a B version of *Bewitched*.[24] "We just made the mistake of listening to people who *thought* they knew what our comedy was about," explained Dick.[25]

Sitting out the first half of the 1966–67 television season, the Smothers Brothers returned to CBS in January—this time with a comedy-variety show. If the structure of the new *Smothers Brothers Comedy Hour* was somewhat old-fashioned, the show's content was, in self-conscious relation to its prime-time setting, nothing less than avant-garde. Blackout sketches attacked U.S. Vietnam policy as well as diverse establishment targets, including the clergy and big business. During the election year of 1968, series regular Pat Paulsen "ran for president," poking fun at both specific candidates and the entire electoral system. Just as NBC had preempted *That Was the Week That Was* during the shank of the Goldwater-Johnson campaign in 1964, CBS refused to allow Paulsen on the air during the weeks immediately preceding the Humphrey-Nixon election.

Brooks and Marsh have characterized the guest stars who appeared on *The Smothers Brothers Comedy Hour* as "predominantly antiwar, left-wing, and outspoken."[26] This may be a bit of an exaggeration; guest performers carrying little or no political baggage, such as Bob Crane, Glen Campbell, and Sid Caesar, were as much a part of the show as its more controversial guests. But the Smothers Brothers did present some faces otherwise not seen in sixties prime time. They included Joan Baez, who dedicated a song to her husband, then serving time in federal prison for draft evasion; the Blackstone Rangers, a street gang from the South Side of Chicago that had organized itself into a kind of Black Panthers version of Up with People; and Pete Seeger, whose unwavering commitment to a variety of political causes had kept him off of commercial television since its earliest days.

Seeger, especially, caused a sensation. The Smothers Brothers had invited him to appear on their season opener in September 1967. The folksinger, who usually performed for relatively small and intrinsically sympathetic audiences, was excited about the prospect of bringing his work to a huge television audience. "All of a sudden here was a breach in the wall of prime time, a very dangerous thing as far as the establishment was concerned," he wrote.[27] Everyone seemed to feel good about the breaking of the seventeen-year network boycott of Seeger, the network, the producers, and even the sponsors patted themselves on the back for their progressive attitudes. Many newspapers, including the New York *Times* and the Los Angeles *Times*, devoted editorial space to praising CBS for its good citizenship in breaking the blacklist.

But the air of reconciliation surrounding the announcement of Seeger's appearance did not survive his performance. The singer had videotaped a rendition of "Waist Deep in the Big Muddy," an antiwar song that he had written in response to the escalating situation in Vietnam. He left Los Angeles fully expecting it to be used on the taped show. Though the rest of Seeger's participation in the episode was telecast, the "Big Muddy" segment was unceremoniously cut by line producers Saul Ilson and Ernest Chambers in response to pressure from CBS Standards and Practices. Furthermore, Seeger only learned that his song had been censored as he viewed the program on the night of the telecast.

The story was reported by *Variety* and brought general press comment. The Honolulu *Star-Bulletin* editorialized, "Is the presidency so teetery that it cannot withstand the musical barbs of a folksinger? And is our democracy so fragile that songs of social protest must be stricken from the public airwaves?"[28] CBS responded with a press release explaining its action by claiming that it didn't want "political controversy on entertainment programs."[29] It is perhaps testimony to the special importance of television in the consciousness industry that CBS saw no inconsistency in the fact that Seeger had recorded "Waist Deep in the Big Muddy" for its Columbia Records division less than a year earlier.

The Smothers Brothers, embarrassed on their left, invited Seeger back for a second appearance in February 1968. This time, with the spotlight of a free-speech issue thrown on the event, Seeger was given a generous twenty-minute segment of the program to do with as he pleased. Performing alone in a spotlight on a dark stage, he began with "My Get-Up-and-Go Has Got Up and Went," a lighthearted, relatively apolitical song about aging. He then broke into a medley of American antiwar songs that spanned the period from the Mexican War to World War I, punctuating the tunes with didactic commentary on their historical contexts. The medley, in turn, acted as an introduction for the featured number that everyone had been waiting for.

"Waist Deep in the Big Muddy" tells a story about a World War II captain who, against the pleas of his enlisted men, leads a patrol into dangerously deep waters—and drowns himself. Lest the allegorical message of the song elude any listeners, Seeger took pains to reiterate it in the final verse:

> Well I'm not going to point any moral
> I'll leave that for yourself
> Maybe you're still walking and you're still talking
> And you'd like to keep your health.
> But every time I read the papers,
> Them old feelings come on;
> We're waist deep in the Big Muddy
> Neck deep! So deep even a tall man is over his head!
> And the big fool says to push on.
>
> © Words and music by Pete Seeger,
> TRO-Melody Trails, Inc.

"I was thinking of Vietnam," Seeger later told his biographer. "On the other hand, I purposely decided I would just let it be an allegory on its own, like the political nursery rhymes. As the years go by, the song may make another appearance and be sung in another context."[30] Though many reluctant CBS affiliates had been embarrassed into carrying the segment by the publicity that the censorship incident had generated, the network's Detroit affiliate, WJBK, owned by the Storer Broadcasting Company, saw fit to turn off the sound during the last verse of "Big Muddy" on the night of the telecast.

To understand why CBS had cut the Smothers Brothers so much slack in the first place, it is necessary to recall that unlike the ill-conceived magic sitcom, the Smothers Brothers comedy-variety hour had come to television as quite a promising property. A midseason replacement for the ossifying *Garry Moore Show*, *The Smothers Brothers Comedy Hour* had miraculously knocked NBC's *Bonanza* out of its perennial first place position in the Sunday 9–10 P.M. slot several times during the winter and spring of 1967. During 1967–68, the show's first complete season, it finished a very bankable eighteenth in the overall Nielsens.

But as with other "topically oriented" prime-time shows, it was proving to be more trouble than it was worth from the network point of view. When the program's ratings showed evidence of decline during the 1968–69 season, CBS grabbed the first opportunity to cancel it. The network cited the late delivery of scripts—a rarely enforced technicality—as the reason behind the move. Though the Smothers Brothers sued and eventually won a cash settlement, the damage was done; *The Smothers Brothers Comedy Hour* was replaced by *Hee Haw* in September 1969. *TV Guide* supported the decision in an editorial titled "Smothers Out: A Wise Decision":

> We are in full accord with the Columbia Broadcasting System in its wise, determined and wholly justified insistence on meeting its responsibilities by retaining the right to preview what it will telecast over its facilities. CBS, however, found out that it could not carry out this duty because the Smothers Brothers, in their arrogance, make it impossible by delaying the delivery of their finished shows. . . . The issue is: Shall entertainers using a mass medium for *all* the people be allowed to amuse a few by satirizing religion while offending the substantial majority? . . . The issue is: Shall a network be required to provide time for a Joan Baez to pay tribute to her draft-evading husband while hundreds of thousands of viewers in the households of men fighting and dying in Vietnam look on in shocked resentment?[31]

Viewed twenty years later in a museum, *The Smothers Brothers Comedy Hour* makes for less than consistently arresting viewing pleasure. The poorly written blackout sketches are mostly hack embarrassments, rarely reaching the level of complexity that one might find on *The Carol Burnett Show*, not to speak of *Saturday Night Live* or *SCTV*. Even the extraordinary guests that the Smothers were able to sign—Bette Davis and Moms Mabley among them—were for the most part wasted on deadly material. It is perhaps little wonder that the Smothers Brothers' comeback attempts on both ABC (1970) and NBC (1975) failed and that, despite the desperate need for programming brought on by cable expansion, *The Smothers Brothers Comedy Hour* has never been syndicated.[32]

Yet, the show does have its moments as a germinating oracle of a peculiar moment in the eclipsing histories of America and its mass culture. Even the slapstick is pure period:

Tom: I have a tickle in my throat.
Dick: There's a great medical authority who gave advice on how to keep from getting sick.
Tom: What's the advice?
Dick: He says not to get caught in the draft.
Tom: Who said this?
Dick: Dr. Spock.[33]

In the same vein, a semiregular feature of the show was "Share A Little Tea with Goldie," with comedienne Leigh French playing the title character. A stoned yenta, Goldie would deliver a barrage of loosely veiled pot and pottie jokes ("Don't you hate it when all you've got left are twigs and stems when friends are due over for high tea?"). These were the first marijuana jokes heard on television—not even Lenny Bruce had dared make one on *The Steve Allen Show*—and they presaged the genre of drug gags that would grow on *Saturday Night Live*, *Fridays*, and other late-night comedy shows a decade later.

On a February 1967 program, the Buffalo Springfield made their only network television appearance ever, performing their hit song "For What It's Worth":

> Paranoia strikes deep,
> Into your heart it will creep.
> It starts when you're always afraid,

Step out of line, the man come and take you away.
Hey, stop, children, what's that sound,
Everybody look what's going down.
© Words and music by Stephen Stills,
Ten-East Music/Cotillion Music, Inc./Spingalo Tunes.

What made the performance especially interesting was the fact that Neil Young, a Canadian member of the band, was having trouble with the Immigration and Naturalization Service at the time. Illegally in the United States, he appeared in front of millions on national television, facing away from the camera—an inexplicable production feature, no doubt, to the show's viewers.

Rowan and Martin's Laugh-In (NBC, 1968–73) was much more commercially successful than *The Smothers Brothers Comedy Hour*, finishing first in the Nielsens in two of its five seasons. *Laugh-In* was the only other comedy program on prime-time commercial television during the late sixties that had any pointed topical content and its stars, Rowan and Martin, developed a special sense of kinship with the Smothers Brothers. When CBS refused to allow the Smothers Brothers to cross networks to appear on *Laugh-In*, Rowan and Martin did a series of unadvertised cameos on a *Smothers Brothers* episode. In tiny, *Laugh-In*-style one-liner bits that were inserted into various parts of the hour, Rowan and Martin offered *explications de texte* of the Smothers Brothers' show. For example, after the pothead Goldie lauds a new household cleanser by exclaiming, "I love my can!" (big laugh from audience), Rowan and Martin suddenly appear, wearing peace symbols on their blazers; Dan says to Dick, "We couldn't even say that on *Laugh-In*."[34]

With its relentless quick cutting and total devotion to visual and verbal one-liners at the expense of any other type of comedy, *Laugh-In* differed in form from virtually any show that had ever been seen in prime time. Though some critics have found the origins of *Laugh-In*'s cubist continuity in the work of Ernie Kovacs, the pace of cutting developed by *Laugh-In*'s creator-producer George Schlatter was so much faster than the meticulous, grandiloquent leisure of a Kovacs sketch that such comparisons are of little value.[35] A minute of *Laugh-In* looks more like a minute of 1980s channel-zapping than a minute of Kovacs or any of the early masters.

150

Whereas the Smothers Brothers had used the conventional structure of a classic fifties comedy-variety show (host, guest, blackout sketch, musical number) and subverted it with the presentation of controversial performers and subjects, *Laugh-In* was an attempt to create a new genre of comedy programming whose aesthetic appeal would be based on videotape-editing gestures rather than on the approximation of vaudeville traditions. Each episode was loosely composed of segments: "The Party," in which the ensemble did the Watusi, pausing every other moment to focus on one of the dancing comedians for a gag line; "Mod, Mod World," which would examine some recent trend or event with a machine-gun series of minisketches; "*Laugh-In* Looks at the News," the weekly news summary that has become obligatory on every TV satire show; the "The Joke Wall," during which comedians pop out of trap doors and windows to deliver one-liners. But most of the show was composed of formless segues: John Wayne, Sammy Davis, Jr., or Richard Nixon inexplicably appearing in front of the camera to say, "Sock it to me" or "Here come de judge"; Joanne Worley sitting on a baby grand, belting out crazed opera cadenzas; a six-second film of a man pedaling a tricycle and falling over; Arte Johnson as the Nazi soldier, saying "Verrrrrrrrry interesting. . . ."

Whereas the Smothers Brothers were self-conscious and even self-congratulatory about their transgressions against TV-industry wisdom, on *Laugh-In* politically loaded remarks were delivered in a casual way:

Goldie Hawn: "I love Joan Baez; I've even got a set of her fingerprints."[36]

Henry Gibson dressed in clerical collar: "My church welcomes all denominations, but especially the five-dollar bill."

Barbara Eden (in a guest appearance): "I went to a parochial school where we really learned the three R's: reading, writing, and rhythm."

Judy Carne: "It's not the hawks or the doves I'm worried about; it's those cuckoos in Washington who are trying to make pigeons out of all of us."

151

Dick Wittington (dressed as a Confederate officer): "Our granddaddy the colonel taught us never to go out with a colored girl—especially to a public place."

Dan: "You know, we only went into Vietnam as advisers. Last week we dropped over 400,000 tons of advice."[37]

Though Rowan and Martin were the show's hosts, *Laugh-In* was dominated by its women comics: Goldie Hawn, playing an updated dumb blonde for the sixties; Ruth Buzzi, the shrewish hag ceaselessly beating Arte Johnson over the head with her handbag in the park; Joanne Worley, the Martha Raye-like bigmouth screaming out jokes and nonsense syllables; and so on. Lily Tomlin was surely the show's greatest comic discovery. Her unbearably nasty telephone operator Ernestine provided the closest thing to an evolved critique of an American corporation that had ever been heard on the airwaves: "This is the Telephone Company. We are not subject to state, local, or federal regulations. We are omnipotent. We handle 84 billion calls a year from everyone, including presidents and the Pope. We don't need the business of scum like you, who owe us $18.34 for your last month's bill."[38] Like so many of the endlessly repeated lines on *Laugh-In* ("Sock it to me!" "Look that up in your Funk and Wagnalls!" "You bet your bippy!" "Beautiful downtown Burbank," and so on), Ernestine's smarmy, snooty "That's one ringy-dingy" found its way into the national language for the proverbial fifteen minutes. "Telephone operators started giving me awards," recalls Tomlin. "I went to presentation dinners. The Federation of Women Telephone Workers gave me a silver trophy."[39] Attempting to domesticate the beast, A.T.&T. offered Tomlin a reported half-million-dollar contract to play Ernestine on telephone company commercials. She refused. Despite the restructuring of the telephone industry from monopoly to oligarchy that has since occurred, reruns of Ernestine retain much of their sting.

The possibility that *Laugh-In* might provide a model for the rebirth of nondramatic comedy in prime time was undermined by the failure of its first clone, *Turn-On*, a 1969 ABC show that lasted exactly one week. George Schlatter, the auteur of *Laugh-In*, was the show's producer; he tried to go himself one better in his new show. Instead of a stand-up comedian as its host, *Turn-On*—quite presciently—used a wisecracking computer. There were no "regular" segments. "*Turn-On* was not really a show," Schlatter told *TV Guide*. "It was an experience, a happening. It was meant to be disturbing. It was provocative, adult, sophisticated. It was environmental comedy."[40] A CBS executive who had rejected *Turn-On* when it was offered to him explained that "it was so fast with the cuts and chops that some of our people actually got physically disturbed by it."[41] The limits of formal innovation had apparently been reached, at least for the time being.

There were other, more conservative attempts at copying the form that Schlatter had introduced on *Laugh-In*. *Hee Haw*, the show that had replaced the Smothers Brothers, was a prime example. Following the cutting pace and segmentation ideas of *Laugh-In*, *Hee Haw* exchanged Schlatter's self-consciously "hip urban" content for a self-consciously "corny rural" metaphor. The Joke Wall became the Corn Patch, with comedians popping up between the stalks with country one-liners, and so on. Though *Hee Haw* was dropped by CBS at the end of its first season, the show moved to Nashville and has remained in production as a syndicated program for twenty years.

Oddly enough, the greatest legacy of *Laugh-In* endures in a show designed neither for prime time nor even for commercial distribution: *Sesame Street* (PBS, 1969–present).[42] *Laugh-In* had proved television's ability to instantly and effortlessly make words, phrases, and ideas current in national culture through humorous repetition. The formula was seized upon by Joan Ganz Cooney, executive director of the Children's Television Workshop, a not-for-profit company funded by Ford Foundation, Carnegie Foundation, and U.S. Office of Education grants. If kids all over the country could learn to say "Sock it to me" to each other, they could also learn to count to ten that way. Like its progenitor *Laugh-In*, *Sesame Street* has been alternately praised for exploiting the possibilities of television as a medium and condemned for siding with the enemy in the war against human attention span.

As the sixties ended, TV comedy was still fumbling for a commercially feasible way to break the cautious mentality that had marked its McCarthyite youth. Magicom premises became increasingly ridiculous as the genre was aesthetically strip-mined. ABC, as usual, defined the limits of depth. *The Flying Nun* (ABC, 1967–70) had Sally Fields, who had only recently achieved fame as Gidget, joining a convent in Puerto Rico where, for reasons alternately attributed to physics and God, she discovers the ability to fly. *Nanny and the Professor* (ABC, 1970–71) was a TV adaptation of Disney's *Mary Poppins*, with Juliet Mills as the magical, mystical housekeeper. *The Partridge Family* (ABC, 1970–74), while not strictly speaking a magicom, was a remarkable "the future has arrived" vision of the American family as a pop-music act.

As the sixties ended, however, the pendulum of sitcom imagination made a swift and decisive swing from magical fantasies to its own version of realistic representation. With the successes in the seventies of shows such as *All in the Family*, *Mary Tyler Moore*, *The Jeffersons*, *Rhoda*, and *Alice*, the genre would rediscover its own roots in ethnic humor and urban settings. The comedy-variety show, meanwhile, had apparently blown its last big chance, though performers as diverse as Richard Pryor, Mary Tyler Moore, Tracey Ullman, and Dolly Parton would try and try again.

Notes

1. William H. Whyte, Jr., *The Organization Man* (New York: Simon and Schuster, 1956), p. 301.
2. See Richard Gehman's three-part series "The Great One," *TV Guide*, October 13, 20, and 27, 1962.
3. The first Alice Kramden, dating back to the character's invention on Gleason's *Cavalcade of Stars* (Dumont, 1950–52), was the shrewish, ascerbic Pert Kelton. Kelton, however, was forced to retire when struck by a heart attack the summer before the show's move to CBS.
4. "The Honeymooners" had begun as a continuing series of five-to-ten minute blackout sketches back in the early fifties as part of Gleason's old Dumont Network comedy-variety show. In 1955–56, the skit was formalized into thirty-minute sitcom episodes. The 1966–70 episodes were twice as long as any previous "Honeymooners" presentations.

5. Rod Serling's *The Twilight Zone* (CBS, 1959–65) was the last weekly anthology drama until the genre was temporarily revived in the mid-1980s.
6. For a detailed analysis of the abrupt collapse of the TV Western, see J. Fred Macdonald, *Who Shot the Sheriff?* (New York: Praeger, 1987).
7. A monumental flop of the kind only desperate ABC was capable of, *100 Grand* was canceled after only three episodes.
8. Tim Brooks and Earle Marsh, *The Complete Directory to Prime Network TV Shows*, 3rd ed. (New York: Ballantine, 1985), p. 836.
9. See *Red Channels* (1950). The book featured dossiers on performers, writers, and behind-the-camera personnel whom it deemed subversives. Listing no author, it was published by *Counterattack*, an anti-Left newsletter.
10. See Brooks and Marsh, pp. 1033–36.
11. Harry Castleman and Walter Podrazik, *Watching Television: Four Decades of American Television* (New York: McGraw-Hill, 1982), p. 189.
12. For a detailed history of the made-for-TV movie, see Alvin H. Marill, *Movies Made for Television* (New York: Da Capo, 1980).
13. *Robert Klein Time* (USA, 1986).
14. *Mr. Ed* actually began as a first-run syndication series, moving to CBS after one season.
15. See Peter Biskind, *Seeing Is Believing: How Hollywood Taught Us to Stop Worrying and Love the Fifties* (New York: Pantheon, 1983), especially Chapter Two, "Us and Them."
16. Other series by Jack Chertok include *The Lone Ranger*, *Sky King*, and *The Girl with Something Extra*.
17. Isaac Asimov, "Husbands, Beware!" *TV Guide*, March 22, 1969, p. 10.
18. *Bewitched*, "Be It Ever So Mortgaged."
19. Kenneth T. Jackson, *Crabgrass Frontiers: The Suburbanization of the United States* (New York: Oxford, 1985), p. 272.
20. Ibid.
21. Authorship credit for *Green Acres* must also be extended to line producer Jay Sommers.
22. As quoted in Dwight Whitney, "Irreverent Is the Word for the Smothers Brothers," *TV Guide*, February 10, 1968, p. 17.
23. David King Dunaway, *How Can I Keep from Singing: Pete Seeger* (New York: McGraw-Hill, 1981), pp. 214–17.
24. Cleveland Amory, review of *The Smothers Brothers Show*, *TV Guide*, February 26, 1966, p. 1.
25. Whitney, p. 16.
26. Brooks and Marsh, p. 774.
27. Dunaway, p. 263.
28. Ibid., p. 264.
29. Ibid.
30. Ibid., p. 252.

31. "Smothers Out: A Wise Decision," *TV Guide* (New York Metropolitan ed.), April 19, 1968, p. A-1.
32. Ironically, the obscure failed magicom that the Smothers had made in 1965–66 has managed to stay alive in syndication; reruns of it have even appeared nationally in prime-time over Nick at Nite cable.
33. *The Smothers Brothers Comedy Hour*, CBS, January 21, 1968.
34. *The Smothers Brothers Comedy Hour*, CBS, February 25, 1968.
35. See, for example, Christopher Sterling and John Kitross, *Stay Tuned: A Concise History of American Broadcasting* (Belmont, Calif.: Wadsworth, 1978), p. 402: "It [*Laugh-In*] was reminiscent of the innovative Ernie Kovaks [sic] of 1955–56 and subsequent specials."
36. *Rowan and Martin's Laugh-In*, April 22, 1968.
37. Ibid., October 28, 1968.
38. Joe Franklin, *Encyclopedia of Comedians* (Secaucus, N.J.: Citadel, 1979), p. 314.
39. D. Hobson, "Lily Tomlin," *TV Guide*, November 14, 1970, p. 38.
40. Richard Doan and Joseph Finnegan, "The Show That Died After One Night," *TV Guide*, May 17, 1969, p. 8.
41. Ibid.
42. For a discussion of *Laugh-In*'s influence an *Sesame Street*, see Erik Barnouw, *Tube of Plenty*, rev. ed. (New York: Oxford, 1982), pp. 436–37.

CHAPTER 5

The Sitcom at Literate Peak: Post-Vietnam Refinements of Mass Consciousness

It is by no means natural for television to represent reality in the way that it does, just as it is by no means natural for language to do so.
—John Fiske and John Hartley, *Reading Television*[1]

What if the next national fad sport was tree climbing? They would build these spas in New York City where they would have trees shipped in from all around the world. People would be connoisseurs of what kind of tree they would climb.
—Michael Stipe, lead singer, R.E.M.[2]

It is perhaps difficult to believe that only a hundred and fifty years ago Ralph Waldo Emerson felt the need to warn Americans against an intellectual dependency on books that could make them into "bibliomaniacs." He urged his country-men instead to make "nature . . . our dictionary."[3] A romantic thinker, Emerson saw Nature (the green world, the actual earth of value) in debate with Culture (the print world, the mind of Europe), and threw his support behind the former in hopes of redressing the emerging industrial era's radical bias toward the abstract symbolization of thought and knowledge. The problems of Man Thinking, however, are not quite those of Man Viewing. The issue of an epistemological balance between the organic and the synthetic remains with us, but the paradigm has shifted. The idea that the printed word constitutes a dangerous distraction from the physical world seems as picturesque today as Thoreau's nineteenth-century complaint about a train of the Fitchburg Railroad intruding "like a comet" upon his solitude at Walden Pond. In the age of television, reading seems almost a pastoral activity. Velocity and noise have left much of the world unpropitious to a reading self. Through all this, the value of reading has not diminished; quite to the contrary, scarcity stimulates worth. Technocrats are perhaps the most voracious readers of all. But a love of reading, an appreciation that savors its demands as much as its rewards, becomes romantic, even nostalgic, in the face of its incompatibility with the routine designs of contemporary life.

Of the many horrors that postmodern culture holds for the relatively few who are able and willing to remain faithful to the traditions of print, none (save perhaps the nuclear holocaust) is quite so depressing as the general and continuing contraction of attention span. An obvious symptom of the collapse of concentration, television is often accused of being its cause. Neil Postman, in *Amusing Ourselves to Death*, even goes so far as to claim that, as a medium, television is structurally inimical to the very processes of rational thought.[4] This blaming of television for the compelling sense of dyslexia that pervades the public arenas of American life is not so much groundless as weightless. Reading makes nonnegotiable demands upon personal attention; television, which does not, is more user-friendly and thus more competitive in a multimedia environment. A preference for reading over TV watching signifies nonconformity not simply because more people spend more time watching television but because anyone with the time and solitude for reading is living anything but an ordinary life in the late twentieth century.

A book, like a telecast, is a transmission system, not a communications system. It can dispense data, but cannot receive it. Feedback must seek a separate vessel of response. Every medium has peculiar traits, and one great advantage of reading over many other, more modern information-consumption techniques is the compelling illusion of extremely intimate rapport between data giver and data getter (that is, book and reader). A novel is a portable memory bank that contains the replayable software of a peculiar consciousness abroad in culture: Oh, to go whaling with Melville, to walk among the pathetic psychopaths of Anderson's Winesburg, to sing the body electric

158

with enchanting Whitman. The satisfaction of reconverting the silent ink words on a piece of paper into images and stories, songs and sense, and, finally, experience is a sweet, personal, individual achievement that is among the perks of human being. Where the book loses its competitive edge these days is in its monolithic demand for long periods of undivided attention. While it is, of course, possible to read sloppily, to fall in and out of synch with the text, to move along turning pages, regardless of one's degree of comprehension, if the activity is to be called reading at all, it requires at least some absolute degree of attention that keeps the eyes penetrating paragraphs, moving across lines, pausing at commas, halting at periods, and so on. This demand for isolation from all other sensory stimuli stigmatizes reading as a peculiar activity in an environment where brash offers of quick-action gratification are made to every human impulse all day long: Start the car. Give me a call. Be all that you can be. Can I have another glass of Coke, please? By contrast, books are slow and take unpredictable amounts of work to understand.

Driving, to name but one contemporary activity, competes with reading for aesthetic shelf space every bit as much as television does. The imperial triumph over space is exercised often and prominently. The excitement of "reading" the world through the windshield—a world full of all kinds of possibilities, including physical beauty, pathos, mechanical breakdown, spontaneous consummation of consumer urge, and even sexual encounter—can be highly stimulating, a seamless web of cubist experience. The car allows the driver to simultaneously penetrate the world and keep it at bay. Unlike reading, driving allows for a high degree of synesthesia. A half a dozen radio formats are available at the fingertips. Conversations that include little or no eye contact can be carried on for hours. Commuters "read" cassettes of Books for the Blind on expressways. Sensory phenomena continually compete for the driver's attention and fracture it: architecture, topography, weather, and proximity to the insane all can make dents in drive-time consciousness.

Watching television is an activity midway between the social isolation of reading and the social hyperboles of driving. Television demands only a share of attention. The text, with or without viewer collaboration, continues. A viewer may receive telephone calls, cook dinner, sit in rapt attention in a dark room, or engage in any number of activities while still receiving enough textual information so that it can honestly be said that he or she has "watched" the program. As a consequence, TV viewing offers itself as the default activity of domestic life. While reading's requirements must be actively met, television allows you to pick your own spots. Is it so strange that people turn on their sets like lamps when entering their homes? After all, television promises and, with erratic quality but astounding quantity, delivers a bottomless supply of emotional, commercial, erotic, and instructional texts for private and social appraisal. Why shouldn't the set be playing? Something good might be on.

As members of a besieged, hardworking minority that is constantly forced to appreciate the scarcity of time and space, many readers regard television in much the same way as free-marketeers regard welfare: each program is seen as a giveaway to people who neither pay for it nor earn it; nothing comes of the handout but a continuing need for more of the same; laziness and passivity are encouraged at the expense of creativity and individuality. Watching television is tolerated as a kind of cultural safety net, a subsidized aesthetic cuisine in which ketchup truly is a vegetable. Cable feeds the audience more calories every day, but satisfaction remains difficult to achieve. The spirit starves in the midst of plenty.

Short of unplugging—and thus denying citizenship in the twentieth century—the viewer is left to experiment with mundane ingredients in a search for nourishment that defies this regime of cultural subsistence. The creating mind, though ghettoized and patronized by the "mass" quality of video transmission, remains prideful of its heritage. Freeing itself from dependence upon the surpluses of the entertainment-industrial complex, the human imagination forages the barks and lichens of a vast and mostly thankless culturescape to gain sustenance from whatever hardy grubs it can lap up.

Hans Enzensberger argues that the main business of television is not so much the selling of specific products as the selling of an existing order.[5] This emphatically German vision of the individual's relationship to postindustrial organization flourishes on the air with great vitality in America. How much of McDonald's mission is selling a hamburger and how much of it is selling a life in which hamburgers are both possible and desirable?[6] In this context, the sitcom, among all genres of mass-culture art, can be seen as a mythopoeic loss leader in the supermarket of national consciousness. Simultaneously more ridiculous ("Who lives like that?") and more realistic ("most people, I guess") than any single viewer might suppose his or her own life to be, situation comedy imbues the banal with potent allegorical force. Structurally didactic, the genre functions as a lighthearted, forgiving guide to the conscience for fans who remain unmoved by the book-thumping polarities of either the fundamentalist clergy or the secular humanist faculty. The millions who do not view television as a tool of either the Devil or Darkness risk only their attention spans. The sitcom rewards them with a morality that is gently taught as a series of lifestyle tips.

Like the epic poem, the novel, and other narrative long forms, the sitcom creates a mythic sense of realism by means of self-reference. If sitcoms often seem alien and frightening to the appreciaters of literary genres, perhaps this is due in some measure to the way in which technological innovation in and of itself becomes a signifier of mimetic legitimacy on television. The progress of technology defines all sense of past and present in situation comedy. On television, Science (as the Prime Mover behind all new consumer goods) functions as God. It bestows favors (VCRs, turbocharged cars) and punishments (everything gives you cancer, nuclear war threatens) in a sometimes logical, often unfathomable way. Consumer goods constitute the Word of Science revealed—proof that it really works. Succeeding generations of sitcoms validate themselves by violating the techno-aesthetic conventions established by their ancestors.

Radio sitcoms—less glamorous and, more important, less fantastic than movies—established disembodied families as vital illusions enduring and recurring right in the home on a week-to-week basis. Following the technological frontier, the radio sitcom migrated to television—lock, stock, and station wagon—during the fifties. *Father Knows Best* was more realistic than a radio sitcom because the Andersons lived in a home that was not a figment of the listener's active imagination, but rather a professionally researched domestic habitat peopled by a demographically justifiable family. *The Dick Van Dyke Show* was more realistic than *Father Knows Best* because the Petries exposed the relatively static quality of the Andersons' life. By acknowledging cultural heterogeneity (Jew, unmarried woman, bohemian) while maintaining the same unspoken white-WASP-male-suburban hegemony that lay at the bottom of Jim Anderson's authority, Rob and Laura mocked the Anderson style while enjoying the Anderson substance, much as the Kennedys had done after eight years of Eisenhower and Dulles. *All in the Family* was more "realistic" than *The Dick Van Dyke Show* because it exposed and implicitly protested that very same hegemony by constantly mocking it as crude, unhip, and downscale. *Happy Days*, in turn, fossilized the explicit political obsessions of *All in the Family* by coolly dismissing the importance of overt political consciousness to personal happiness. As is the case with automobile marketing, the latest model anachronizes last year's model by defining a new state of the art.

Despite the smooth year-to-year mechanical continuity of network self-promotion, a choppy sense of history emerges from long-term televiewing. Programming formats rise and fall: Westerns, big-money quiz shows, and talent-scout auditions came, came on strong, went, and, of course, may come again. Golden ages abound: the comedy-variety show of the early fifties, the live anthology drama of the late fifties, the prime-time family-saga soaps of the eighties. Golden ages, however, imply the existence of silver, bronze, and leaden ages bracketing them. Independent stations and cable networks, which rely on reruns for most of their programming, celebrate the television past, proclaiming shows to be "classics," even canonizing their properties with ritual festivals: twenty *Twilight Zones* in a row; an evening of *Perry Masons*; a *Mary Tyler Moore*-athon. Conversely, the networks are irrevocably committed to the future: next fall, next week, tomorrow, in a half hour. The shows used to be better and are going to get better; the present is always the worst time to be watching television.

As the viewer pans a forty-channel spectrum, history goes into its dance. Programs casually materialize from every phase of television evolution. A brand new sitcom, the product of a multimillion-dollar investment, may very well have to compete with a twenty-year-old episode of a long-dead series whose overhead costs are only a memory. A skeptical viewer—perhaps even a member of a demographically desirable group—may prefer the "classics," or least feel the urge to return to them after sampling the contemporary product, but the prevalence of such an aesthetic among Nielsen families could play havoc with the American economy.

This opportunity offered by television to cruise the time warps of the postbomb world by remote control has already created new experiences of collective memory for the viewer. The children of black-and-white families are not bound by the same code of manners as the children of *The Cosby Show* and *Family Ties*. The sitcom aliens that visit white, middle-class earthling-Americans mutate with the decades and networks: *My Favorite Martian* (CBS, mid-1960s, alien as buddy), *Mork and Mindy* (ABC, late 1970s, alien as lover), *Alf* (NBC, mid-1980s, alien as sarcastic houseguest). *The Phil Silvers Show* (CBS, 1955–59) is fictively set in its own time—a post-Korea, second-term-Eisenhower present. This places it fictively after *M*A*S*H* (CBS, 1972–83). However, the language and cosmos of *M*A*S*H* are not only post-*Bilko* but post-Vietnam and even, at times, post-Watergate. *The Honeymooners*, though explicitly set in the fifties, is so laden with Gleason's autobiographical vision of his Great Depression childhood that the Kramdens, far from dreaming of a move to the suburbs, are still working on getting a telephone and a television. (They don't even have a radio!) It has always been the privilege of drama to stylize historical time in the heightened world of the stage, but it has rarely been the privilege of the viewer to redecorate at will.

The cubist possibilities of televiewing will no doubt continue to expand as remote-control technology is further refined. Early television took inspiration from radio and theater: comedy-variety put vaudeville in the living room, and anthology drama aspired to the "seriousness" of Broadway. By the sixties, however, television had utterly abandoned the "live stage" metaphor in favor of the sitcom and the action-adventure hour, narrative genres owing much to the popular storytelling traditions of the novel and the movies. There is no guarantee, however, that this dominance will last forever. Split-screen viewing is already on the market. Some cable operations, including VH-1 and The Weather Channel, have essentially abandoned Network Era structures such as "shows" and "series" in favor of monolithic programming formats, imitating the course taken by radio stations in the fifties after storytelling had moved to television. Direct-sales services such as the Home Shopping Club and the Consumer Value Network have eliminated all forms of programming except commercials. The viewer may still turn on CBS to see an episode of *Cagney and Lacey*, *Dallas*, or some other weekly narrative drama featuring recurring recognizable characters. But the viewer typically turns on MTV to view MTV, a single endless "program" splintered into revolving and evolving three- and four-minute segments. As viewing conditions shift, attention span continues to fracture and recombinate; new textual forms create new human responses. A character generator spits out press clips from Reuters even as Lucy draws a reluctant Ethel into another harebrained scheme.

With the decline of three-network hegemony (a process that began with the push toward mass cablization in the early seventies), it is perhaps logical that network serial genres such as the sitcom, the crime show, the doctor show, and the lawyer show have displayed increasing literacy. A smaller audience always may be assumed to be a more homogenous audience. Homogeneity inspires frankness—a form of truth—which usually makes for better drama. The prime-time TV series, much like a play, novel, or movie, is a self-conscious work of fiction that cannot help but offer a portrayal of what Enzensberger calls the "existing order." There is not a moment of network television that fails to resonate with dozens of corporately approved decisions about plotting, dialogue, marketing strategy, or any of a thousand matters of creative production. At the peak of network dominance, the problem was always the same: get more viewers. The most inoffensive, in such a quandary, is always most beautiful. Since that time, however, the problem has been changing: get viewers who are more like each other. The compromises of least-objectionability begin to yield to the strong metaphors that are possible when a preacher is speaking to the converted.

If commercially successful, one TV show may significantly revise an "existing order" that has been casually portrayed in a given genre for years. This happened to the sitcom during the early seventies when three revisionary programs became major hits almost at once: James Brooks and Allan Burns's *The Mary Tyler Moore Show* (CBS, 1970–77), Norman Lear's *All in the Family* (CBS, 1971–79),[7] and Larry Gelbart and Gene Reynolds' *M*A*S*H* (CBS, 1972–83).

Updating the representation of American life to more precisely reflect dreams that could be sold to new classes of consumers, these shows retooled the sitcom as an engine of mass appeal at a moment when the genre was suffering the stasis of its long commercial success. The black-and-white world of the fifties family had already been obviated by the full-color sixties. The witches and genies had cast their spells twice too often. *The Monkees* has never cracked the Top Twenty-five, dying after three seasons, leaving no spin-offs. Lucy, Doris Day, and Andy Griffith could not sustain prime time with their fixed-income audiences. For the first time in the history of telecast, the networks were faced with the problem of creating programming that would attract people who had been watching television all their lives. CBS, whose Program Research Department had so thoroughly dominated the sixties that the network was number one in the ratings every season of the decade, was right on top of its game. Jed Clampett yielded to Archie Bunker; Eva Gabor to Mary Tyler Moore; Captains Nelson and Healy to Captains Pierce and McIntyre.

Though subsequent cycles of obsolescence and legitimacy have blossomed and gone to seed since *Mary Tyler Moore*, *All in the Family*, and *M*A*S*H* left the spotlight of prime time, the shows endure in syndication as a kind of period triptych of seventies America, constituting the sitcom at its literate peak during the last days of three-network hegemony. There was a sense while watching these shows that whether one liked them or not, somehow they could not be goofed on in the same way as virtually all the sitcoms that preceded them. For a viewer who had experienced a childhood of intense, wide-eyed viewing and an adolescence of spiraling alienation, television that neither invited contempt nor hid beneath it was a fresh, even disconcerting phenomenon. The shows could succeed or fail from episode to episode or from line to line, but even in failure they demanded to be judged on their own merits, not on the merits of the past performance of their medium or genre. Sitting on an aesthetic cusp between precable innocence and postcable cynicism, these three series drove the sitcom to the brink of respectability as an art form. Perhaps it was the psychic tension brought on by the very prospect of such maturity that precipitated the genre's subsequent collapse into retrograde nostalgia.

Legs . . . Wife . . . Woman

The television production studio known as MTM Enterprises was founded as a corporate partnership by Grant Tinker, Mary Tyler Moore, and Arthur Price in 1970 for the sole purpose, its founders claim, of producing *The Mary Tyler Moore Show*. In any event, MTM delivered quite a bit more than it had originally promised. *The Mary Tyler Moore Show* turned out to be but the first in a string of state-of-the-art sitcom hits that would include *The* (Chicago-set) *Bob Newhart Show*, *Rhoda*, and *WKRP in Cincinnati*. Switching genres in the late seventies, the studio followed with *Lou Grant* and *The White Shadow*, two politically liberal, if aesthetically conservative, hour-long drama series. By the eighties, *Hill Street Blues* and *St. Elsewhere*, with their radically decentralized personae, breathless ironies, and freewheeling recognitions of post-Darwinian agnosticism, had redefined such time-honored teleforms as the cop show and the doctor show. Successful MTM shows have generally distinguished themselves not so much for astounding mass ratings but rather for a consistent ability to capture the viewing attentions of the well-educated, a segment of the audience that is often less than thrilled by the offerings of the nation's major cultural medium. There isn't another TV studio in Hollywood with a comparable track record.[8] MTM artists have left the company to produce such upscale favorites as *Taxi*, *Brothers*, and *L.A. Law*.

While Norman Lear was becoming a household word in the early seventies as the behind-the-scenes mastermind of *All in the Family*, *The Jeffersons*, *Maude*, and a half dozen other immensely popular sitcom portrayals of an American family that had survived the sixties to become eternally obsessed with race relations, menopause, inflation, and the defense budget, MTM was creating a post-1960s comedy of manners in which the nuclear family was conspicuous only by its absence. Allan Burns and James L. Brooks, who created *The Mary Tyler Moore Show*, had originally imagined Mary as a divorcée. A crusty CBS, however, was still hitting the Nielsen Top Ten with wacky widows in 1969 (*Here's Lucy*, *The Doris Day Show*), and the network did not believe the fans were ready to accept a sitcom heroine who had renounced sacred vows. Mike Dann, then head of CBS programming, had made it clear to the studio that his own research had conclusively proven that there were three types of people Americans didn't want to see in situation comedy: people from New York, people with mustaches, and people who were divorced.[9] In this first of its many censorship battles, the fledgling studio, seeing little choice, capitulated to network pressure.

Mary arrived at the WJM-TV newsroom in September 1970 not as a rebounding divorcée, but rather as a never-wed single going through the growing pains of bouncing back from a broken long-term romance.[10] Had network censorship unwittingly served the muse? A divorced Mary Richards would have advertised the show's hipness, raising the painful specter of sitcom pretense. But a single Mary simply placed the character in a familiar tradition of sitcom career girls. As it turned out, the significance of *The MTM Show* would lie not so much in Mary's reason for being "on her own" as in her ability to survive—and even flourish—without the benefit of nuclear-family support or structure. Mary left the small exurban community of her birth and became a one-member household in the big city, securing an entrance position in a high-tech service industry. The demographic drums were beating. Woodstock Nation became Planet of the Singles; the Age of Soup-for-One had begun.

Audience research proved a handmaiden to mythopoeic conceit. In the fifties, Mary had come to television as the Hotpoint Girl, dancing her way through mazes of gleaming white appliances. Later, on *Richard Diamond, Private Detective*, she played Sam, the otherwise unseen pair of legs who served as secretary. It was not until the 1960s that she finally evolved from primitive, iconic sexual totem into an upbeat, contempo sitcom human being. Yet, as late as 1966, the final spring of *The Dick Van*

Dyke Show, Mary-Laura was still forsaking career development in favor of domesticity and traditional maternity. Though more fully rounded than Margaret Anderson and quite a bit brighter than Lucy, her limitations remained more prominent than her possibilities. A mere four seasons later, a new Mary—Mary-Mary—was having none of that. No longer stuck with Dick Van Dyke in static suburban New Rochelle, Mary resurfaced as an ambitious, eligible, girl-on-the-make in neogenteel Minneapolis, lifestyle capital of the northern Midwest. The trope of this midlife career change was a watershed event in American teleculture.[11]

Innovation was highlighted by continuity. Mary-Laura had been a creature of the New Frontier, a walking, talking, occasionally dancing signifier of the coming post-Ike ruling elite; white wine and aerobics were just around her corner. Hubby had a good, even glamorous job in the national consciousness industry, while wife tended to modernly furnished single-unit detached dwelling and progressively brought-up child. A Jew and an unmarried woman were among the frequent guests in their home. They attended racially integrated social functions. They had reverence for The Arts, though they understood on which side their bread was buttered.

The Mary of the seventies took an apartment for herself in the city, was friends with a Jew, and held a quasi-administrative position in the provincial consciousness industry. In the signature montage of each episode, we see Mary, new mass woman of the stagflation era, in a variety of semicute poses enjoying the urban delights of Minneapolis: Nicollet Mall, the IDS Center, Lake of the Isles. These images are balanced by a single exquisite shot—the shot of the seventies—in which she reads the price on a package of plastic supermarket meat and looks up at the gods in exasperation.

The long-suffering TV career woman is redeemed in the beautiful but familiar, capable but human, compassionate but logical Mary Richards. Mary transcended not only the model moms of the *Donna Reed* and *Leave It to Beaver* era but also the more recent efforts at widowed career women (*The Lucy Show*, *The Doris Day Show*) that had replaced them. If Mary had an immediate ancestor it was probably *That Girl* (ABC, 1966–71). But unlike Ann Marie (Marlo Thomas), Mary didn't need a steady boyfriend to define her sexual identity and dispose of it as a textual issue. As if to emphasize the point, Mary had an affair with *That Girl's* eternal fiancé, Ted Bessell—and broke it off quite casually after only a few episodes.

On *The Mary Tyler Moore Show*, the nuclear family, once the energy-giving center of the sitcom universe, is thoroughly eclipsed by what has since come to be known as the support group. Rhoda Morgenstern (Valerie Harper), who, like Al Jolson in *The Jazz Singer*, had forsaken New York ghetto life for the lure of the American West, was the perfectly imperfect *upstairsnik* for a splendid Midwestern *shiksa* like Mary. Though stylistically at odds—Mary was a perky optimist, and Rhoda, a *kvetching* whiner—the two shared points of view on the meat-and-potatoes issues of the heart. Their emotional solidarity served to underline the trendy, pretentious silliness of their married downstairs neighbor and landlady, Phyllis Lindstrom (Cloris Leachman). In a grand reversal of sitcom aesthetics, the single women enjoy an active, fulfilling relationship while their married friend is the odd one out. The traditionally pathetic sitcom spinster—Sally Rogers, Ann Sothern, *Our Miss Brooks*—is rehabilitated into a happy, healthy consumer target: the single-female household.

Mary's friendship with her coworker Murray Slaughter (Gavin MacLeod) introduced the notion to the genre (and perhaps to prime time in general) that a relationship between a woman and a man could be nonsexual without being asexual. In a fifties or sixties sitcom, if a married man was even seen talking to an attractive single woman, it was grounds for his wife to pack a suitcase and go directly to her mother's house for the duration of the episode. But Murray's wife, Marie, didn't seem to mind; in fact, in her rare series appearances, she is decidedly friendly toward Mary. Sitting next to each other at twin desks, the homely aging family man and the attractive single woman become indispensable allies in the office wars of WJM-TV. In a violation of sitcom taboo, their friendship is sufficiently complex so as to contain, rather than avoid, a sexual dynamic. In "The Slaughter Affair," Marie suspects that Murray is having an affair with Mary, while he is actually moonlighting to buy her an anniversary gift. This episode is a sitcom standby: Lucy suspected Ricky and a chorus girl; Samantha suspected Darrin and a female client. But in "Murray in Love," Murray actually admits to Mary that he loves her. Convinced that his passion is unrequited, he assures her that he knows nothing can come of it, and he will simply have to handle it. In another episode, Murray and the other male regulars trade screen realizations of their fantasies of being married to Mary. As is the case with the Mary-Rhoda friendship, a shared sense of irony emerges as the bottom-line factor in contemporary simpatico, overpowering all other forces.

Lou Grant (Ed Asner), the newsroom boss, is a transitional figure from the pretelevision past. His early life as a newspaper reporter on the streets of Detroit and his time on the front during World War II excite a romantic career vision in Mary, a generational prisoner of the cosmetically sterile but ethically tawdry TV era. The aging print journalist gains Mary's unflagging respect as he exercises solid subjective moral authority over the plastic, relativistic atmosphere of the video newsroom. Preferring Jack Daniels' to white wine, an American handshake to a Mediterranean embrace, and the goddamn truth to a few lousy ratings points, Lou is, at once, heroic for surviving, even prospering, across a technological cusp, and ever so slightly pathetic for having been reduced to practicing the great democratic art of journalism behind the mindless media facade of a TV anchorman. He functions as a father figure to be sure, but his marital problems (culminating in midseries divorce), his bottle, and his less than superhuman capabilities in the face of crisis prevent the specter of Robert Young from rearing its condescending head. Mary's independence is not compromised by Lou's paternalism.

Ted Baxter (Ted Knight) was among the show's self-conscious sitcom innovations, though the opportunities for generic subversion offered by the self-centered, arrogant, narcissistic, incompetent anchorman were never fully realized. Though universally disliked, he is rarely ostracized from the group. His moral superiors (that is, just about everyone) tease him, but he rarely gets the joke and, making more money than any of them, he suffers little. True hate, as one can find it in almost any gesellschaft workplace, remains an emotion beyond the purview of the sitcom. By the same token, Ted's potential is never allowed to reach its precipitate. In one episode, he is offered a job as the host of his own game show in New York. Though he has consistently throughout the series displayed greediness, lack of loyalty, and vulgar ambition at every opportunity, Ted miraculously responds to Lou's speech on the noble calling of journalism ("You're an anchorman!") and turns down the Big Life with the Big Money in the Big Town, preferring to stay with his "friends" at WJM. The centrist ideological tendency of situation comedy is tested by this episode and shown to be alive and well. Ted's midseries marriage to the kindhearted but dopey Georgette (Georgia Engel) is similarly disappointing in that it further humanizes him.

Sue Ann Nivens (Betty White) is a more successful attempt at generic subversion. A kind of anti-Mary, a Ted with a brain and a sharp tongue, her arrogance and meanspiritedness grow not out of pathetic lack of sensitivity, but rather out of purposeful design. On WJM's screen-within-a-screen Sue Ann is the smiling Happy Homemaker, baking angel food cakes, darning hard-to-mend stockings, making planters out of everything—a chirping oracle of practical domestic wisdom. But she knows one side of the proscenium arch from the other, and when the show is over, she chucks her apron and garlic press, and reveals her true self. Sexually forthright, she claims to pick up sailors (in Minneapolis!) and even hectors Lou for a night in heaven. More than just talk, Sue Ann makes her share of conquests, including Phyllis' husband, Lars ("The Lars Affair"). Her swaggering and bravado makes the neurotically discreet Mary extremely uncomfortable, a condition that for one such as her is far more severe than it sounds.

In his taxonomy of television fiction modes, James W. Cheseboro has classified The Mary Tyler Moore Show as a "mimetic communication system" in which "the central character is 'one of us,' equally intelligent and equally able to control circumstances."[12] Mary's heroic quality is her innate reflex to seek the golden mean, a time-honored trait among sitcom personae. Rhoda is self-deprecating; Mary is modest. Phyllis is trendy; Mary is up-to-date. Sue Ann is into one-night stands; Mary likes to date. Georgette marries Ted; Mary is not that desperate. However, Mary's ameliorative sensibility is not made sacred. This is made quite clear in "Chuckles Bites the Dust." Chuckles the Clown, host of the WJM late-afternoon kiddie show, is crushed by an elephant while dressed as a peanut as he makes a personal appearance in a circus parade. No one can resist making jokes about Chuckles' hyperbolically poetic demise. Traditional alliances and enmities are shuffled as Lou, Ted, Murray, and Sue Ann all throw one-liners into the face of death. Mary is horrified and lets everybody know. Her moralistic patronizing isolates her from her friends, leaving the viewer disoriented at this unconventional state of affairs. In the climactic scene, however, the response of the group is redeemed at Mary's expense. As the minister eulogizes Chuckles' contribution to Western civilization, Mary bursts out laughing in front of the assembled throng. Her pomposity has blinded her from the wisdom of the group's sublimation of the fear of death, and now she must pay with personal embarrassment. This time *she* learns the middle way.

The Mary Tyler Moore Show and the MTM sitcoms that would follow take place in a white, middle-class, metropolitan America in which idealistic urges and ironic reflexes create a confusion of lost hopes and found ambitions. For a decade before *The Big Chill* was released, the survivors of the same fallen post-1960s world were evident in the MTM shows. Rhoda (still following Jolson's path) returns to New York. She gets married, but soon gets divorced and turns her attention to career development. As for Phyllis, her husband Lars the dentist dies. As cocky and incompetent as ever, she moves away to San Francisco to start over; in a tasteful confusion of art and life, the series is canceled within a year.

Bob Newhart, the "button-down" humorist of the pre-Beatles world, reemerged in the 1970s as a sitcom therapist with a Ph.D. in psychology, offering therapy to Chicago's neurotic paying customers. No one seems to make any progress, least of all Bob, who must doggedly return to his stylish Gold Coast apartment each evening only to find Bill Daily (once an astronaut on *I Dream of Jeannie*, now a civilian airline navigator) raiding his frost-free refrigerator in a bourgeois reprise of Ed Norton's assault on Ralph Kramden's icebox in the *The Honeymooners*. Bob's wife, Emily (Suzanne Pleshette), has a teaching career to worry about, offering her husband no better solace than the admonition, "Physician, heal thyself."

Like WJM in Minneapolis, *WKRP in Cincinnati* is staffed by attractive, reasonable, even admirable people, with the

Ted-like Herb Tarlek (Frank Bonner) thrown in just to keep things honest in the MTM style. Despite such excellent personnel—or perhaps because of them—WKRP (like WJM) is a loser in the (fictional) ratings. One can suppose that WKRP's program director, Andy (Gary Sandy), was meant to be a kind of male Mary: attractive, bright-eyed, bushy-tailed, ethical, modest, ambitious (but not to a fault). The character, however, lacked an issue, such as was implicit in the feminist thrust of Mary's independence, and never found direction. Despite his good looks and good heart, Andy got lost in the glare of Loni Anderson's sudden pinup stardom and the more exotic personalities of the station's disc jockeys, Dr. Johnny Fever (Howard Hesseman) and Venus Flytrap (Tim Reid). The perky center would not hold.

The sitcom, which for many people had epitomized all that was distasteful and moronic in television—and in mass culture in general—achieved a kind of maturity in the early and middle 1970s, though this golden age was not to last out the decade.[13] If Norman Lear had abruptly revealed himself as the Émile Zola of a genre that had previously seemed to be devoid of a dynamic social conscience and if $M*A*S*H$ had gingerly given the lie to the McCarthy-era belief that politically pungent transmissions would not be well received in Peoria, the contribution of the MTM shows to this vital period of sitcom development was a new configuration of social relations. With divorce rates soaring, the family was in retreat. In MTM America there were few marriages (and some of these ended in the lawyer's office). There were even fewer children. Among all the MTM sitcom characters, only Phyllis, who proved herself a fool in every other way, was raising a child on screen. Even Bob and Emily Hartley, two successful middle-aged professionals with an apartment that reeked of equity, seemed uninterested in perpetuating the race. Dating, formerly an activity reserved for teenagers, became a way of social existence for adults. Even the divorced Lou Grant "went out."

Money was shown to be tougher to come by for MTM Americans than it had been for fifties sitcom squires like Jim Anderson or Ward Cleaver. But Mary gradually achieves upward mobility, rising from associate producer (still making coffee) to producer of *The Six O'Clock News* and moving from her relatively modest studio apartment in an old subdivided neighborhood house to a one-bedroom unit in a downtown high-rise. A relatively genteel life was still available to those who were willing to work hard for it. The coherence of this baby-boom vision of adulthood depends in great degree on a faith that there is no inherent contradiction between gentility and hard work, a belief that is always popular among rising middle classes. In short, what is now called the "yuppie" had been predicted, perhaps partially created, by the studio that had chosen a meowing housecat for its symbol.

At the end of the 1976–77 season, having finished out of the Top Twenty-five for the first time in its seven-year production run, *The Mary Tyler Moore Show* took itself off the air in a farewell episode in which a new owner buys WJM and fires everyone in the newsroom—except Ted. The basic unfairness of the world is reiterated as the grand punch line of the comedy. Irony proves more powerful than justice. Institutions are heartless and cold, but what can a modern professional do but chalk it up on the old resumé and seek the protection of another job with another institution? In the years that followed, MTM virtually abandoned situation comedy, turning its attention instead toward hour-long drama series. The studio's wholesale pullout from the genre helps explain the abrupt sitcom retrenchment that ensued.

Polarized Sources

The second of the three sitcoms that significantly contributed to the revision of prime-time mythology in the early 1970s was Norman Lear's *All in the Family*. The difference in style between it and *The Mary Tyler Moore Show* reflects a tradition of pop-culture social-class stereotypes: the bourgeoisie is soft-spoken, rational, successful, and fair-minded (*Father Knows Best, Donna Reed, Leave It to Beaver*); the lower classes are loud, emotional, static, but, despite their bluster, decent at heart (*The Life of Riley, The Honeymooners, The Phil Silvers Show*).

Lacking the grace, poise, taste, or elegance of *The Mary Tyler Moore Show*, *All in the Family* brashly presented itself as the breakthrough that situation comedy had been waiting for since radio days. Here was the series that would finally bring something like realism to sitcom representationalism: black people would not only exist but would be called "coloreds" (though never "niggers") by the white star. Jews would not only say words like "bar mitzvah" and "oy, oy, oy" to get laughs, but would be called "Hebes" (though never "kikes") by the Christian star. Women and men would not only engage in Lucy-Ricky "battles of the sexes," but some of them would do so with ideological motives. Homosexual envoys would visit the sitcom planet. A genre pathetically circumscribed by taboos that had been in decay since Edward R. Murrow gave the raspberry to Senator Joe McCarthy on *See It Now* would break free into forbidden territory and make use of the expanding public dialogues provoked by Vietnam and the recent civil rights struggles on the home front. The News, which had already begun to exert direct influence on action-adventure crime shows such as *Dragnet '67* and *The Mod Squad*, was finally making its weight felt in situation comedy, the most intimately banal of prime-time genres.

ABC had languished in last place since the advent of network telecast, and Lear logically went to the "third network" first, hoping that the very boldness of his stroke would catch the fancy of hungry programmers plotting an escape from the Nielsen basement. Such was the fear, however, that the opening of Archie Bunker's mouth might also be the opening of a Pandora's box of American sociopolitical neuroses that the network passed up the opportunity, rejecting the show as too controversial. Lear went next to CBS, where he found a friendly patron in network president Robert Wood. Though at the peak of its ratings dominance, CBS was beginning to understand the vulnerability of its aging, downscale Andy Griffith–loving audience in the dawning era of boomers, yuppies, and HBO. Could a comedy set in the black hole of what was still being called "the generation gap" reach those hard-to-get but got-to-have viewers between eighteen and thirty-four?

All in the Family was ready to go into production as early as 1969, but was America ready for it? The CBS front office kept the series in cautious abeyance for over a year as research teams studied the reactions of test group after test group.

Meanwhile, *Here's Lucy*, *Gunsmoke*, *Mayberry R.F.D.*, *Hee Haw*, and *The Doris Day Show* all remained in the Nielsen Top Twenty during 1969–70. A bird in the hand, conservatives argued. Demographics in the bush, marketing visionaries replied. Mike Dann, the network programming chief who that very same year had nixed Mary's etiological divorce, surely held doubts about a program promising to pack every line with potentially objectionable social problems; September passed as the debate raged on. *All in the Family* was finally inserted into the prime-time lineup in January as a midseason replacement for *To Rome with Love*, a faltering retrograde sitcom starring John Forsythe as a schoolteacher with two daughters from Iowa who takes a job at an American school in Rome after the death of his wife. With *All in the Family*, the fans were promised respect for their post-1960s maturity; the industry was promised a quality mass audience delivered by a quality product.

The *All in the Family* in-house controversy at CBS must have made *The Mary Tyler Moore Show* seem like a relatively safe project, especially once the divorce issue had been disposed of in the network's favor. *Mary* was well along in development, rapidly approaching its September 1970 premiere, when Allan Burns and James Brooks, the show's creators, were invited by CBS brass to a sneak preview of Archie Bunker on a VCR in executive offices. Burns recalls the screening: "We were feeling pretty good about it [*The Mary Tyler Moore Show*], cocky about it. We felt it was going to be *the* show. Then we sat down and watched *All in the Family* and we came out with very mixed feelings. We were very impressed that something was going to be that competitive with us. To be honest, we thought it was going to steal a lot of wind from our sails."[14]

Burns's apprehension was correct. While *Mary* quietly found an audience that would make it a very respectable number twenty-two in the ratings for 1970–71, Archie Bunker grabbed an unprecedented share of headlines, catapulting *All in the Family* to a number-one finish during its first full season. The show would remain the highest-rated series on all of TV for five consecutive years, an unprecedented Nielsen achievement. Moreover, from 1970–71 to 1975–76, it was the only series on television to achieve a rating of more than thirty, a projection that imagined its audience at close to 50 million each week.

As is usual with a big TV hit, *All in the Family* found its way either directly or by cultural osmosis into the remote nooks and crannies of the American consciousness. A national dialogue developed over Lear's comic drama. Every racist, ethnocentric, sexist, and sexual preferentialist epithet provoked another newspaper column or magazine article. Churchmen, political activists, television-haters and industry operatives debated the merits of the program. The sitcom had lost its innocence, everyone agreed, but were we looking at a fulfilling new relationship or a rape? Was *All in the Family* a sorely needed airing of America's dirty laundry that would help purge the culture of long-term and lingering sins? Or had the dominance of the middle way of implicit tolerance been broken, effectively valorizing the bigot, no matter what the auteur's intention? Had the working class been slandered with hardhat hyperbole? Or were the fears of the great ignored masses of wage earners finally finding expression in the medium they had carried on their backs to cultural dominance?

Not since the days of Chester A. Riley and Ralph Kramden had the hoi polloi made such waves in prime time. Historian George Lipsitz has written, "The presence of ethnic, working-class situation comedies on television network schedules seems to run contrary to the commercial and artistic properties of the medium. Television delivers audiences to advertisers by glorifying consumption, not only during commercial breaks but in the programs themselves. The relative economic deprivation of ethnic working-class households would seem to provide an inappropriate setting for the display and promotion of commodities as desired by the networks and their commercial sponsors."[15]

One thing that differentiated *All in the Family* from its 1950s predecessors was that while it was emphatic about being a working-class sitcom, it was equally emphatic about *not* being ethnic. Though Norman Lear freely told the press that Archie had been modeled after his own Jewish father and that the show itself was a kind of autobiographical exploration of his Queens childhood, the Bunkers were presented to the American public as declassé Protestants, the kind of people one was more likely to meet in Quincy, Illinois, than on Queens Boulevard. A decade earlier, Carl Reiner had been forced to revise his autobiographical *Head of the Family* into the compromises that rendered *The Dick Van Dyke Show*. Lear, through his own savvy, had taken a British sitcom about Cockney intolerance (the BBC's *Till Death Do Us Part*), reimagined it as a confessional memoir of lower-class New York Jewish family life (à la Neil Simon and Woody Allen), and realized it on prime-time network television as a mass-marketable Middle American allegory.

Archie Bunker, a warehouse loading-dock worker, was television's first explicitly WASP hourly wage earner. As Lipsitz points out in his study of working-class sitcoms, earning one's living with one's hands had traditionally been associated with hyphenated ethnicity in the sitcom: in *Mama* (CBS, 1949–56), Papa Hansen, head of the Norwegian-American household, was a carpenter; in *The Goldbergs* (CBS, 1949–51; NBC, 1952–53; Dumont, 1954), Jewish-American Jake Goldberg was a tailor; in *The Life of Riley* (NBC, 1949–50, 1953–58), airplane riveter Chester A. Riley was an Irish-American who followed his job from Brooklyn to Los Angeles. All three of these series, perhaps not coincidentally, were adapted for television from other media and other decades: *I Remember Mama*, a Depression novel by Kathryn Forbes, had played on stage and screen before coming to television. *The Goldbergs* and *Riley* had both been successful radio sitcoms.

As these shows came to the ends of their long production runs in the late fifties, blue-collar ethnic families disappeared from prime time. The only remaining working-class characters were servants who were typically treated as honorary members of bourgeois families: Hazel, Grindl, Mr. French of *Family Affair*, and so on. By the same token, black families disappeared from prime time during the mid-1950s as well, with only an occasional servant left in the picture. After the cancellations of *Amos'n'Andy* and *Beulah* in 1953—again, both originally had been radio sitcoms—no sitcoms concerning black Americans appeared on the air at all for fifteen years. From the late fifties until the end of the sixties, domestic situation comedy narrative was thoroughly dominated by professional, college-educated WASPs.

All in the Family, though certainly the most successful, was not the only sitcom to break the blue-collar boycott during the 1970–71 television season. *Arnie*, starring Herschel Bernardi, had premiered on CBS five months earlier. The differences between the two programs are salient. Arnie Nuvo (!), like Archie Bunker, is a loading-dock worker. In a kind of stagflation-era reprise of *The Beverly Hillbillies*, however, Arnie achieves instant and innocent upward mobility when he is miraculously kicked upstairs to become the executive head of the Product Improvement Division of the Continental Flange Company. The Greek-American Nuvos—dad, mom, junior, and sis—undergo severe sitcom class dislocation, striving to keep continuity between their former lives as simple, earthy, ethical proles and their unfolding American Dream adventure among the managerial classes. They run into snobs (that is, villains), but in most cases upper-class folks turn out to be, well, just folks, and everything works out in a way that implies the triviality of class differences as compared to the bottom-line issues that bind all classes together (such as God and country). Arnie even remains in close touch with one of his old loading-dock friends, Julius (Tom Pedi), a relationship allowing him the dual advantages of a sentimental attachment to his working-class good old days as well as a direct conduit to what the boys on the loading dock are up to.

Lear, however, supplied no such *deus ex machina* to lift Archie Bunker out of loading-dock Hades to the Olympus of white-collar bourgeois security. Archie drove a cab part-time on weekends, got laid off, suffered inflation, got mugged, lost his home-owner's insurance, and went on strike. If Ralph Kramden's obsession with get-rich-quick schemes at least implied an active faith in the American Dream, Archie Bunker seemed to harbor no such illusions; he just watched television. The Bunker-Kramden comparison is hardly gratuitous. Lear seemed to take special pleasure in rehabilitating classic *Honeymooners* episodes with doses of his new sitcomic social realism: Archie faces the company physical; Edith gets a job, despite Archie's opposition; Archie has a reunion with an old buddy who has "made it big." Gleason had done all three of these plots on *The Honeymooners* in 1955–56. But whereas the Kramdens were merely the playthings of cruel and ironic gods, the Bunkers were post-Zola citizens of a neurotic industrial state. As such, they were caught in a hopeless tangle of social corruption: economic exploitation,

179

racism, sexism, xenophobia, and worse. Gleason's bus driver did not complain that black Americans were getting what was rightfully his. Ralph Kramden lived in an atemporal vacuum where it was just him, the money, and fate; now if only fate would finally give him a break. In contrast, Archie shlepped the baggage of mass man through an incomprehensible clutter of social contexts.

Though the Bunkers own their own home, it is worth noting that they have no car. As with the religion question, this bit of information creates a prismatic confusion of significances, this time mostly regional in character. Not owning an automobile in New York City is one thing; not owning one almost anywhere else in America is quite another. Though the taxicabs and even the sidewalks of New York are full of well-to-do people who don't bother to keep automobiles, beyond the Hudson such deprivation is usually a sign of early adolescence, physical disability, terminal lumpenproletarian despair, or some combination thereof. The Bunkers were not rich, but the question of how poor they were was left in the eye of the beholder.

In 1974, Horace Newcomb wrote,

The furniture is not the plush modern with which television viewers have always been familiar. It is old, worn, without style. The comforts are those of use, rather than of design, and the easy chair sits before the television set waiting for Archie to occupy it. The dining area is in the living room. Upstairs the bedrooms are bastions of privacy, but as in any crowded situation privacy is often ignored. The bathroom—there is only one—is another point of contention, and serves both as a battleground for the two families in the home and as a symbol of Archie's social prudery. He does not allow anyone to mention 'going to the bathroom.'[16]

A Texan of Mississippi heritage, Newcomb's perception of the economic status of the house at 704 Hauser Street surely reflects that of most viewers. But once again, the New York City setting acts as a distorting filter on the Bunkers' class position. One toilet or a "dining area in the living room" will suffice to carry a family considerably further up the class scale in New

York City than elsewhere in North America. From the point of view of many New Yorkers, the mere fact that the Bunkers live in a detached single-family dwelling is enough to bestow upon them the middle-class status of *alrightniks*.

The Bunker household, despite Lear's self-consciously up-to-date content, came to form as a Greek theater dedicated to the American mysteries that had reasserted themselves so abruptly in the sixties. Archie, the enemy of liberal secular humanist values, emerges as a pathetically displaced person. Everything he knows is right is wrong. The nurturing, orderly *gemeinschaft* of his youth ("Guys like us, we had it made. . . .") has dissolved into an impudent, humiliating *gesellschaft*. He has worked hard and has done what was expected of him. But where is his reward? Being given away by the government to racial strangers, sexual deviants, and ideological insurgents.

Despite Lear's claim to have made his Jewish father the model for "Protestant" Archie, the character more sharply reflects the profile of the ethnic Catholic blue-collar worker that Kevin Phillips describes in his 1970 book *The Emerging Republican Majority*.[17] There is very little other than the name Bunker that is Yankee about Archie, perhaps least of all Carroll O'Connor's characterization, which more readily evokes a caricature of the Irish. Though O'Connor imbues the character with simultaneous doses of prudery in his pronouncements and vulgarity in his demeanor, Archie maintains an abiding faith that traditional, institutional authority is always to be trusted over individual organic desire. This mind-set is a hallmark of what Phillips calls the "social conservative." A decade before it happened, Phillips predicted that the defection of socially conservative urban Catholics from the Democratic to the Republican party might one day help elect a Ronald Reagan to the presidency. Though in the signature montage, Archie sings, "Mister, we could use a man like Herbert Hoover again,"[18] it's hard to imagine him as anything but a New Deal Democrat who has switched allegiances away from the party during its post–Lyndon Johnson drift to the McGovern left.

Ironically, as written, it is left to Archie's emphatically McGovernite Polish-American son-in-law, Mike Stivic (Rob Reiner), to bear the standard of the Pope of Rome over the course of the more than 200 episodes that compose the series. A fallen Catholic to say the least, Mike advocates every modernist position from the theory of evolution to abortion on demand, finding a way to flaunt a secular humanist's agnosticism even in the most unlikely of conversations. Archie and Mike, represented as Protestant and Catholic, are stereotypes struggling to avoid themselves: if Archie evokes a Kevin Phillips post–Great Society Catholic social conservative, then Mike is even more suggestive of a post-Woodstock Jewish graduate student.

The women in the Bunker household are far less suggestive of ethnic, political, and religious stereotypes. Their texts are primarily gender and age. Edith (Jean Stapleton) is a lower-middle-class hausfrau devoid of the resentment and rage that gave Alice Kramden the courage to withstand and combat the insufferable bluster of Ralph. Edith instead generally bears the burden of Archie's ego in the service of family harmony. She is morally superior to Archie by dint of the impeccable instincts of her heart, but this only serves to make her more of a martyr as she waits on Archie hand and foot. Edith transcends racism not by ideological decision, but rather through an innocent, unabashed, organic love of her fellow human beings. This is most prominently manifested in the friendship she develops with Louise Jefferson, her black next-door neighbor. While their husbands, Archie and George, are social prisoners of prideful petty prejudices, Edith and Louise borrow cups of flour, exchange casserole dishes, and shoot the breeze over the kitchen table in utopian innocence. The righteousness of their congeniality is affirmed by its practicality.

Stapleton, who had been playing downscale, middle-aged "neighborhood" women since the Hollywood adaptation of *Damn Yankees* in 1958, possesses Edith utterly, as O'Connor possesses Archie. Mugging, wincing, and double-taking, always crossing with heavy feet, Stapleton and O'Connor create a sitcom marriage on the scale of the Ricardos. Archie is always ready with a wisecrack, but his quickness is undermined by the malapropism it is likely to contain. Edith seems dense and dim-witted, but her slowness is redeemed by the spiritual purity of *un coeur simple*. The broadstroke excesses of their performances are so emphatically theatrical—*All in the Family* is truly a television approximation of a stage play—as to appear quaint on post-1960s color equipment. The nostalgic ambience of Lear's precinematic, almost Victorian teletheater is so busy and tight with players and props and doors and staircases that it serves as an aesthetic counterweight to the borderline pretentiousness of the show's self-consciously progressive narrative didacticism.

Archie, though the center of viewer attention, is by no means the persona of *All in the Family*. Instead, Lear's omniscient narrative sensibility serves that function. Unseen, but never unfelt, the Lear zeitgeist continuously intervenes to point out Archie's errors and thus, by indirection, its own vision of the brighter day. Optimism is invested in youth. Mike and Gloria (Sally Struthers), though riddled with minor faults, are the heroes of *All in the Family*. Their "liberal" views are consistently presented as centrist and reasonable, while Archie's "conservative" views contain obvious and glaring flaws of logic and/or character. Edith's heart of gold is precious, but her subservience to a rigid, constraining role-destiny makes her something less than a model for social evolution.

Archie's animus is mitigated by the fact that he is the sole breadwinner in a house of four adults, a relevant reminder to any high-minded middle-class viewers who may be watching that a contempt for hardhatism does not change the fact that workers like Archie are the people who make civilization and culture possible. We do not see Archie punching the clock or hoisting boxes, day-in and day-out, expending his life. We do, however, see Mike reading and otherwise preparing for an academic career under the roof that Archie has been paying off for so many years with his sweat and diligence. Mike's notorious energy at the dinner table comically epitomizes the situation, as Archie watches his wages (or at least what Uncle Sam, Albany, and City Hall have not already grabbed) disappear into the bottomless pit of his "Meathead" son-in-law.

The Stivics are first and foremost people of *Kultur*, spending their leisure time with books and concerts, parks and museums; Archie settles for a can of beer at the TV set while Edith scans *Woman's Day* for exciting yet economical recipes. Sexually, Mike and Gloria revel in the satisfaction of their mutual desires, while Archie covers a leering prurience with phony piety and Edith breaks into uncontrollable giggling at the mention of undergarments. "Which future for you, gentle viewer?" is what

All in the Family asks its audience. The Stivics' friends—hippies, feminists, gays, draft resisters, academicians—enrage Archie, but typically serve to point out just how mainstream Mike and Gloria really are. This is, perhaps, the punch line of Lear's situation comedy. America's future belongs to the tolerant and eclectic; Archie Bunker's days are numbered.

Direct and spiritual spin-offs of *All in the Family* peppered prime time for most of the seventies. *Maude* (CBS, 1972–78) starred Beatrice Arthur as Edith's "limousine liberal" cousin from haute suburban Tuckahoe. The most daring of the Lear shows in terms of content, it became a yardstick with which the parameters of prime-time content could be measured during the mid-1970s. Materializing on CBS only two years after the *Mary* divorce controversy, *Maude* was already on her fourth husband in the series pilot (which appeared as an episode of *All in the Family* in the spring of 1972). Over the next half-dozen seasons, she would have an abortion on a two-part episode not carried by all affiliates; go through menopause, including hot flashes, right in front of the camera; and blithely cop a set of political attitudes that placed her firmly in the political territory dividing George McGovern and Simone de Beauvoir. *All in the Family* had revived a dead subgenre with its working-class setting, but *Maude* was even more radical an innovation in that it invaded the familiarly innocent milieu of the Andersons, the Cleavers, the Nelsons, and their like—the upper middle-class suburban living room—with the charged rhetoric of race, class, and political polarization. Maude dispensed birth-control advice with the same gusto with which June Cleaver had once proffered brownies.

Perhaps Lear's greatest impact on sitcom development was the return of the black family to prime time, a development that he almost single-handedly engineered. The first of the Lear black sitcoms was *Sanford and Son* (NBC, 1972–77), which starred Redd Foxx, a comedian whom Malcolm X once called "the funniest man I ever met."[19] Once again, Lear used a British sitcom, *Steptoe and Son*, as a formal model for American content. The show, coproduced with Bud Yorkin, was set in the home of a Watts junk dealer. It created the tone and style of black prime-time "dozens" humor that would become the definitive feature of a popular new subgenre—the black situation comedy—that would flourish for over a decade.

Just as Paul Henning had created a mirror image of *The Beverly Hillbillies* in *Green Acres* in the sixties, Lear moved the entrepreneurially successful Jeffersons out of Archie Bunker's Corona section of Queens into a "deluxe apartment in the sky"[20] on the Upper East Side of Manhattan. *The Jeffersons* (CBS, 1975–86) became a smash hit that would outlast *All in the Family*. George, as the owner of a chain of dry-cleaning shops, would find himself displaced in a world of phony middle-class manners, simultaneously coveting acceptance and resisting the sacrifice of his instincts and background. Louise, like Edith, would have an easier time of it, unblinded by male ego and more ready to accept the world as it presents itself.

Other big Lear successes during the seventies included *Good Times* (CBS, 1974–79), concerning a poor black family in a Chicago public housing project; and *One Day at a Time* (CBS, 1975–84), a lower-middle-class white divorcée bringing up two girls in Indianapolis. In all of his shows, Lear's message is clear: a culture of human progress traceable to the Enlightenment and the French Revolution continues to grow. The dislocations it causes are a small price to pay for its benefits. Furthermore, the American family, united by bottom-line love, is capable of absorbing the shocks of constant or sudden changes. Ignorance, not evil, is the enemy, and time is on our side.

As usually happens to a long-running series, *All in the Family* began to disintegrate after more than a half-dozen years on the air. Actors and writers—their pockets full of prime-time loot and their financial futures secured by syndication deals—began to yearn for fresh projects as satisfying plot permutations became increasingly elusive. This process was particularly painful in the case of *All in the Family*. In sitcoms such as *The Beverly Hillbillies* and *Bewitched*, shows that had elements of the absurd built right into their structure, periods of decay late in their production runs often provided particularly fecund episodes; an unlikely realism gave way to a kind of seedy, primitivistic surrealism, which in turn mingled freely with science fiction.[21] The final year of the *Hillbillies*, for example, included a multiepisode plot line that had the Clampetts mistaking a grunion run at a Southern California beach for an invasion of aliens from outer space. Late *Bewitched* episodes are rife with time travel and even the animation of fictional characters. But Lear had invested so much in the creation of a generically fresh realism for the sitcom that *All in the Family* merely became wooden and ordinary as the blush went off the rose.

All in the Family's exhaustion accelerated into a nervous breakdown when Archie put together the money to buy Kelsey's Bar, eventually changing it and *All in the Family* into *Archie Bunker's Place* (CBS, 1979–83). Archie's sudden and casual promotion into the petite bourgeoisie after all those years of social-realist financial aggravation and class stasis seemed utterly gratuitous. Archie, like Jed Clampett, had found his version of a gusher in the front yard. Though small-business ownership was not portrayed as any waltz into a Beverly Hills mansion, Archie had crossed over the American Jordan from wage work into entrepreneurship, sapping the sitcom of a powerful tension it had spent years building.

Also, during these later episodes, Lear seemed increasingly interested in exploring Jewish themes in the show, which he had allegorized into a Protestant household a decade previously. After Mike finally finished his dissertation and he, Gloria, and little Joey had moved away to California, the Bunkers adopted Edith's half-Jewish niece, Stephanie Mills (Danielle Brisebois). Archie's business partner at Archie Bunker's Place was Murray Klein (Martin Balsam). Suddenly, the series had one and a half Jewish characters. Just as Carl Reiner had found a way to bring *The Dick Van Dyke Show* back to some of the Jewish themes that had been lost in its WASP-ization (as in the "Buddy's Bar Mitzvah" episode), Lear too seemed to move wistfully in this direction as the series went through its final years of production.

With Edith's death (a *fait accompli* in the opening episode of the 1980–81 season), the show lost its last important link to the Bunker living room, an American locus that now sits, reconstructed, in the Smithsonian Institution. Lear filled the bar with a host of new characters who provided broadside targets for Archie's familiar prejudices: an Irish cook (Anne Meara), a Puerto Rican busboy (Abraham Alvarez), a Jewish accountant (Barry Gordon), a black housekeeper (Barbara Meek). The sting, however, had gone out of the bee. Archie had already learned so many lessons about the brotherhood and sisterhood of mankind over a decade of episodes that he almost seemed to be caricaturing himself when complaining about "your coloreds," "your gay homosexuals," or "your women of the female persuasion."

Perhaps it was the failure of Lear's more formalistically radical projects that led him to try to keep Archie alive as a sounding board for his political agenda into the Reagan era. During the late seventies he had produced several half-hour series that truly tested the limits to which the sitcom had been pushed. These experimental shows included *Mary Hartman, Mary Hartman* (a self-reflexive satiric synthesis of afternoon soap opera and prime-time sitcom), *Fernwood 2-Night* (a talk-show spoof set in Mary Hartman's Ohio hometown), and *All That Glitters* (a sci-fi soap opera set in a society where all traditional Western gender roles are reversed). Despite Lear's stunning Nielsen track record, none of the three were accepted by the networks and he was forced to put them into first-run syndication; none achieved truly national coverage. The parameters of reform were thus defined, always a painful event for a person of liberal sensibility.

Whereas both *The Mary Tyler Moore Show* and *M*A*S*H* took themselves off the air while they were still able to produce rich, cosmologically expansive episodes, *Archie Bunker's Place* devolved into a period piece during the early eighties as sitcoms such as *Three's Company*, *Soap*, and *Family Ties* became the stylistic cutting edges of the genre. Ironically, all of these shows, though clearly retreats from Lear's gung-ho didacticism, owe much to the innovations that Lear had pioneered in the early seventies. Despite *All in the Family*'s agonizing demise, the show had redefined the sitcom's "existing order"—its rhetoric, its metaphors, and even, to some degree, its spirit—in ways that have made the substance and style of all subsequent sitcoms directly or indirectly traceable to those revisions.

A Land War in Asia

Both *The Mary Tyler Moore Show* and *All in the Family* were portents of larger studio-based aesthetics that would be expressed and refined in spin-offs and imitations for years to come. The meowing pussycat that closed every *Mary* episode came to symbolize a baby-boom-based urban professional television gestalt that would survive MTM's abandonment of situation comedy to flourish in the company's upscale designer soap operas (*Hill Street Blues, St. Elsewhere*) during the eighties. Meanwhile, Norman Lear had established himself as the sitcom's first media-personality auteur. On the basis of his reputation as a behind-the-scenes television artist, he gradually emerged as a leading citizen's voice in American liberalism during the eighties. The man who gave the world Archie Bunker rose to challenge the Reverend Jerry Falwell during the conservative salad days of the Reagan presidency.

M*A*S*H, however, though every bit as culturally ubiquitous as these other two sitcoms, never spawned any family of spin-offs (*AfterMASH* was the one stillborn attempt) or even inspired any obvious imitators of its aesthetic or ideological style. The studio that produced it, 20th-Century–Fox Television, had for years been a nuts-and-bolts supplier to the networks. Its hits, including such shows as *Room 222*, *Peyton Place*, and *Batman*, were diverse in character, leaving Fox without a distinctive public face. Moreover, *M*A*S*H* was dominated by different key collaborators at various junctures in its production history, and its authorial background never became household knowledge.

In a medium dominated by formulas based on such antiart concepts as "least-objectionability models" and "audience special-effort quotients," it is perhaps difficult to see what William Self of 20th-Century–Fox Television saw in Robert Altman's film that made him believe it could be built into a successful commercial television series in the early 1970s. For starters, the film's script had been written by Ring Lardner, Jr., a veteran victim of the McCarthy blacklists. Moreover, Lardner and Altman's movie had contained a wide-ranging selection of contemporary TV taboos, including four-letter words, nudity, blood-splattering open-heart surgery, and—perhaps most shocking—personae given to nihilistic musing. These could have hardly seemed attractive features at a time when CBS was still scoring well with *My Three Sons* and *The Glen Campbell Goodtime Hour*. Yet, with the corporate debate raging over how to win the hearts and pocketbooks of the burgeoning new audience of those between eighteen and thirty-four, Self managed to get a green light for development from the marketing visionaries at CBS.

Self's first move was to put a solid Tinseltown citizen, Gene Reynolds, in charge of the potentially volatile production. Reynolds' credits included work as a child star in over forty MGM films (he was, among other things, one of the boys in *Boys' Town*), and behind-the-scenes credits in such baroque sitcoms as *Hennesey* (which concerned a military doctor) and *The Ghost and Mrs. Muir*. Reynolds, in turn, went off to England to try to convince his old friend Larry Gelbart to come home to American television for the purpose of collaborating with him on the new Fox series. Offering Gelbart assurances of artistic freedom—and encouraging him by pointing out the exciting possibilities signaled by the very existence of the MTM and Lear projects—Reynolds persuaded Gelbart to accept the offer and the two began the job of developing *M*A*S*H* for television.

Unlike *All in the Family* or *Mary Tyler Moore*, *M*A*S*H* was a TV adaptation of a property that already enjoyed currency in American mythology. The 1970 feature film *M*A*S*H*, a boldly antiwar comedy released during the height of American engagement in Vietnam, had starred Elliott Gould, Donald Sutherland, and Sally Kellerman.[22] Gould and Sutherland, as Drs. "Hawkeye" Pierce and "Trapper" John McIntyre, had brought hedonistic American college-boy and summer-camp pranksterism into the misery of the Korean peninsula during the early 1950s with gratifying results. By maintaining their adolescence in the midst of the relentless firestorm, they managed to keep an American spirit of rebellious independence alive. Whitmanian reverences for fellow feeling, intoxication, and orgasm were revealed as ample to the task of personal survival against the mindless, steely thud of bureaucracy, blood, shrapnel, and death.

The movie had caused something of a sensation, both by winning profits for its backers and an Academy Award for the once-scorned Lardner. Though it is by no means unusual for Hollywood films to inspire sitcomic adaptations, typical examples of this phenomenon in the past had included such lighthearted fluffcoms as *Gidget* and *The Farmer's Daughter*—shows that hovered comfortably near zero on the least-objectionability Richter scale. War? Death? Amputation? Ambiguous attitudes toward the U.S. Army, the United States of America, and legal authority itself? No one had yet attempted a sitcom that evoked the moods and messages of E. E. Cummings' *The Enormous Room* or Ernest Hemingway's *A Farewell to Arms*. Was there room in the sitcom genre for the presentation of the myth of Sisyphus? Oh, Lucy, what were they trying to do to you?

Larry Gelbart's resumé made him perhaps an unlikely candidate to become the leading creative force behind what would become one of the most formally and rhetorically daring TV series. As a radio writer, Gelbart had cranked out one-liners for the likes of Fanny Brice, Baby Snooks, and Danny Thomas on *The Maxwell House Comedy Hour* on NBC radio. His only visit to Korea occurred in 1951, as a gag writer on tour with the Bob Hope USO show. Pioneering in the TV gold rush of the early fifties, Gelbart found clients for his jokes among variety-show personalities such as Red Buttons, Pat Boone, and Celeste Holm. In what was surely the early highlight of his television career, he had shared writers' quarters with Neil Simon, Mel Brooks, and Woody Allen on the writing staff of *Your Show of Shows*.

Like Simon, Gelbart made his escape from television via Broadway, scoring big with the musical comedy *A Funny Thing Happened on the Way to the Forum* in 1962 (the very same year that Newton Minow had called television "a vast wasteland"). Eventually choosing London for a self-imposed exile from what he had come to view as the Hollywood–Madison Avenue shlock factory, Gelbart found more satisfying work in the relatively less constrained environments of British television and film during the sixties.

A conversation with Larry Gelbart sheds some light on his decision to return to Hollywood and again become a voice in American culture. An admirer of Arthur Miller, Gelbart was an artist who had felt the sting of McCarthyism as a young writer during the fifties. Though personally unscathed, "I had seen people around me hurt—and that hurt," he recalls.[23] Hawkeye's frequent and freewheeling jabs at McCarthy, MacArthur, and all things right of Eisenhower can be viewed in this context as the belated revenge of a generation of popular artists for the stifling effect that witch-hunting, blacklisting, and a political meanspiritedness toward art and artists had placed upon its development.

"Gene came over and we worked out the pilot in London," Gelbart continues. "We knew we had something right away; the question was, Would it play? Then Gene and Burt [Metcalfe] took care of casting on the Coast while I tied up loose ends in England."

"One early problem we faced," according to Gene Reynolds, "was how to simplify the film, how to make the story 'television-size.' The movie had featured three heroes: Hawkeye, Trapper, and Duke the Southerner. We knew that was too much for a half-hour show. For a while we even considered going with one hero, Hawkeye, and cutting both of the others. But then we figured Hawkeye needed an equal to talk to—so we just dropped Duke."

In the movie, Duke starts out as an equal member of the heroic trio of free spirits he forms with the two other doctors. However, Hawkeye, a New Englander, and Trapper, a westerner, become alienated from Duke when he reveals racist attitudes toward a black medic named Spearchucker Jones, whom they import for the M*A*S*H unit's football team. Racism is rejected by Hawkeye and Trapper as weak, stupid, and evil; the racist character is exiled from the brotherhood of hedonists. Duke was the obvious choice to be cut. To maintain him in the sitcom, the show's creators would have had to do one of three things: rehabilitate him, make him into a kind of Archie Bunker (a doctor!), or ignore the issue. Having already exposed themselves through so many open windows of audience objectionability, Gelbart and Reynolds decided to punt on this most volatile American issue of all. Instead, all-purpose villainy, including a naive belief in racial stereotypes, would be invested in the whining, sniveling, incompetent Major Frank Burns.

At least one important new character was added to the cast. Corporal Maxwell Klinger, the reluctant draftee from Toledo, would spend most of his eleven seasons with the 4077th bucking for a Section 8 in skirt and heels. Klinger was originally conceived by Gelbart as a one-shot character for the

191

show, written into the third episode with a half-page bit. "Larry based him on Lenny Bruce's story of how he got out of the navy by impersonating a WAVE," claims Reynolds.

Despite the obviousness of the show's politically loaded obsessions, it is difficult to get most of the people involved in *M*A*S*H* to discuss the show's political content—or even the possibility that it had any. The hesitation of most television producers to speak frankly on such issues points to a legacy of McCarthyism that continues to cast a shadow over American popular culture. Silence by *M*A*S*H*'s producers—coupled with strong ratings—probably went a long way toward protecting the series from censorship during its production run and in keeping it alive and healthy in off-network syndication. When pressed, the auteurs tend to deflect the politically controversial aspects of *M*A*S*H*'s antiwar, antimilitarist statements to other sources of potential objectionability, especially gore and sex. For example, asked if he had ever run into political censorship at CBS, Reynolds replied, "The network had a number of reservations. For one thing, there was some sentiment to not allow any operating-room scenes. The movie had been full of them, with blood spurting all over the place. One CBS official claimed he had seen people walk out of the theater during those sequences. But we knew we had to have O-R scenes and convinced them."

John Rappaport, a *M*A*S*H* associate producer and writer, claims that sex was always a bigger issue with network censors than was politics. As a veteran contributor to content groundbreakers ranging from *All in the Family* to *Rowan and Martin's Laugh-In*, Rappaport had much experience in this regard. Reynolds, however, bristles even at this suggestion. "We were not a licentious show," he insists. "People sent us scripts all the time which had Hawkeye and B. J. doing all kinds of things with the nurses that we would have never had them do. We're just a good 'gang comedy.' We had a lot of terrific characters played by a lot of talented actors—real professionals who worked very well together."[24]

Larry Gelbart, whose career plans were less tied to prime-time network television, doesn't quite remember it that way: "We were battling with Standards and Practices all the time. In fact I'd say that many of the episodes that centered on the doctors' troubles with the military brass were metaphorically drawn from our own conflicts with the CBS brass."

Gelbart, feeling an urge to make new use of the commercial credibility he had won with the success of *M*A*S*H*, left the series after the 1975–76 season to pursue other projects, including *United States* (NBC, 1980), an experimental ratings-dead proto-dramedy starring Beau Bridges and Helen Shaver as a sitcom couple without a laughtrack. Gelbart did better at the movies with the smash film *Tootsie*, whose script he wrote in collaboration with Murray Schisgal and Elaine May. In retrospect, the Gelbart years at *M*A*S*H* seem painted with relatively broad brushstrokes as compared to what followed.

In the early episodes, Hawkeye was a borderline alcoholic, driven by his painful circumstances to swill the beakers of medical-school moonshine that he and Trapper cooked in their test-tube distillery. Like Phil Silvers' Sergeant Ernie Bilko or Ernest Borgnine's Commander Quint McHale, Alda's Captain Benjamin Franklin ("Hawkeye") Pierce depended on a sharp, deviant, yet above all humane imagination to outmaneuver the vigilant but bumbling, insensitive, incompetent brass of the U.S. armed forces. Hawkeye was separated from these earlier military sitcom noncom conmen not only by rank and class but by a desperate sense of mission in his battles with the bureaucracy. An unrepentant sensualist with a romantic vision of himself and his friends, Hawkeye willingly works within a system that he finds insane, asking only the single condition that he be permitted to retain control of his own soul. The only problem with this arrangement is that he is never completely convinced that the other side is capable of keeping the bargain or even knowing that it has been made.

Carrying the legacy of James Fenimore Cooper into the postbomb world, Hawkeye is a sitcom version of what Norman Mailer had called "the new American frontiersman" of the postbomb world in his 1959 essay "The White Negro." Like the heroes of Jack Kerouac's novels, Hawkeye is torn between the responsibilities thrust upon him by the unfeeling authorities and his urge to celebrate his erotic capacity to laugh and love.

Captain Pierce combines the organic earthiness of the military sitcom's traditional working-class sergeants—Bilko, McHale, Carter (*Gomer Pyle*), O'Rourke (*F Troop*)—with the imagination, wit, and values of a well-educated, highly articulate young physician from an unpretentious small town in Maine. Though living in the fictive fifties, Hawkeye speaks in the tones of a survivor of the sixties. His fear and hatred of the war and of the dehumanizing bureaucracy that wages it create in him a harmony of self-interest and social conscience. The aims of his endless sitcom schemes are not merely to extract privileges for himself from the army—the Bilko model—but to shelter the psychologically vulnerable, including himself, from the horror and the horror-making apparatus. A sixties hero in a seventies sitcom set in the fifties, Hawkeye's hedonism leads him not toward an obsession with personal material gain, but rather to an ethics-based social sensibility. One imagines an eighties sitcom hero such as Alex Keaton (Michael J. Fox) of *Family Ties* laughing at Hawkeye, not with him. Look at all the dumb chances he takes for the sake of others.

Trapper John (Wayne Rogers), while an ideological ally to Hawkeye, provides a stylistic contrast to his sardonic wit. Trapper, and later B. J., are pensive Ethels to Alda's expressive Lucy, acting as sounding boards for Hawkeye and as confederates in his schemes. Lieutenant Colonel Henry Blake (McLean Stevenson), the 4077th's reluctant commanding officer, dreams of returning to his midwestern medical practice, his country club, and even his unfaithful wife. His is a synthesis of familiar sitcom CO's. As inept as *McHale's Navy*'s Captain Binghamton, he is every bit as sympathetic as *Bilko*'s Colonel Hall. Father Francis Mulcahy (William Christopher), the camp's all-purpose religious adviser, betrays signs of Ethical Culture beneath his Catholic collar in his admiration for the godless Samaritan surgeons. Company clerk Corporal "Radar" O'Reilly (Gary Burghoff) is a shy Iowa farm boy trying to find his manhood in the middle of a war. Like Father Mulcahy, Radar is put off by Hawkeye's bawdiness, but not so much so that an alien style blinds him from the heroic substance of Hawkeye's humor in a world where the will to laugh is the will to live.

Ideologically, all of the above are united in a secular humanist popular front against the military martinets. Major Margaret

194

("Hot Lips") Houlihan (Loretta Swit) and Major Frank Burns (Larry Linville) are presented as flag-waving, hyperpatriotic "regulation" creeps. Constantly exposing themselves as hypocrites and shameless brown-nosers, Hot Lips and Frank are little more than wooden stereotypes in the early episodes, straw men for the righteous, progressive-thinking prankster-surgeon heroes. Reynolds calls Hot Lips and Burns in the pre-1977 episodes "obstacles which Hawkeye and Trapper could bump into."

The camp public-address system ("Due to incoming wounded, tonight has been canceled.") is the show's ironic narrator, a disembodied arbiter of the fate of all concerned. Nothing can stop the relentless human tragedy, which has no respect for poker games, romance, a bottle on a cold night, or unbearable fatigue. The army itself, pursuing no comprehensible object in a conflict whose meaning is vague and abstract (but whose meaninglessness is only too readily available), occasionally shells the 4077th by accident. A wounded North Korean soldier stumbles into the camp, showing equal mystification at the purpose of the war as he is healed by the good doctors. Beneath the military uniforms on both sides stand hapless civilians who continually reassert their right and ability to seek happiness—with a joke, with a kiss—in a nightmarish combat zone that is as dangerous to the soul as it is to the body. Hawkeye's bottomless supply of wisecracks in the face of all this makes the Alda character a kind of self-reflexive marginal narrator. Like Groucho in a Marx Brothers film, he is such a magnet for audience identification that every close-up of him suspends dramatic development and becomes direct address to the viewer.

M*A*S*H went through many transitions as the production team, the cast, and the culture that had bestowed Nielsen success upon it continued to change throughout the seventies. Gelbart had pushed for formal experiments, cajoling the network to try episodes without laughtracks and to present black-and-white half-hours on its "full color" schedule. His last and, by his own estimation, finest episode depicted the regulars as they were interviewed for a mock 1953 newsreel documentary. In a scene recalling Whitman's Civil War poems, Father Mulcahy tells the camera about warming his hands on a cold morning in the heat rising from the dead bodies. This kind of poetic stab at the eternal and universal distinguished Gelbart's equally didactic situation comedy from the sometimes clumsily energetic headline sensationalism of the Norman Lear shows. Collectively, Gelbart and Lear, though different in style, had done a remarkable job of carrying the ideological mantle of Adlai Stevenson into the popular imagination of an increasingly conservative decade.

Early *M*A*S*H*, running on television concurrently with the war in Vietnam, is indeed of an ideological piece with *All in the Family*. But after the fall of Saigon and the departure of Gelbart, *M*A*S*H* came to be dominated by its new executive producer, Burt Metcalfe, and its ever more-powerful star, Alan Alda. As a result, the concerns of the series increasingly inhabited MTM territory.[25] Interpersonal relationships gradually shoved American foreign-policy issues to the textual margins; a sixties revisionist history of the fifties gave way to a seventies revisionist history of the sixties. The ways in which cast changes were handled were perhaps the most visible reflections of this shift.

Many of the regulars, their pockets stuffed with *M*A*S*H* money, set off to find starring vehicles of their own. Between 1975 and 1979, McLean Stevenson, Wayne Rogers, Larry Linville and Gary Burghoff all left the show, taking Colonel Blake, Trapper John, Frank Burns, and Radar with them. The replacements for these characters were not merely new actors in the old roles, or substitute stereotypes, but, instead, a set of completely new characters who added accruing layers of social complexity to the narrative.

To replace Frank Burns as the odd-doctor-out, Metcalfe came up with Major Charles Emerson Winchester, a snooty Boston blue-blooded surgeon who had little patience for the antics or ideas of his egalitarian tentmates. Metcalfe tailored the role for actor David Ogden Stiers and handed it to him without an audition. "Frank Burns had become the convenient, easy joke—a totally cartoon character," recalls Metcalfe. "Winchester would embody everything Frank Burns did not; he'd be a fine surgeon, a formidable adversary for Hawkeye, with a bit of William F. Buckley in him that separated him from the rest of the guys." If Burns had been a vulgar redneck racist, Winchester was merely ethnocentric in a WASPish kind of way. If Burns was a sexual hypocrite (a married man, he was pretentiously pious in public, but apt to jump on Hot Lips whenever he thought no one was looking), Winchester expressed a sincere Victorian reverence for women. An articulate appreciator of the fine arts, a man of *Kultur*—Winchester, while not exactly the stuff of sitcom heroes, stood head and shoulders above the whining, repulsive Burns.

Captain B. J. Hunnicut (Mike Farrell) takes Trapper's cot on the simpatico side of the tent. Farrell's B. J., far from the devil-may-care playboy of Wayne Rogers' Trapper, is a tragically absent husband and father—a serious idealist rather than a skirt-chasing cynic. His one brief camp romance is characterized by intense self-reexamination and even self-recrimination, both major themes of the later *M*A*S*H*. B. J. generally and genuinely appreciates Hawkeye's sense of humor, but he is also capable of telling Hawkeye when to get off, of letting him know when he has gone too far, when his pranks have become insensitive or even cruel. He becomes a conscience for Hawkeye, who, during the Gelbart years, was himself the paragon of conscience.

After Henry Blake wins his release from the army (he promptly dies when his helicopter is shot down on the first leg of the journey back home), Colonel Sherman Potter (Harry Morgan) becomes the camp's new commanding officer. Potter, a Missouri-born doctor and an army lifer with credentials going back to World War I, does the most to defuse the volatile polarization between the army regulars and the reluctant draftees that had powered Altman's film and the Gelbart TV episodes. Potter's revulsion at war and his sense of humor are capacities that had been previously reserved strictly for the antimilitary forces. Harry Morgan, giving the role equal doses of Harry Truman and sitcom papa, is a TV veteran whose career parallels that of the medium itself. Having played Officer Bill Gannon, Jack Webb's sidekick on the late-sixties *Dragnet* revival, Morgan retains the arguable distinction of having been a regular in both the most politically conservative and the most politically liberal series ever to appear on the networks.

Of equal importance to the new characters are the changes that take place among the surviving cast members. Hawkeye kicks the beaker and learns a few lessons about sexism as Alan Alda becomes the nonconformist whom Middle America can trust during the seventies. Alda, who had called the early Hawkeye "a sexual Archie Bunker," asserted his newly gained authorship rights by gradually clamping down on Hawkeye's libido. Like President Jimmy Carter, the post-1976 Hawkeye may have shown signs of "lust in his heart," but an emerging sense of guilt, born out of a new definition of sexual politics, begins to prevent him from acting too impetuously upon it. A committed crusader for the ill-fated equal-rights amendment during the late seventies, Alda found himself the darling of women's magazines, from *Good Housekeeping* to *Ms.* By 1977 he had become so popular that he finished second only to John Wayne in the Performer Q survey, a statistic that pointed to a strong polarization of the national audience in matters of gender propriety.[26]

M*A*S*H's supporting characters evolved as well. Father Mulcahy, though a Catholic priest, develops nonpriestly emotional traits, doubting his calling in selected episodes and even surviving a near brush with romance. Klinger, taking over as company clerk after Radar's departure, takes off his dress and finally accepts the immutable reality of his hitch in the army. Some of the most poignant of the later episodes involve the sexually born-again Hawkeye's relationship with the most changed character of all, Margaret (no longer "Hot Lips") Houlihan, who gradually sheds the cardboard stereotype of the military iron maiden and becomes a three-dimensional, at times even sympathetic, human being.

Margaret's transition comes in the wake of her marriage to Lieutenant Colonel Donald Penobscott, which falls apart during the couple's Tokyo honeymoon and eventually ends in divorce. Hawkeye had lusted after her since the earliest episodes—since the movie, since the novel!—but this crude passion is resolved in a climactic moment for the entire series when the two of them are pinned down under enemy fire, convinced of their impending deaths. They fall into each other's arms, their mutual fear of mortality wiping away the years of rivalry and animosity. They make love. Waking the next morning—still alive—they realize that they simply don't have much more to give each other physically. The tension that has been separating them for years is spent in a single night. A gulf has been bridged; they become friends. Nothing like it had happened on a situation comedy before.

Appropriately enough, a shrink, Captain Sidney Freedman (Alan Arbus), was added to the cast, filling the role of modern confessor that eluded the sincere but hopelessly outdated Father Mulcahy. Psychological introspection established itself as *M*A*S*H*'s primary text during the late seventies. Personal madness replaced the insanity of the bureaucracy as the main villain, though the former was still often spurred by the latter. Appropriately enough, the final episode, a two-and-a-half-hour extravaganza, finds Hawkeye· over the psychotic borderline as the Treaty of Panmunjom is signed. It seems as if the tiny cell of humanity within him that contains his sense of humor, his compassion, and his reason will fall one episode short of surviving the war. Despite all, however, *M*A*S*H* is a comedy. The test of valor in the 4077th is the ability to remain a wiseguy under any circumstances. With the help of his friends, Hawkeye passes this test one last time. He proclaims his sanity and the series ends.

Verbal Scores Plummet

During the first three decades of national commercial tele-cast, the bulk of program production consisted largely of works derived from older arts, especially radio, theater, and cinema. The success in the 1970s of prime-time sitcoms such as *The Mary Tyler Moore Show*, *All in the Family*, and *M*A*S*H* constituted the flowering of this protovideo aesthetic. All the things that had upset English teachers so deeply about *I Love Lucy*, *Bewitched*, and *Gilligan's Island* had been addressed and improved in these sitcoms and their spin-offs. Did not Mary, Archie, and Hawkeye display rich characterization? Had not witty repartee supplanted cardboard one-liners? Were not racism, sexism, generational conflict, war and peace, existential malaise, and finding the right apartment issues of sufficient depth to engage contemporary literati? Was there not, in each case, evidence of a humane soul at the narrative rudder? Even if the very existence of the commercials had blackballed the genre from admission to the genteel country club of fine arts, situation comedy at least had demonstrated a heretofore unseen civility. During the previous quarter century of *I Married Joan* and *Mr. Ed*, *Petticoat Junction* and *Hazel*, *F Troop* and *I Dream of Jeannie*, who would have thought the savage capable of even this?

But as so often happens in the bomb world, positivist visions of spiraling progress drop without warning into craters of entropy. If the waning of the literate sitcom was sudden, the hasty decline of a developing art form was nothing new to television. In the early fifties, Caesar, Berle, and Kovacs had knocked on the door of Chaplin, Keaton, and Lloyd, but were denied space in the pantheon of American mass-culture clowns as their genre went into abrupt commercial free-fall before they could bring it to maturity.[27] Barely a decade after its premiere, the comedy-variety show was already fading from view; the silent cinema, by contrast, had flourished for more than thirty years before its technological double cross at the hands of the talkies. Similarly, Rod Serling and Paddy Chayefsky had self-consciously aspired to the status of Tennessee Williams and Arthur Miller during the golden age of live teleplays, but they too had barely transcended midculture when their genre—anthology drama—was abruptly canceled by the networks.

The producers of *The Mary Tyler Moore Show*, *All in the Family*, and *M*A*S*H* saw an opening for their work in the industry's confusion over baby-boomer marketing strategy at the end of the 1960s. They accepted the formal terms of the network sitcom—thirty minutes in four segments, audience response track, ultraslick production values, and so on—and rushed in to attempt the neat trick of a literate comedy of manners in a genre that had become synonymous with the decline of literacy. Playing against the sitcom's historical barrenness, they proved that content—in the form of broad-brushstroke writing—could energize even the most banal of forms.

Though their artistic and commercial success was astounding, it did not bring about the sitcom millennium. Far from signaling the dawning of a new age, the literate sitcoms of the seventies were destined to be remembered as yet another of TV's golden ages. By the end of the decade, Garry Marshall's self-conscious return-to-normalcy trilogy—*Happy Days, Laverne and Shirley*, and *Mork and Mindy*—had replaced the litcoms at the top of the Nielsen heap. More importantly, the Marshall shows soon established themselves as the state-of-the-art models to be imitated.

Anxiety-provoking problems such as generational polarization, racism, and U.S. foreign policy were washed away by the cartoon Levittownism of the Cunninghams. Meathead's rebelliousness on social issues gave way to The Fonz instructing America's youth on the advantages of holding a library card. The urbane chitchat of Mary and Rhoda was drowned out by the high-decibel shrieking of Laverne and Shirley. The brazen political didacticism of *Maude* deteriorated into the painfully cute reports on human frailties that Mork delivered to Orson from Boulder, Colorado, at the conclusion of *Mork and Mindy* each week. The no-exit hell of Hawkeye Pierce brightened into the Southern California lifestyle options of Jack Tripper.

M*A*S*H may have been the most enduring sitcom of the three, and *All in the Family* certainly got the most press, but most of what has survived of the seventies sitcom renaissance can be traced to MTM Enterprises. In the eighties, sitcom attention shifted away from single people (MTM's specialty) and back toward the genre's traditional center: the family. Family and "family values" shows such as *Diff'rent Strokes, The Facts of Life, Silver Spoons*, and *Family Ties*, and later *The Cosby Show, Who's the Boss?* and *Growing Pains* defined the state of the art. Meanwhile, however, series such as *Taxi, Cheers*, and *Brothers*—shows whose production teams were rife with MTM veterans—continued the litcom tradition, making it into a kind of prestigious, if commercially limited, subgenre. *Brothers* a pay-cable-only sitcom that aired on Showtime, may point the way to the litcom's future. Though many MTM alumni have worked on these shows, the studio itself pretty much abandoned the sitcom by the end of the seventies (*Newhart* is the notable exception) in favor of another genre—the upscale prime-time soap opera.

It has been on series such as *Hill Street Blues, St. Elsewhere*, and *L.A. Law* that novelistic television has strived to survive on the networks in the remote-control and cable era. Full of allusion, disjunction of expectation, love, death, and financial problems, these shows simultaneously manage to imitate the form of channel zapping and still tell stories by condensing narrative sequences into tangentially related dramatic units that rarely last beyond a few minutes in length. On *Hill Street*, the officers sit together in the precinct room, get their orders for the day, jump into their cars and zigzag across the episode, meeting each other at key junctions and separating again. On *L.A. Law*, created and produced by *Hill Street*'s Steven Bochco, the partners' meeting serves a similar function in a similar structure. On *St. Elsewhere*, Bruce Paltrow, John Masius, and Tom Fontana employ a slightly different structuring device. The characters, confined for the most part to the interior of the hospital building, cross each other in the halls. As they do, the camera reverses fields, following a different character into a different narrative line. As with the Bochco programs, the severity of the segmentation is softened by the immediacy and richness of the segment's content. The early TV playwrights, still tied to a theatrical model, had complained about condensation and segmentation. The writers of the nighttime soap operas—*Dallas* and *Dynasty* included with those above—have exploited these very qualities to advantage. When a show like *St. Elsewhere* is really cooking—balancing three, four, or even five engaging subplots of variable comic and tragic intensity while maintaining broad narrative unity—it becomes potentially as interesting as constantly changing channels with the remote-control button. In each case, a viewing situation is created in which no image need outlast its welcome; the "attention-span problem" has been circumvented. Little such imaginative action is seen in the eighties sitcom: Diane Chambers of *Cheers*, a knotted web of cultural pretenses and survival instincts, is a Mary for her times; *The Golden Girls* is issue-oriented and pleasantly overacted in a Norman Lear sort of way; the cast of *M*A*S*H* is doing IBM commercials. But shows such as these no longer define the existing order. The phenomenal success of *Family Ties* and, more emphatically, *The Cosby Show* demonstrated that the problems of raising those darned kids would rule the genre once again.

Perhaps the brevity of adult wit in sitcom history was technologically predetermined. In the late seventies, as cable snaked its way down the American boulevard, television began to mutate further and further away from the recognizable traits of the literature-conscious arts that had spawned it. MTV has, to a great extent, replaced "movies," "shows," "series," and other such quaint narrative units with brief and emphatically storyless "videos." The Weather Channel ungraded what traditionally had been a three-minute segment on the local news into a permanent twenty-four-hour-a-day telethon, marrying meteorology to show business in ways that precable viewers could not have forecast. The reruns, movies, sporting events, prayer meetings, and informational services that have crowded the burgeoning spectrum are joined by local character-generators inviting the viewer to look for a job, a used car, a new television set, or even a cure for obesity or alcoholism.[28] The new services brought by cable television, whatever their purposes, have become new forms of home entertainment, making the broadcast networks just three increasingly undistinguished blips among thirty-five or forty.

Considering the innovative intensifications of commercialism offered by cable, even the stodgiest of English teachers may remember the Network Era—those years during which virtually the whole population was watching one of three narrative images—with some fondness. At least people viewed whole "shows" in those days; at least Aristotle's prescription for "a beginning, a middle, and an end" was respected, even if ineptly. The ancient TV shows, media historians are likely to remind us, actually made use of such time-honored devices as setting, characterization, conflict, and climax, even if execution, when judged against the literary canon, was relatively clumsy. But the doom of Aristotelian television is already assured. The eight or ten hours it takes to read most novels gives way to the two or so hours it takes to see most movies, which gives way to the thirty to sixty minutes it takes to watch most TV shows, which gives way to the three to five minutes it takes to witness a rock video, which gives way to the two to ten seconds it takes to recognize an image, tire of it, and hit the remote-control button for another.

Multichannel remote-control cable television is a domestic technology bound to achieve the ubiquity of indoor plumbing in advanced capitalist societies. It fights the traditional urge for narrative continuity that ruled TV watching during the medium's infancy. Why look at anything for longer than the duration of its allure, when dozens more *imagi mundi*—all of them bouncing and shifting through endless permutations—seductively tickle the fingertip? Viewer becomes editor-collagist as every set becomes a bottomless inkwell of footage.

With the installation of cablebox wireless remote control, the hapless couch potato is retooled into an insatiable Platonist: PBS penguins roosting on the ice floes. Boxcar Willie is a guest on *Nashville Now*. Lucy smuggles a giant provolone cheese onto an airplane by disguising it as a baby. The House is holding hearings. A rerun of a college basketball game; I think I know the score. Kill cockroaches with sonic waves. Could that really be Deputy Dawg? A new show—does the star cue psychosexual responses? A different Lucy episode arrives from a neighboring market. It's the one where Lucy goes to the eye doctor and gets a glaucoma test that impairs her vision just before she's supposed to do a dance number down at the club with a professional jitterbug. Whole minutes of dueling Lucies: a woman with a real baby sits down next to Lucy; the jitterbug, wearing a zoot suit, calls Lucy a "chick"; Fred and Ethel reluctantly agree to help; Ricky's anger sends him into Spanish. I pray to the god of HBO; oh no, not *The Black Stallion* again! This guy is either the Herbalife guy or the guy who tells you how to become a millionaire by taking over bad mortgages. *The PTL Club* without Tammy or Jim? No thanks. Sally Jessy Raphael—the poor woman's Phil Donahue. Didactic *Starsky and Hutch*: a Soviet ballerina falls in love with Hutch and defects to the West Coast. Julia Child is adding butter. Mark Goodman is announcing concert dates for incomprehensible pop bands. Fred Flintstone is yelling for Wilma. Can the linear narrative development of any show possibly be as rich as the cubist montage afforded by channel changing? Sitting through an entire thirty-minute episode of *The Mary Tyler Moore Show*, *All in the Family*, or *M*A*S*H* is, by contrast, an evening at the opera. The well-wrought urn is smashed into a thousand shards.

An invisible expense hiding among the modern necessities of the monthly electric bill, television isn't fattening, and unless you sit bathing in its radiance, it probably won't give you cancer. Spending time with the set, however, is unlikely to improve a viewer's self-image. While watching unaccompanied, it is not difficult to find in oneself a lonely, alienated, pathetic three-dollar bill who, unable to cement meaningful relationships with real human beings, dotes upon the unresponsive packaged attractions of video images. When watching with friends, the thought recurs at random intervals that intelligent, sensitive people who really cared about each other might find something more interactive to do. When watching with family, fundamentalist warnings on the future of this living arrangement lurk like an evil cloud over the set. Control, no matter how remote, is all the more appreciated in such painfully low-prestige contexts.

A 1985 episode of *Steven Spielberg's Amazing Stories* indicates that the implications of remote control have not escaped one of Hollywood's craftiest marketing geniuses. Titled "Remote Control Man," the *Amazing Story* concerns a henpecked wimp who, in the *Twilight Zone* tradition of finding cameras that take pictures of the future and stopwatches that freeze the world in suspended animation, comes into possession of a truly postmodern television set with a remote-control unit that allows the viewer to turn actual TV characters into so-called real people. Turned off by a shrewish wife who has let herself go, he tunes in a lithesome aerobics instructor to come forth from the set and replace her. After a night of elevated pulse rates, Remote Control Man requests breakfast of his new and agile special friend, only to learn that, in this age of specialization, TV exercise professionals do not perform kitchen duties. Whipping out the old remote, he zaps up June Cleaver (played, as ever, by Barbara Billingsley), who is, of course, no Jane Fonda, but sure can cook. Before the half hour is up, he trades in his spike-haired son for Gary Coleman,[29] gets Lyle Alzado to save him from criminals, and similarly conjures Ed McMahon, Jim Lange, La Wanda Page, Richard Simmons, and a host of others, generic and specific, from the bowels of the teleworld. This *Amazing Story*, by imitating the sensation of channel-changing in the body of its text, might well serve as a prototype for a new subgenre of sitcom meant specifically to combat the growing tide of spectrum grazing.

The proliferation of remote control presents a direct threat to the entertainment-industrial complex as we know it. The happy union of laziness and commercial attendance has been rent asunder. The inertia that has bound the viewer to sit still for so much has been broken. But there is already solid evidence that Madison Avenue is on the case. No longer satisfied to monitor its test sample at intervals of fifteen minutes, the A. C. Nielsen Company now makes a continuous record of all channel movement. The ratings exist, after all, to measure the quantity of heads present for the commercials, and these new home video technologies threaten those numbers by posing the dual challenges of "zapping" (changing channels every time the action pauses for a word from our sponsor) and "zipping" (hitting the fast-forward scan button while watching taped shows on a VCR). Whatever programming solutions the industry finds to these problems are likely to contain new existing orders and new comic visions of American personality and culture.

Notes

1. John Fiske and John Hartley, *Reading Television* (New York: Methuen, 1978), p. 17.
2. As told to Barry Walters, "Visions of Glory," *Spin*, October 1986, p. 56.
3. Ralph Waldo Emerson, "The American Scholar" (1837).
4. See Neil Postman, *Amusing Ourselves to Death* (New York: Elizabeth Sifton, Viking, 1985), especially Chapter Two, "Media as Epistemology."
5. See especially Hans Magnus Enzensberger, *The Consciousness Industry* (New York: Seabury, 1974).
6. See Ray Kroc, with Robert Anderson, *Grinding It Out: The Making of McDonald's* (Chicago: Regnery, 1977).
7. I am treating *Archie Bunker's Place* as a spin-off, rather than a change of name, of *All in the Family*.
8. See Jane Feuer, Paul Kerr, and Tise Vahimagi, eds., *MTM "Quality Television"* (London: British Film Institute, 1984).
9. Chris Bryars, *The Real Mary Tyler Moore Show* (New York: Pinnacle, 1977), p. 88.
10. It was not until 1975 that Norman Lear, always the politician, decisively cracked the divorcée persona barrier with *One Day at a Time*.
11. "A CBS offical claimed that if Mary were a divorcée, people would think she'd divorced Dick Van Dyke, 'and nobody divorces Dick Van Dyke,'" according to Bryars, p. 89.
12. James W. Cheseboro, "Communication, Values, and Popular Television Series," in *Television: The Critical View*, ed. Horace Newcomb, 3rd ed. (New York: Oxford, 1982), p. 13.

13. "In the area of comedy it is fair to say . . . that these [the mid-1970s] were television's 'Golden Years.'" Horace Newcomb and Robert S. Alley, *The Producer's Medium* (New York: Oxford, 1983), p. 4.
14. Quoted in Newcomb and Alley, p. 174.
15. George Lipsitz, "The Meaning of Memory: Family, Class, and Ethnicity in Early Network Television Programs," *Cultural Anthropology*, 1:4 (November 1986), p. 355.
16. Horace Newcomb, *TV: The Most Popular Art* (New York: Anchor/Doubleday, 1974), p. 219.
17. Kevin P. Phillips, *The Emerging Republican Majority* (New Rochelle, N.Y.: Arlington House, 1970); see especially the sections on northern Catholic blue-collar support for George Wallace in the 1968 presidential election.
18. "Those Were the Days," lyrics by Lee Adams; music by Charles Strouse. Copyright © 1971 by New Tandem Music Company, Los Angeles.
19. Malcolm X and Alex Haley, *The Autobiography of Malcolm X* (New York: Grove Press, 1965).
20. "Movin' On Up," lyrics and music by Jeff Barry and Ja'net Dubois. Copyright © 1975 by Belfast Music.
21. This concept should be attributed to J. Hoberman, who, commenting about a program on a local New York City television station that shows a continuous loop of a burning log all night each Christmas Eve, wrote, "With *The Yule Log*, day-to-day life in America has transcended surrealism and broken through to science fiction." J. Hoberman, "Medium Cool Yule," *Village Voice*, December 26, 1976, p. 129.
22. Altman's film, in turn, had been adapted from Richard Hooker's novel *M*A*S*H* (New York: William Morrow, 1968). Hooker is actually Dr. Richard Hornberger, who had served with a MASH unit in Korea.
23. These and all comments by Gelbart, Reynolds, and Metcalfe, unless otherwise noted, were made during telephone interviews conducted by the author in October 1985.
24. "Gang comedy" is a standard sitcom formula in which emphasis is placed on the building-up of a repertoire of interacting characters, rather than the featuring of a single star personality. By design, all military sitcoms lend themselves to the gang-comedy format.
25. It is worth noting that in 1977, Gene Reynolds, Gelbart's original collaborator, joined MTM Enterprises to produce *Lou Grant*. However, he remained a "creative consultant" to *M*A*S*H* until the series left the air. Alda took a "creative consultant" credit as well.
26. A Q-score is a measure of performer popularity based on sample group questionnaire testing that is done each year by a company known as Performer Q of Port Washington, New York.

27. There were, of course, notable exceptions. Red Skelton lasted through the sixties, as did Jackie Gleason; and Carol Burnett even managed to hold a comedy-variety hour through the seventies. But these few exceptions, when measured against the ubiquity of comedy-variety during the early days, only serve to prove the rule; by 1960, the fate of the genre was sealed.
28. In 1981, for example, I found a job teaching at Cornell University on the classified ad service of Cerrache Cablevision, Ithaca, New York.
29. This may not be as "amazing" a story as it seems. The white-parent–black-child relationship achieved conventional status in the early eighties. See *Diff'rent Strokes* and *Webster*.

CHAPTER 6

Postscripts

Risus in ore stultis abundat.

The velocity of movement in trend and style on commercial television is so great that a writer can hardly hope to bring out a truly up-to-date book on the subject. I have focused in this book on three decades of television comedy: the fifties, sixties, and seventies. What follows is merely a short sketch of some developments that have taken place in the wake of this thirty-year period.

The Sitcom: The End of CBS Hegemony

During the latter part of the seventies, just at the time that cable was making its first significant market penetrations, CBS lost the commercial and artistic hegemony that it had historically held over TV situation comedy. The network's proud stable of relatively erudite didacticoms, including such successful properties as *The Mary Tyler Moore Show*, *All in the Family*, *Rhoda*, *Good Times*, *Maude*, *One Day at a Time*, *Alice*, *The Jeffersons*, and *M*A*S*H*—every last one had been a Top Ten finisher—gradually ended production and went their separate ways into the public-opinion research bazaars of local syndication.[1]

As is the fate of all TV programming styles, what had once been an attractive, innovative aesthetic became conventional, institutionalized, and finally all too familiar. But CBS programmers remained enamored of the success they had achieved with these sitcoms of social concern. A decade earlier, the network had gambled by canceling still popular ruralcoms, such as *The Beverly Hillbillies*, *Petticoat Junction*, and *Mayberry R.F.D.*, in order to make way for the Lear and MTM shows, in the quest for younger and more cash-fluid viewers. By 1979, *All in the Family* had replaced *The Beverly Hillbillies* as CBS's all-time sitcom ratings winner, and unlike the *Hillbillies*, it was a prestigious critical hit to boot. The network was reluctant to part with it. With hundreds of episodes already in syndication and three of its four original stars gone, the once vital program was allowed to mutate into *Archie Bunker's Place*, extending its run for another four seasons. As late as 1982, CBS was still trying *All in the Family* spin-offs: the short-lived *Gloria* brought back Sally Struthers in the role of Archie's daughter, now abandoned with child by Meathead, who has run off to join a California commune. What had started out as sitcom social realism was wandering into *The Twilight Zone*.

With so many sitcom content battles seemingly won during the first half of the seventies, it was only natural that some producers would turn their attention to tinkering with the very form of the genre. Three of the attempts that made it to the air involved the cross-fertilization of the sitcom with the hanging serial format of a Monday-through-Friday daytime drama. Norman Lear produced two experimental soap operatic sitcoms: *Mary Hartman, Mary Hartman* (syndication, 1976–78), a hyperbolically turgid suds spoof, and *All That Glitters* (syndication, 1977), a show that took place in an unspecified world (or future) in which all traditional gender roles are reversed. Neither was able to win a buy order from any of the three networks, despite Lear's stunning prime-time track record. The one soapcom that did achieve national success was produced by a Lear protégée, Susan Harris, who had written the famous two-part "Maude Gets an Abortion" episode. But her show, *Soap* (ABC, 1977–81), was weekly, not daily, and it quickly tempered the Learesque topics of its early episodes, such as homosexuality and race relations, with increasing doses of magicom shtick: an alien from outer space, a demonic possession, evil twin doubles, and so on. The boundaries of sitcom experimentation were thus fixed and a period of retrenchment ensued during which ABC, for the first time, would become the most popular and most profitable network.

Having rejected *All in the Family* back in 1969, ABC had found itself up the sitcom creek in the wake of Lear's spectacular successes. In 1973–74, for example, ABC counterprogrammed *The Partridge Family*, its only Top Twenty sitcom, directly against *All in the Family*. This turned out to be a kamikaze mission, resulting in the cancellation of one of the network's most popular series. That same year, ABC scheduled *The Brady Bunch* (1969–74) against Lear's NBC hit *Sanford and Son* and got exactly the same result.

Attempts by ABC to clone the Lear style were similarly disastrous. In 1972–73, the network tried a show titled *The Corner Bar*, produced by Alan King and Howard Morris. Its cast was multiracial and multiethnic, with a gay character and a hard hat thrown in just for good confrontation. The network was so high on the concept that after an initial ratings failure, it laid out the money to reshoot and recast the show, giving *The Corner Bar* a second (ill-fated) shot the following fall. *A Touch of Grace* (1973), produced for ABC by Carl Reiner (his first sitcom since *The Dick Van Dyke Show*), likewise went nowhere. A transformation on the "generation gap" model of *All in the Family*, it starred Shirley Booth, late of *Hazel*, as a "hip" senior citizen, recently widowed, who moves in with her conservative daughter and son-in-law. Both shows met their doom even as Archie Bunker was ascending into Nielsen heaven. Castleman and Podrazik attribute the failure of the ABC didacticoms to the inability of their writers to create the sustained intensity of credible confrontational dialogue that was the hallmark of Lear and his studio.[2] ABC finally did get an actual Norman Lear sitcom in 1975. The show, *Hot L Baltimore* (1975), was a controversial adaptation of an off-Broadway play that included a gay man and a prostitute among its series regulars. Lasting only several months, it turned out to be one of Lear's few network failures.

After thirty years as the humble "third network," however, ABC would yet have its day. As is the fate of any fad, trend, philosophy, economic theory, or school of art, the socially conscious sitcom reached its point of saturation and began to suffer entropic demise. ABC, by virtue of its failure to create any

211

confrontational hits, was more than ready for this development with a new wave of emphatically nonconfrontational sitcoms that were custom-made for what *Time* magazine (via Tom Wolfe) was now calling "the Me Decade."

Under its new programming chief, Fred Silverman (whom the network had raided from corporate top-heavy CBS), ABC began to dominate the sitcom—and for a brief period all of television—with such hits as *Happy Days* (1974–84), *Welcome Back, Kotter* (1975–79), *Laverne and Shirley* (1976–83), *Three's Company* (1977–84), and *Mork and Mindy* (1978–82), all of which were obvious, even self-conscious retreats from the blunt, polarized dialogue and political topicality that had characterized the CBS hits of the earlier part of the decade. Garry Marshall, a softspoken liberal who preferred to accentuate the positive with nostalgic visions of a pre-1960s past, won control of the dramatic conversation from the feisty, contentious Lear and established himself as the genre's hot new auteur.

A kind of artistic melancholia overcame situation comedy after the passing of its moment of paraliterate glory. Lear cut off day-to-day involvement with on-line sitcom production, preferring instead to become directly involved in national politics as a founder of People for the American Way, a liberal interest group. He was little more than a front-office desk jockey at his new company, Embassy Communications, which was grinding out such sweet stuff as *Diff'rent Strokes* and *The Facts of Life*. MTM Enterprises, meanwhile, seemed to lose interest in the genre it had been founded to produce, abandoning situation comedy to explore new frontiers in hour-long serial teledrama with such shows as *Hill Street Blues* and *St. Elsewhere*. The military sitcom retreated from the pungent critique of authority in *M*A*S*H* to the lame Sad Sack slapstick—this time with women—of *Private Benjamin*.

The genre contracted around its recently won freedoms. Marshall's *Happy Days*, armed with the force of post-1960s hindsight, turned away from polarization to revisit the fifties midwestern milieu of *Father Knows Best*. The suburbopastoral Cunninghams of *Happy Days*, though fictive contemporaries of the Andersons, enjoyed the advantages of living color. Residing in a racially segregated, crime-free, culturally homogenous neighborhood of spacious single-family homes, they gradually replaced the fussing and fighting inner-city Bunkers as TV's state-of-the-art sitcom family. In 1976–77, *Happy Days* broke *All in the Family*'s string of five straight number-one seasons, scoring a whopping 31.5 in the Nielsen ratings. Because of the fragmentation of the mass audience that has subsequently been brought about by cable, few series would ever again finish a season with a rating above 30.

Ron Howard starred in *Happy Days* as Richie Cunningham, the teenaged center of narrative focus. Howard, who had last crossed the national stage as Sheriff Andy Taylor's little boy Opie, returned to sitcom work as the quintessentially white middle-class high school student with the big Howdy Doody smile. Though every bit as much the bright-eyed all-American burger eater as Bud Anderson, Ricky Nelson, or Wally Cleaver, Richie often expressed romantic desires that transcended the stuffy Victorian courtship rituals that passed for making out on the old fifties domesticoms. Despite all his dates, Bud had never talked much about getting laid; Richie's intentions, on the other hand, were clear.[3] In the years dividing *Happy Days* from its antecedents, lust, as casually expressed by characters such as Hawkeye and Meathead, had become an acceptable emotion for heroic sitcom men.

If Bud and the other Andersons had depended almost solely on Father for the wisdom to grow by, Richie looked to a more generationally ambiguous figure known as the Fonz (Henry Winkler). In many ways a startling TV sellout of the mythically alienated bikers and gearheads that had been made famous by Marlon Brando and James Dean in the fifties cinema, the Fonz—not Richie's father, Howard Cunningham—became the program's omniscient, omnipotent guide to righteous American living. Though sporting biker clothes and possessed of legendary sexual charisma (as we are so often reminded), the Fonz emerges as a bizarre post–Archie Bunker Jim Anderson, offering Richie and the viewing audience advice on everything from the importance of staying in school to the evils of racial prejudice. An episode in which the Fonz took out a library card provides a startling example: the American Library Association, noting an immediate upsurge in library card applications following the telecast, substituted the *Happy Days* episode for the 16mm film it had been using for years to promote library usage among schoolchildren.[4] As Marshall himself put it, "*Leave It to Beaver, Father Knows Best* were about nice men saying, 'Be nice.' Can't do that anymore; nobody listens. Now I got a guy with a leather jacket and black boots who says, 'I can beat you up. I can ride a bike better than you, I do a lot of things better than you, and I get girls, and I'm kind of a rebel, but, also, be nice.' It's the same message, only it's coming from a more modern voice."[5] By the final season of the series, still wearing his leather jacket, the Fonz fulfills his apparent role destiny and becomes a schoolteacher. It was as if the alienation that had powered the rebel biker figure of the early fifties had been cleansed from the black leather jacket, leaving an empty semiological slug that in turn was reanimated by Marshall with the energies of devout citizenship.

Even more so than *Happy Days*, D. L. Taftner's *Three's Company* became a symbol, perhaps a whipping boy, for the sitcom's regression from literate bourgeois complexity to the less subtle aesthetic currents that would yield such critically despised subgenres as the back-to-the-fiftiescom and the jigglecom. *Three's Company* seemed nothing less than smug in the way it exploited so many of the content breakthroughs of the early seventies without taking any chances of its own. The show owed its pointedly "daring" concept—a man sharing an apartment with two women—to the battles fought and won by Lear and Gelbart. Its young, sitcomically hip, yuppified characters lived by grace of the valorization of middle-class unmarrieds that had taken place on the MTM shows.

Chrissy (Suzanne Somers) and Janet (Joyce DeWitt) take Jack (John Ritter) as their roommate in a three-bedroom Southern California garden apartment. This, however, is just a tease, as none of the members of the sitcom household become anything more than just good friends. The running gag of the show is that Chrissy and Janet have told the frumpy landlord that Jack is gay so as to create a facade of pre-1960s propriety. Ironically, it had taken the introduction of actual gay characters on episodes of *All in the Family* and *Maude* to establish a commercially acceptable discourse that would allow Jack to falsely claim to be gay (the clinically ominous term "homosexual" is never used). Beyond that, the lie is concocted by the roommates in order to convince the landlord that there is no hanky-panky going on in the apartment—which, of course, there isn't in the first place.

Three's Company's airhead indifference toward the sense of public advocacy that had become the hallmark of the Lear, MTM, and *M*A*S*H* shows was complemented by a similarly *derrière-garde* method of representation. For one thing, the show was not principally language-oriented. Though it was thoroughly ornamented with thin double entendres, its main sources of humor were visual and physical, in contrast to the verbal, characterization-based scripts that had become the measure of sitcom sophistication during the early seventies. John Ritter, as energetic and proficient a pie-in-the-face, trip-over-the-sofa comic as had been seen on television since Lucille Ball, functioned on *Three's Company* as a sitcomic version of a burlesque funnyman, poking his nose into Suzanne Somers' *décolletage* and going cross-eyed and weak-kneed for the camera. This emphasis on slapstick left little time or context for complex conversation.

While "youth" had only recently carried its own set of political connotations in situation comedy, especially in the Lear shows, the young characters of *Three's Company* were without identifiable political opinions or outlooks. The polarization of the generations, which had taken place along clear political-cultural lines between Archie and Meathead, was reworked into an apolitical style conflict by Taftner. Jack, Chrissy, and Janet were hip enough not to fetishize sex, and thus, they were healthy and admirable. Their landlord, Mr. Roper (Norman Fell), was unhip because he could not be casual about sexual matters. The correlation between casualness toward sex and psychological health was accentuated by the fact that Mr. Roper's sexual prowess was constantly put in question by Mrs. Roper (Audra Lindley). Mr. Furley (Don Knotts), the new landlord after the *The Ropers* got their own spin-off, was even less casual toward sex and sexuality and thus even less psychologically healthy. Playing a "traditional bachelor" from the pre-1960s world, Don Knotts creates a funhouse grotesque of Jack: Barney Fife on the planet of the California singles. With his *Playboy* smoking jacket and hair pomade, he is the pathetic antithesis of Jack, a modern, all-natural single guy who knows how to score in the "enlightened" contemporary environment. Men in their fifties, Mr. Roper and Mr. Furley are easily convinced that Jack is gay, because they are unable to conceive of the idea that a "normal" man might share an apartment—and friendship—with women who were not doing his sexual bidding. The audience, which can see this only too clearly, is congratulated for living in the liberated future.

If *Happy Days* had settled on a new set of standards for family relations, and *Three's Company* had done the same for singles, series such as *Carter Country* (ABC, 1977–79), *Diff'rent Strokes* (NBC, 1978–87), *Benson* (ABC, 1979–86), *Gimme a Break* (NBC, 1981–87), and *Webster* (ABC, 1983–87) presented a picture of an integrated post–civil rights movement America, where racists were implicitly disposed of as pathetic outsiders who were denying themselves the warmth and love of membership in the interracial extended families of the new "postracist" America. *The Jeffersons* (CBS, 1975–86), though an ancient *All in the Family* spin-off, was particularly well suited for this new trend in black situation comedy. The story of a nouveau riche black family living among wealthy whites in a luxury high-rise, the show was Norman Lear's most racially integrated and longest-lasting program. Tom and Helen Willis, the Jeffersons' in-laws, were the first integrated couple ever to appear as regular characters in a television series.

The black sitcoms of the late seventies and early eighties seem to have been created with the idea of fostering a sense of reconciliation between whites and blacks after the riots and public atrocities that TV viewers had witnessed on The News during twenty years of sustained civil rights agitation. *Carter Country* (small-town southern police station) and *Benson* (the governor's mansion) show interracial friendship growing out of interdependence at the workplace. *Diff'rent Strokes*, *Gimme a Break*, and *Webster* take this concept into a more intimate realm by presenting interracial parenting fantasies. But watching these shows, it is also easy to get the impression that enough has been done to correct what are now being catalogued as problems of the past. American institutional racism has been atoned for, and like prudery in the age of the sexual revolution, it is shown to survive only as a pitiable character flaw of the unhip and the out-of-step. Painfully abundant evidence to the contrary, though aired daily on The News, rarely finds its way into the scripts.

By the last years of the eighties, the nuclear-family sitcom was back on top of the ratings, even though, according to the Census Bureau, such families had become increasingly rare: among the have-nots, teenage pregnancies and single-parent households had risen dramatically; among the haves, career-oriented men and women were increasingly putting off marriage until later in life or forgoing it completely; the divorce rate was settling in at about one out of every two marriages. If the Andersons had been an idealized version of a "normal" American family, the Keatons of *Family Ties* and the Huxtables of *Cosby* were like families of gods in a nation of latchkey children.

In Gary David Goldberg's *Family Ties* (NBC, 1982–present), Mike and Gloria Stivic, the liberal boomers of *All in the Family*, come back from the ashes of the Norman Lear world as the solidly married, solidly middle-class Steve and Elyse Keaton, with their son Alex (Michael J. Fox) as an articulate, dressed-for-success teenage Archie Bunker.

The Cosby Show (NBC, 1984–present), surely the greatest hit of the 1980s, is a kind of upside-down *Amos'n'Andy*, offering a vision of a well-to-do inner-city black family living a life utterly compatible with the values and goals of the suburban middle classes. The program achieves the family warmth, solidarity, and love of *Father Knows Best*, while giving the lie to the idea that such transcendental domesticity is the province of any one racial group.

Growing Pains (ABC, 1985–present), the next great nuclear-family sitcom hit of the eighties, was a clone of *The Cosby Show*. Its kicker? The family is white.

Comedy-Variety: No More Vaudeville

Comedy-variety, barely hanging on in prime time, could offer little relief from the dull self-congratulatory neoconservatism that cast a pall over the sitcom during the late seventies. Sketch comedy was reborn as the province of late-night NBC shows such as *Saturday Night Live* and *SCTV Comedy Network*. Stand-up comedy, virtually absent from prime-time television for over a decade, at long last found a suitable format for presentation in the uninterrupted, uncensored "comedy concerts" offered by premium cable services, especially HBO and Showtime.

There have been only a few attempts to resuscitate comedy-variety as a prime-time enterprise since 1975. All were instant failures. In 1977, for example, NBC, the network that seemed to have adopted such an "anything goes" policy toward *Saturday Night Live*, announced the premiére of a new comedy-variety hour starring Richard Pryor. The advertising stakes, however, are so much greater in prime time that the network was unwilling to apply its "late-night" standards. *The Richard Pryor Show* triggered so many censorship squabbles that it was canceled after only five weeks.

Pryor, perhaps the greatest stand-up artist in the history of American comedy, would have indeed been a welcome addition to network TV during a season whose Top Three Nielsen finishers would be *Laverne and Shirley* (ABC), 31.6; *Happy Days* (ABC), 31.4; and *Three's Company* (ABC), 28.3. But the star took a suitably cavalier attitude toward prime-time pieties, refusing to sacrifice his personality on the altar of least-objectionability. In the tradition of Lenny Bruce's appearance on Steve Allen in 1959 and Pete Seeger's appearance with the Smothers Brothers in 1969, the problem of censorship became the self-reflexive subject of *The Richard Pryor Show*. In the first sketch of the very first episode, Pryor was to appear "nude from the waist up, commenting that he had lost nothing in his battles with the network censors, this followed by a pan down his body in which he appeared to be both completely nude *and* emasculated (he was actually wearing a body stocking)."[6] The sketch was deleted from the telecast by the network, thus setting the tone for *The Richard Pryor Show*'s short relationship with NBC.

The opening show's sight gag was not the only thing that set off least-objectionability alarms in Rockefeller Center. Charley Hill, a Native American stand-up comedian, made a rare network appearance as one of Richard's guests: "I'm an Oneida from Wisconsin. We used to be from New York, but we had a real estate problem. The Pilgrims came to this land 400 years ago as illegal aliens; we used to call them whitebacks. Don't you hate it when people come over and just never leave?"[7]

218

A *Twilight Zone*-ish sketch finds Pryor entering a gun store. As he walks through the shop, each of the pistols and rifles recounts anecdotes about murders they have committed. Finally, after listening to a nostalgic account of World War II by a Luger, he leaves without making a purchase. The sketch aired and predictably inspired a National Rifle Association letter-writing campaign that reminded the network, in no uncertain terms, about the constitutional right to bear arms.

Jokes about Pryor's sex life, many unabashedly washing America's racial dirty laundry, abounded. The following lines, for example, were delivered in a sketch that took the form of a "roast" for Pryor: Victor Dunlop reminisced, "Richard was born in Peoria, where today half the kids in town call him 'superstar'; the other half call him 'daddy.' I'm glad Richard is married now; I can send my kids to school without being frightened." Marsha Warfield said, "Richard is a real humanitarian. He's raised a lot of money for needy students. In fact, he's paid half the girls at Hollywood High School to keep their mouths shut. I dated Richard for a while, but I wasn't his type: I wasn't beautiful, I wasn't sexy, I wasn't white." Sandra Bernhard observed, "Richard has settled down and become a real family man. In fact, he's given everything he has to his children: a flat nose and big lips."

By the show's fifth week, both artist and censor had given up on each other and the series was canceled. On the final program, guest star Robin Williams remarked, "This man is a genius. Who else can take all the forms of comedy—slapstick, satire, mime, and stand-up—and turn them into something that will offend everyone?" The show's rating were not high enough to win it any saviors in high places; it had been counterprogrammed against *Happy Days* during the height of the *Pax Fonzie*.

In 1978, Mary Tyler Moore, who had voluntarily canceled her own sitcom only a season earlier, attempted to return to television in a new, hour-long series. *Mary*, which premiered on CBS that September, presented none of the censorship problems of *The Richard Pryor Show*. A "backstage sitcom," it was a curious hybrid of comedy-variety and situation comedy in the tradition of certain early TV shows, such as *The Jack Benny Show* and *Burns and Allen*. Mary played the part of Mary McKinnon, the star of a comedy-variety hour; the singers, dancers, and comedians who performed on "the show" all played themselves. But it was such a bland collection of Tin Pan Alley hoofing and belting that it was off the air by the second week in October. For Mary, genre had proved thicker than stardom. The following March, CBS repackaged the show as *The Mary Tyler Moore Hour*, eliminating the self-reflexive narrative frame. But once again, the sketch material was pablum and the show could not find viewers. There seemed to be no happy medium for comedy-variety: it was either too objectionable for the censors or not objectionable enough for the audience.

Yet another glancing blow to comedy-variety came in 1979, when *The Carol Burnett Show*, the last surviving prime-time comedy-variety hour, a show that had been airing since 1967, was canceled. Burnett, who had been continuously performing sketch comedy on national television since her debut on *The Garry Moore Show* some twenty years earlier, had watched the genre crumble around her for more than a decade and became its last great exponent. Her show, a mixture of blackout sketches, stand-up routines, songs, and even musical production numbers, was something right out of the Berle-Caesar-Gleason era. But it had not placed among the Top Twenty-five programs since 1972, and CBS, which had been carrying the show as a gesture toward older viewers, finally gave it the ax in the show's eleventh season.

Andy Warhol claimed that *The Carol Burnett Show* was his favorite TV series because it was immune to the repetitive trends and fashions that otherwise ruled network programming.[8] Indeed, as the last of the old-time comedy-variety shows, it had the rare privilege of defining generic form with its own content. The show's most popular sketch, "Ed and Eunice," for example, presented a type of family comedy all during the seventies that was completely oblivious to *All in the Family*, *Happy Days*, or any other trend-setting hit.

Eunice Higgins, a beleaguered blue-collar housewife from Raytown, U.S.A., was probably Burnett's most original and complete character. Eunice, who dreams of status and celebrity, is saddled with a good-for-nothing husband, Ed (Harvey Korman), and an unforgiving mother (Vicki Lawrence), a blue-haired biddy whose mission in life is to remind Eunice of her shortcomings. The relentless bickering of the family over the most trivial of matters—Jell-O flavors!—somehow manages to toe the line of hyperbole and strike a terrible note of banal reality deep in the American heart. There was something indescribably "normal" about this family in which everyone was eating each other's heart out.

One "Ed and Eunice" sketch concerned the death of Eunice's Aunt May, who "died while watching *The Mike Douglas Show*." It is Saturday afternoon, and Ed is anxious to get home in time to catch a Bugs Bunny cartoon:

Ed: When is this funeral gonna be over?
Eunice: It will be over when it is over and I would thank you not to give us all the rush act today. There are gonna be plenty of other Saturdays for you to watch TV. Now shut up and sit down!

Strewn with the flotsam and jetsam of day-to-day mass-culture life, the "Ed and Eunice" sketches revealed much about the soul of supermarket-coupon, hair-curler, laundromat America. References and allusions to popular movies, TV shows, and brand-name consumer products somehow serve to ground the ridiculous and encourage the willing suspension of disbelief. In literature, only Don Delillo has been able to work successfully in this territory.[9]

Eunice is unlike any sitcom character of the period. She is a woman at odds with herself. Though very much a creature of the world of hamburger strips and K-Marts, she has visions of something classier. Ironically, Eunice, television's great "mass" woman, believes in *Kultur*. She senses that somewhere in America there are educated, intelligent people who know about art and style and fashion and don't holler at each other all the time. Furthermore, she believes that she is one of them but is trapped by cruel fate in a life that she is better than. In one episode, Ed, a hardware salesman, receives a free promotional dinner-for-two at the fanciest restaurant in town. Eunice's Mama, of course, comes along; the psychoverbal consequences of not taking her would be too much to consider. At the elegant restaurant, Eunice's chance to mingle with Raytown's elite turns into a nightmare of embarrassments:

221

Mama doesn't know how to use a pepper mill. Ed orders a burger and fries. (The sophisticated Eunice prefers "beef bro-shetty.") When a strolling violinist visits the table, Ed hides his head in his lap, afraid that "that fiddle player was gonna pull out a tambourine and ask for money."

"You two absolutely refuse to recognize any nice thing in life!" Eunice shouts in exasperation at her masscult husband and mother. But this only opens things up for a good old-fashioned family fight. Finally, the maître d' arrives and asks them all to leave. The parting shot is a portrait of Eunice at the door to the dining room. Her look of mortification is pathetic and overpowering, an aesthetic counterweight to the slapstick gags that dominate the body of the sketch. It is not a happy ending; but then again, "Ed and Eunice" was no sitcom.

Many viewers and critics had hoped that cable television, by cracking the three-network, commercial, tale-telling oligarchy, would produce a more eclectic mix of programming. Some new genres, in fact, have been created. Professional programming aimed at physicians is offered by the Lifetime network; drug companies and investment houses advertise. ESPN offers magazine shows targeted at leisure affinity groups, such as surfers, bodybuilders, and fishing enthusiasts; commercials for surfboard waxes, Nautilus clubs, and fishing equipment foot the bill. But the major effect of cable television on existing genres has been not so much to explore new heights of artistry as new depths.

The "B" sitcom, a concept that many would have once thought of as redundant, has taken real form on cable and in the vastly expanded market of first-run syndication. Shows such as *Check It Out*, *Sanchez of Bel Air*, *The New Gidget*, and *One Big Family* formed the avant-garde of this movement. Each of these sitcoms involved the remarketing of a star or a concept that had long ago sunk past the interest level of the major networks.

Don Adams, the star of *Check It Out*, is a prime example. He achieved national fame during the late sixties as the star of *Get Smart*, a sitcom spoof of the spy craze that had begun with the James Bond movies and then migrated to television with shows such as *I Spy* and *The Man From U.N.C.L.E.* After the cancellation of *Get Smart* in 1970, Adams' star quickly faded. His 1972 NBC sitcom, *The Partners*, in which he played a cop, was an instant failure. By the mid-1970s his network appearances were limited to guest shots on *The Love Boat*. Voices for cartoon characters followed, and he even put in a short stint as the host of a syndicated game show before virtually disappearing from television by 1980. With the lower stakes of cable advertising, however, Adams' name recognition—though no longer high enough to interest the networks—once again became a bankable commodity. In 1985 he resurfaced on USA cable network as the star of *Check It Out*, reprising much of his familiar *Get Smart* shtick as the manager of a supermarket. *Check It Out*'s greatest distinction is its cheap, tawdry, obviously "subnetwork" level of production. A typical episode is so dominated by cost-conscious talking-heads shots that *Check It Out* makes *Three's Company* look like a Jean Renoir movie.

Similarly, *Sanchez of Bel Air* is a remarkably shlocko synthesis of minor marketing ideas and bare-bones production values that could never hope to reach network air but found national exposure on cable. A Chicano reworking of *The Beverly Hillbillies* via *The Jeffersons*, the Sanchezes are a Los Angeles family that hits the big money and moves in among the Anglos. Their next-door neighbor in swank Bel Air is none other than Bobby Sherman, a teen throb of twenty years ago both in so-called "real life" and in the sitcom. In *The New Gidget* we have an adaptation of a failed sitcom, *Gidget* (ABC, 1965–66), which itself was an adaptation of a moderately successful series of Hollywood movies about a California teenager who becomes enamored of funky surf culture without sacrificing her God-given right to remain a middle-class suburban brat. The Gidget of the eighties is, of course, an entrepreneur, with her own travel agency. *One Big Family* digs up Danny Thomas, who started performing situation comedy as the star of *Make Room for Daddy* in 1953 and who has failed in his every network comeback attempt since, this one included. The bargain-basement remarketing of properties such as Don Adams, Bobby Sherman, Gidget, and Danny Thomas gives a new dimension to the idea of "reruns" in the cable era.

The News, meanwhile, has also proliferated. As in radio, whole channels have sprung up devoted to nothing else but it. CNN Headline News keeps the stories at around two minutes or less. Ted Turner's other news channel, CNN In-Depth, might go as long as five. The News seems worse when there is lots of it; things mellow on days when pieces about whale birthdays and junkyard sculptors appear. Corporations argue about permissible percentage levels of toxicity as the ecostructure disintegrates in unfathomable poisons. Who is going to fix that hole in the ozone layer? Will the Pope recognize Israel, even in a crowded room? Clergymen of the Right and Left run for president on the advice of God. Compassion, no longer a human emotion, is a theoretical problem for insurance companies. AIDS testing. Drug testing. IQ testing. BMW. Chevrolet. Toyota. Cancer research. Heart attack. Vehicular homicide. Friends, it's a dangerous world. Why not stay at home and watch television, preferably with a healthy friend? "The battle for the survival of man as a responsible being in the Communications Era," wrote Umberto Eco, "is not to be won where the communication originates, but where it arrives."[10]

Notes

1. *M*A*S*H*, especially, became an extraordinary evergreen; in certain cable jurisdictions it could still be seen as many as four or five times a day, almost a decade after its cancellation. *Mary* did less well, her rerun appeal generally not extending past the limits of the largest metropolitan centers. By the eighties, some stations were showing *Maude* after midnight; contemporary prime-time sitcoms had become so unrepentantly tame that *Maude's* abortions, multiple divorces, menopause flashes, and frank dialogue had now become remarketable as risqué, controversial "late-night" material, even though the series had originally aired at 8 P.M. Eastern back in 1972.
2. Harry Castleman and Walter J. Podrazik, *Watching TV: Four Decades of American Television* (New York: McGraw-Hill, 1982), p. 254.
3. It should be noted that episodes made during the first season of *Happy Days* are distinctively different from those of the nine seasons that followed. During the first year, Richie was extremely shy, the Fonz was only a minor character, and the treatment of sex on the show was hardly distinguishable from *Father Knows Best*.
4. As quoted in Horace Newcomb and Robert S. Alley, *The Producer's Medium* (New York: Oxford, 1983), p. 249.
5. Ibid., p. 234.

6. Tim Brooks and Earle Marsh, *The Complete Directory to Prime Time Network TV Shows*, 3rd ed. (New York: Ballantine, 1985), p. 712.
7. This and all other quotations from the series are drawn from *The Richard Pryor Show*, produced by Burt Sugarman, NBC, October 20, 1977.
8. Private conversation, New York, 1973.
9. See Don Delillo, *White Noise* (New York: Viking, 1985).
10. Umberto Eco, *Travels in Hyper Reality*, trans. William Weaver (New York: Harcourt, Brace, Jovanovich, 1986), p. 142.

Bibliography

Books

Adams, Joey, with Henry Tobias. *The Borscht Belt*. New York: Bobbs-Merrill, 1959.

Barnouw, Erik. *Tube of Plenty*. New York: Oxford, 1975; rev. ed., 1982.

Berle, Milton, with Haskel Frankel. *Milton Berle: An Autobiography*. New York: Delacorte, 1974.

Biskind, Peter. *Seeing Is Believing: How Hollywood Taught Us to Stop Worrying and Love the Fifties*. New York: Pantheon, 1983.

Brooks, Tim, and Earle Marsh. *The Complete Directory to Prime Time Network TV Shows*. 3rd ed. New York: Ballantine, 1985.

Bruce, Kitty (ed.). *The Almost Unpublished Lenny Bruce*. Philadelphia: Running Press, 1984.

Bryars, Chris. *The Real Mary Tyler Moore Show*. New York: Pinnacle, 1977.

Castleman, Harry, and Walter Podrazik. *Watching TV: Four Decades of American Television*. New York: McGraw-Hill, 1982.

————. *The Schedule Book: Four Decades of Network Programming from Sign-on to Sign-off*. New York: McGraw-Hill, 1984.

Conrad, Peter. *Television: The Medium and Its Manners*. Boston: Routledge and Kegan Paul, 1982.

Czitrom, Daniel J. *Media and the American Mind: From Morse to McLuhan*. Chapel Hill: University of North Carolina, 1982.

Delillo, Don. *White Noise*. New York: Viking, 1985.

Dunaway, David King. *How Can I Keep from Singing: Pete Seeger*. New York: McGraw-Hill, 1981.

Eco, Umberto. *Travels in Hyper Reality* (trans. William Weaver). New York: Harcourt, Brace, Jovanovich, 1986.

Eisner, Joel, and David Krinsky. *Television Comedy Series*. Winston-Salem: McFarland, 1984.

Eliot, T. S. *Christianity and Culture*. New York: Harvest, 1968.

Emerson, Ralph Waldo. "The American Scholar." 1837.

Enzensberger, Hans Magnus. *The Consciousness Industry*. New York: Seabury, 1974.

Feuer, Jane, Paul Kerr, and Tise Vahimagi. *MTM "Quality Television."* London: British Film Institute, 1984.

Fiedler, Leslie. *What Was Literature?* New York: Simon and Schuster, 1982.

Fisher, Seymour, and Rhoda Fisher. *Pretend the World Is Funny and Forever.* Hillsdale, N.J.: Erlbaum, 1981.

Fiske, John, and John Hartley. *Reading Television.* New York: Methuen, 1978.

Fitzgerald, F. Scott. *The Great Gatsby.* New York: Scribners, 1925.

Flake, Carol. *Redemptorama: Culture, Politics, and the New Evangelism.* New York: Anchor, 1984.

Franklin, Benjamin. *Autobiography and Other Writings* (ed. Russel B. Nye). Boston: Houghton Mifflin, 1958.

Franklin, Joe. *Encyclopedia of Comedians.* Secaucus, N.J.: Citadel, 1979.

Ginsberg, Allen. *Howl and Other Poems.* San Francisco: City Lights, 1956.

Gitlin, Todd. *Inside Prime Time.* New York: Pantheon, 1983.

Goldman, Albert. *Ladies and Gentlemen—Lenny Bruce!* New York: Random House, 1971.

Harrington, Michael. *The Other America.* New York: Macmillan, 1963.

Himmelstein, Hal. *Television Myth and the American Mind.* New York: Praeger, 1984.

Hooker, Richard. *M*A*S*H.* New York: Morrow, 1968.

Howe, Irving. *World of Our Fathers.* New York: Simon and Schuster, 1976.

Hurst, Jack. *Nashville's Grand Ole Opry.* New York: Abrams, 1975.

Jackson, Kenneth T. *Crabgrass Frontier: The Suburbanization of the United States.* New York: Oxford, 1985.

Kerouac, Jack. *On The Road.* New York: Viking, 1957.

———. *The Subterraneans.* New York: Grove, 1958.

Knight, Arthur, and Kit Knight. *The Beat Journey.* California, P.: The Unspeakable Visions of the Individual, 1978.

Krassner, Paul (ed.). *Best of "The Realist."* Philadelphia: Running Press, 1984.

Kroc, Ray, with Robert Anderson. *Grinding It Out: The Making of McDonald's.* Chicago: Regnery, 1977.

MacDonald, J. Fred. *Television and the Red Menace: The Video Road to Vietnam.* New York: Praeger, 1985.

———. *Who Shot the Sheriff: The Rise and Fall of the TV Western.* New York: Praeger, 1987.

Mailer, Norman. "The White Negro," *Advertisements for Myself.* New York: Putnam, 1959.

———. *An American Dream.* New York: Dial, 1965.

Malcolm X, and Alex Haley. *The Autobiography of Malcolm X.* New York: Grove, 1965.

Malone, Bill C. *Country Music U.S.A.* Austin: University of Texas, 1968.

Marill, Alvin H. *Movies Made for Television.* New York: Da Capo, 1980.

McLuhan, Marshall. *The Gutenberg Galaxy.* Toronto: University of Toronto, 1962.

McNeil, Alex. *Total Television: A Comprehensive Guide to Programming.* 2nd ed. New York: Penguin, 1984.

Medvedev, Roy. *Khrushchev* (trans. Brian Pearce). New York: Anchor, 1983.

Modleski, Tania. *Loving with a Vengeance: Mass-Produced Fantasies for Women.* Hamden, Conn.: Archon, 1982.

Nabokov, Vladimir. *Lolita.* Greenwich, Conn.: Fawcett Crest, 1958.

Newcomb, Horace. *TV: The Most Popular Art.* New York: Anchor, 1974.

———, (ed.). *Television: The Critical View.* 3rd ed. New York: Oxford, 1982.

———, and Robert S. Alley. *The Producer's Medium.* New York: Oxford, 1983.

O'Connor, John E. (ed.). *American History/American Television.* New York: Ungar, 1983.

Paul, Sherman. *Edmund Wilson: A Study of Literary Vocation in Our Time.* Urbana: University of Illinois, 1965.

Phillips, Kevin. *The Emerging Republican Majority.* New Rochelle, N.Y.: Arlington House, 1970.

Pope, Alexander. *Poetry and Prose of Alexander Pope* (ed. Aubrey Williams). Boston: Houghton Mifflin, 1969.

Postman, Neil. *Amusing Ourselves to Death.* New York: Elizabeth Sifton, Viking, 1985.

Reiner, Carl. *Enter Laughing.* New York: Simon and Schuster, 1958.

Rosenberg, Bernard, and David Manning White. *Mass Culture: The Popular Arts in America.* New York: Free Press, 1957.

Roth, Philip. *Goodbye, Columbus and Five Short Stories.* Boston: Houghton Mifflin, 1959.

———. *The Professor of Desire.* New York: Bantam, 1977.

Seldes, Gilbert. *The Public Arts.* New York: Simon and Schuster, 1956.

Sorensen, Theodore. *Kennedy.* New York: Harper and Row, 1965.

Sterling, Christopher, and John Kitross. *Stay Tuned: A Concise History of American Broadcasting.* Belmont, Calif.: Wadsworth, 1978.

Toll, Robert. *Blacking Up.* New York: Oxford, 1974.

———. *The Entertainment Machine.* New York: Oxford, 1982.

Waldmeir, Joseph, J. (ed.). *Recent American Fiction.* Boston: Houghton Mifflin, 1961.

Watt, Ian. *The Rise of the Novel.* Berkeley: University of California, 1957.

Weissman, Ginny, and Coyne Steven Sanders. *The Dick Van Dyke Show.* New York: St. Martin's, 1983.

Whitman, Walt. *Leaves of Grass 1855* (ed. Malcolm Cowley). New York: Penguin, 1959.

Whyte, William H., Jr. *The Organization Man.* New York: Simon and Schuster, 1956.

Wilk, Max. *The Golden Age of Television Comedy.* New York: Delacorte, 1976.

Wills, Garry. *The Kennedy Imprisonment.* Boston: Atlantic Monthly, 1982.

Zimmerman, Paul D., and Burt Goldblatt. *The Marx Brothers at the Movies.* New York: Putnam, 1968.

Periodicals

"A Good Bomb?" *New York Times*, September 30, 1984.

Adams, Val. "Newhart to Star in CBS-TV Show." *New York Times*, July 11, 1960.

Amory, Cleveland. Review of *The Smothers Brothers Show*. *TV Guide*, February 26, 1966.

Asimov, Isaac. "Husbands, Beware!" *TV Guide*, March 22, 1969.

Boyer, Paul. "The Cloud over Culture." *New Republic*, August 12–19, 1985.

Cawelti, John G. "The Concept of Formula in the Study of Popular Literature." *Journal of Popular Culture*, 3 (1969).

Doan, Richard and Joseph Finnegan. "The Show that Died After One Night." *TV Guide*, May 17, 1969.

"Comedy on Television: A Dialogue." *Television Quarterly*, Summer 1963.

Czitrom, Daniel and David Marc. "The Elements of Lifestyle." *Atlantic Monthly*, May 1985.

Doan, Richard and Joseph Finnegan. "The Show That Died After One Night." *TV Guide*, May 17, 1969.

Frank, Waldo. "Seriousness and Dada." *1924*, 3 (1924).

Gehman, Richard. "The Great One." *TV Guide*, October 13, 20, and 27, 1962.

Gutis, Philip S. "Suburbia Reexamined at Hofstra Conference." *New York Times*, June 15, 1987.

Hoberman, J. "The Show Biz Messiah." *No Rose*, 1:2 (Spring 1977).

———. "Love and Death in the American Supermarketplace." *Voice Literary Supplement*, November 1982.

———. "Ralph and Alice and Ed and Trixie." *Film Comment*, September–October 1985.

Hobson, D. "Lily Tomlin." *TV Guide*, November 14, 1970.

Kanfer, Stephen. "The Buckle on the Borscht Belt." *Gentleman's Quarterly*, 55:8 (August 1985).

Lipsitz, George. "The Meaning of Memory: Family, Class, and Ethnicity in Early Network Television Programs." *Cultural Anthropology*, 1:4 (November 1986).

Macdonald, Dwight. "A Theory of Mass Culture." *Diogenes*, 3 (1953).

Mintz, Lawrence. "Stand-up Comedy as Cultural and Social Mediation." *American Quarterly*, 37:1 (Spring 1985).

"Smothers Out: A Wise Decision." Editorial. *TV Guide* (New York Metropolitan ed.), April 19, 1968.

Walters, Barry. "Visions of Glory," *Spin*, October 1986.

Whitfield, Stephen. "Richard Nixon as Comic Figure." *American Quarterly*, 37:1 (Spring 1985).

Whitney, Dwight. "Irreverent Is the Word for the Smothers Brothers." *TV Guide*, February 10, 1968.

About the Author

David Marc is Assistant Professor of American Studies at Brandeis University. He is a frequent contributor of articles on mass media to *The Village Voice* and *The Atlantic*, and is the author of *Demographic Vistas* (1984).

Index to Television Comedy Series

231

General Index